Russia's Legal Fictions

Law, Meaning, and Violence

The scope of Law, Meaning, and Violence is defined by the wide-ranging scholarly debates signaled by each of the words in the title. Those debates have taken place among and between lawyers, anthropologists, political theorists, sociologists, and historians, as well as literary and cultural critics. This series is intended to recognize the importance of such ongoing conversations about law, meaning, and violence as well as to encourage and further them.

Series Editors:

Martha Minow, Harvard Law School
Elaine Scarry, Harvard University
Austin Sarat, Amherst College

Narrative, Violence, and the Law: The Essays of Robert Cover,
    edited by Martha Minow, Michael Ryan, and Austin Sarat

Narrative, Authority, and Law, by Robin West

*The Possibility of Popular Justice: A Case Study of Community Mediation
    in the United States,* edited by Sally Engle Merry and Neal Milner

Legal Modernism, by David Luban

*Surveillance, Privacy, and the Law: Employee Drug Testing and the Politics
    of Social Control,* by John Gilliom

Lives of Lawyers: Journeys in the Organizations of Practice,
    by Michael J. Kelly

Unleashing Rights: Law, Meaning, and the Animal Rights Movement,
    by Helena Silverstein

Law Stories, edited by Gary Bellow and Martha Minow

*The Powers That Punish: Prison and Politics in the Era of the "Big House,"
    1920–1955,* by Charles Bright

*Law and the Postmodern Mind: Essays on Psychoanalysis and
    Jurisprudence,* edited by Peter Goodrich and David Gray Carlson

Russia's Legal Fictions, by Harriet Murav

RUSSIA'S
LEGAL FICTIONS

Harriet Murav

ANN ARBOR
THE UNIVERSITY OF MICHIGAN PRESS

Copyright © by the University of Michigan 1998
All rights reserved
Published in the United States of America by
The University of Michigan Press
Manufactured in the United States of America
⊗ Printed on acid-free paper

2001   2000   1999   1998   4   3   2   1

A CIP catalog record for this book is available from the British Library.

Library of Congress Cataloging-in-Publication Data

Murav, Harriet, 1955–
    Russia's legal fictions / Harriet Murav.
       p.   cm.
    Includes bibliographical references (p.   ) and index.
    ISBN 0-472-10879-4 (acid-free paper)
       1. Russian literature—19th century—History and criticism.
    2. Russian literature—20th century—History and criticism. 3. Law
    and literature.   I. Title.
    PG3015.5.L3M87   1998
    891.709'355—dc21   97-45272
                                                              CIP

For Sam, David, Penelope, and Sissela

Contents

Acknowledgments

Research for this publication was supported by grants (in 1989 and 1992) from the International Research and Exchanges Board, with funds provided by the U.S. Department of State (Title VIII program) and the National Endowment for the Humanities. None of these organizations is responsible for the views expressed. My colleagues in Moscow, Olga Borovaia and Sergei Lezov, provided invaluable leads, tips, and general assistance. A quarter-long fellowship during 1991 at the Humanities Institute at the University of California at Davis enabled me to present an initial stage of my work in an interdisciplinary setting. Austin Sarat gave his enthusiastic encouragement to the project. I wish to thank my research assistants, Victoria Shinbrot and Anna Kaladiouk, for their patient and able help. I'm also grateful to the anonymous readers at the University of Michigan Press for their insightful comments. Thanks are due to the staff of the Interlibrary Loan Department at the UC Davis Library, who supplied me with hard-to-find newspapers, journals, and monographs crucial to this study. Finally, my love and thanks to my husband, Bruce Rosenstock, for the innumerable conversations about and readings of the manuscript, for his support, and best of all, for his unflagging interest in the project.

Introduction

Much has been written in recent years about the relation between law and the realm of fiction, narrative, and rhetoric.[1] We have been told that law is vulnerable to the same contingencies of interpretation as any other written text and is as dependent on the master narratives of its time and place as any other cultural artifact.[2] Legal scholars have called for more storytelling in legal practice and for more attention to the way that stories are told. Telling stories promotes "empathy" and understanding for others.[3] While some of the Russian literary canon appears in debates about law and literature, almost no attention is given to the specific legal context in which these works were written, or to the rich legal culture of nineteenth-century Russia. Russian lawyers were profoundly aware that they were telling stories. With the exception of several histories of the law and legal institutions, very little has been said about Russian law and literature, perhaps in part because Russia is seen as outside the pale of the Western legal tradition.

The conflict between the Russian writer and the law is a well-known and even celebrated feature of Russian literary life in the past two centuries. This conflict plays a crucial part in the quasi-political,

---

1. See, for example, Peter Brooks and Paul Gewirtz, *Law's Stories: Narrative and Rhetoric in the Law* (New Haven, Conn.: Yale University Press, 1996); and Austin Sarat and Thomas R. Kearns, eds., *The Rhetoric of Law* (Ann Arbor: University of Michigan Press, 1994).

2. For an argument that emphasizes a particularly Nietzschean perspective on legal meaning, see Sanford Levinson, "Law as Literature," in *Interpreting Law and Literature: A Hermeneutic Reader,* ed. Sanford Levinson and Steven Mailloux (Evanston, Ill.: Northwestern University Press, 1988), 155–73.

3. See, for example, Kim Lane Scheppele, "Forward: Telling Stories," *Michigan Law Review* 87 (1988): 2073–98; and Richard Delgado, "A Plea for Narrative," *Michigan Law Review* 87 (1988): 2411–41. For a critical view, see Toni M. Massaro, "Empathy, Legal Storytelling, and the Rule of Law: New Words, Old Wounds?" *Michigan Law Review* 87 (1988): 2099–3153. Massaro is particularly critical of the call for more individualized justice. For an attack on the whole movement, see Richard Posner, *Law and Literature: A Misunderstood Relation* (Cambridge, Mass.: Harvard University Press, 1988).

public, and moral role that has been much touted as the defining characteristic of the Russian writer since the first part of the nineteenth century.[4] With one exception, the authors to be discussed in this study—Sukhovo-Kobylin, Akhsharumov, Suvorin, and Dostoevsky in the nineteenth century and Solzhenitsyn and Siniavskii in the twentieth—were all put on trial. All of these authors write about some aspect of their arrest, trial or investigation, and imprisonment. How they address their confrontation with the law is one of the basic issues that we will explore: how the writer imagines and represents the law and legal language and authority.

But to focus exclusively on a single moment of conflict is to fall prey to the writer's own self-mythologizing.[5] Furthermore, the question of the writer's response to and representation of the law addresses only one side of the equation. Another dimension is how the law imagines and represents the writer, the literary text, and the process of writing. As the work of Dominick LaCapra and Susan Stewart has shown, the literary trial encapsulates a set of assumptions about literary language, authorship, and meaning. Stewart's *Crimes of Writing: Problems in the Containment of Representation* discusses "specific cases of forgery, literary imposture, pornography, and graffiti," focusing attention on law as writing, primarily by showing its susceptibility to "temporality and interpretation."[6] According to Stewart, these "crimes of writing" reveal what law tries to conceal in its self-creation as transcendent discourse. *Crimes of Writing* simultaneously investigates law in distinct domains, juxtaposing distinct historical time periods in order to delineate a wide-ranging problematic. Stewart's work enables us to see how the literary trial, not only in the cases she describes, but in other instances, such as censorship and libel, opens up a series of questions about, to use her language, meaning, subjectivity, and the law. When a written text is the scene of the crime, when the crime is an act of speech, the trial is an investigation into the nature of authorship. How does the law define the relation between the legal subject, the defendant, the

---

4. For a discussion of the Russian writer's public role, see Donald Fanger, "Conflicting Imperatives in the Model of the Russian Writer: The Case of Tertz/Sinyavsky," and Gary Saul Morson, "Commentary: Traditions and Institutions," in *Literature and History: Theoretical Problems and Russian Case Studies*, ed. Gary Saul Morson (Stanford, Calif.: Stanford University Press, 1986), 111–34, 263–74.

5. For more on the Russian writer's self-mythologizing, see David Bethea, *Joseph Brodsky and the Creation of Exile* (Princeton, N.J.: Princeton University Press, 1994), 11–12.

6. Susan Stewart, *Crimes of Writing: Problems in the Containment of Representation* (Durham, N.C.: Duke University Press, 1994), 3.

subject who is writing, and the personae that emerge from the literary text? A confrontation ensues about who the author is, whether his or her intentions can be deduced from the literary work, how the text ought to be interpreted, and who is to be held responsible. We will examine two literary trials, Aleksei Suvorin's in 1866 and Andrei Siniavskii's in 1966, for what they reveal about these issues.

Law, Narrative, and Authority

To the question of how the writer imagines the law and how the law imagines the writer must be added a more general and more basic question about what legal and literary authority are. In *Beginnings*, a study of the European novel, Edward Said emphasizes that to author means to found and generate. Any author claims a certain authority in order to create a literary work. In so doing, the author may borrow, modify, or violate already existing rules governing how particular types of literature are to be written, what sort of language may be used, for example, or what topics may be addressed. Two works that occupy a prominent place in this study—Dostoevsky's *A Writer's Diary* and Solzhenitsyn's *The Gulag Archipelago*—reveal how authors dispense with the conventions governing literary genres. In each work, languages, styles, genres, and disciplines are crossed: fiction, history, law, medicine, autobiography, and journalism form one vast heterogeneous narrative. Both Dostoevsky and Solzhenitsyn emphasize the significance of their role as specifically literary authors. How they and the other writers in this study define the unique features of the literary in distinction from other forms of discourse will be explored in the chapters that follow.

According to Said, the ability to create and sustain a fictive realm constitutes the literary author's authority. This definition suggests that the literary author's authority has no consequences in the real world of real authorities, who can enforce their laws with violence, if need be. A gap opens up between a purely literary realm in which a certain authority is exercised and the world of social relations, law, politics, and power, where a wholly different kind of authority makes itself felt concretely.

However, the disjuncture between what writers do and what lawmakers and law enforcers do is not as wide as it may at first appear. The authority of the law does not only depend on the force that lies behind it. The American legal scholar Robert Cover writes that for every nomos, there is a narrative. "No set of legal institutions or prescriptions exists apart from the narratives that locate it and give it meaning."[7] What grounds the law—understood not as an externally imposed system of social control, but as a meaningful system—is the sense that it is consonant with the fundamental values of the dominant culture. James Boyd White, one of the founders of the law-and-humanities movement, similarly defines law as a "social and cultural activity," in which language and persuasion serve not only the ends of particular individuals, but more importantly serve to build community.[8] My discussion of law and narrative shifts the emphasis away from community and focuses more on relations of power. I examine how language and narrative are implicated in relations of power, by tracing, for example, the question of distance between author and reader. Storytelling may serve to include more and more listeners and speakers and thus help to create or make visible more communities, but stories can also reinstate forms of exclusion or mask acts of violence.[9]

Both the law and the literary work are actively engaged with the foundational narratives that a culture tells itself. As Robert Weisberg puts it, law and literature can both be seen as part of the "formal archeology of a culture."[10] Definitions of the normal and the abnormal, gender roles, attitudes toward the body, pleasure, and sexuality, questions of national identity, political beliefs, constructions of self and other, and relations between high and low all go into the way a case is made and decided. Reading about a case is like reading a palimpsest, in which layers of cultural constructions are revealed. To give an example, for Dostoevsky and other observers, the question as to whether a little girl was "tortured" by her father—the crucial question in the Kronenberg case of 1876—is transformed into the question of what is Russianness. My analysis of Sukhovo-Kobylin, charged with the murder of his French mistress, examines the legal documents of his case, the letters

---

7. Robert Cover, "The Supreme Court 1982 Term, Forward: Nomos and Narrative," *Harvard Law Review* 97, no. 4 (1983): 4, and see generally the entire article, 4–68.

8. James Boyd White, *Heracles' Bow: Essays on the Rhetoric and Poetics of the Law* (Madison: University of Wisconsin Press, 1985), x.

9. For a discussion of how the construction of the "people" in the American Constitution depends on slavery but conceals its dependence, see Gayatri Chakravorty Spivak, "Constitutions and Culture Studies," in *Legal Studies and Culture Studies: A Post Modern Critical Theory*, ed. Jerry D. Leonard (New York: State University of New York Press, 1995), 155–73.

10. Robert Weisberg, "The Law-Literature Enterprise," *Yale Journal of Law and Humanities* 1, no. 1 (1988): 67.

and memoirs of prominent observers, the study of everyday behavior of the aristocratic circle to which Kobylin belonged, and the literary works that he authored, in order to expose the anxieties and obsessions of Russian elite culture in the middle of the nineteenth century.

The fundamental narratives and metaphors that I spoke of earlier do not have the same meaning for all the members of the society and therefore are subject to change and contestation. I explore the specific forms in which these narratives appear in Russian public life, and the interrelation between the construction of authorial and political legitimacy in several key instances. One such narrative, which is found, of course, not only or even primarily in Russia, figures the ruler as father. I examine how the writers construct their own authority in relation to this figure, fashioning themselves as lawgivers, both legitimate and illegitimate, as fathers, and sometimes as sons.

In emphasizing how literary authors may figure themselves as rulers, and may construct their own personal stories as larger-than-life foundational narratives, my readings depart significantly from Bakhtin's theory of the novel as a disruptive force. Readers are no doubt familiar with Bakhtin's concepts of carnival and the novel; I rehearse them in order to show how my approach incorporates these concepts but also departs from them. For Bakhtin, authoritative discourse, that is, the language of politics, morality, religion, "the word of the father," enter the novel only to be parodied. He sees a fundamental struggle at work in language itself, whereby the centripetal forces that unify, organize, and stabilize language "operate in the midst of heteroglossia," that is, in the midst of a multiplicity of languages that tend to fragment and de-stabilize authoritative discourse. The novel actively incorporates heteroglossia by stylizing and parodying the already accepted official language of the surrounding culture.[11] Insofar as the novel exerts a destabilizing effect on language, judgments, and meanings, it corresponds to the social phenomenon of carnival and serves as the literary form of carnival.

Bakhtin's "carnival" is important for this study, but only if we open up the boundary that places the novel and carnival on one side, and authoritative language and official culture on the other. In the chapters that follow, law and literature are not made to settle neatly on

---

11. M. M. Bakhtin, "Discourse in the Novel," in *The Dialogic Imagination*, ed. Michael Holquist, trans. Caryl Emerson and Michael Holquist (Austin: University of Texas Press, 1981), 314.

opposite sides of the boundary, law on the side of order and unity, and literature on the side of carnival and play. Law is not all fixity, abstraction, and limit, and literature is not all open-endedness and multivalence. I trace carnival not only in the realm of literature, but in the realm of the law and the social world, examining the responses of sometimes unwilling participants in it. When the loss of individual identity and the boundaries that separate one body from another is not spontaneous, but forced, the carnival is no longer joyful, as Michael André Bernstein has written.[12]

Literature, and the novel in particular, can also "lay down the law."[13] Dennis Miller in *The Novel and the Police* and John Bender in *Imagining the Penitentiary* both argue that the "representational techniques of the novel" show how the behavior of individuals can be monitored and controlled.[14] Both connect narrative omniscience with Foucault's panopticon, emphasizing the link between knowledge and power. Miller stresses that even when characters in novels resist the police, the policing functions are assumed by the larger community in the world of the novel and also taken up, as we have just seen, by the very structure of the novel. For Foucault, power is not primarily an external force located in specific political or social institutions but is dispersed throughout society in numerous institutions and social practices that invisibly shape the self.[15] It is Miller's contention that far from disrupting these subtle and yet all-pervasive forms of power, the novel sustains them.

In contrast, I am concerned primarily with specifically legal and political forms of power and authority insofar as they figure in the literary author's construction of his or her own authority. The more

---

12. Michael André Bernstein, "When the Carnival Turns Bitter: Preliminary Reflections Upon the Abject Hero," in *Bakhtin: Essays and Dialogues on His Work,* ed. Gary Saul Morson (Chicago: University of Chicago Press, 1986), 99–121.

13. I take the phrase from J. Hillis Miller, "Laying Down the Law in Literature: The Example of Kleist," in *Deconstruction and the Possibility of Justice,* ed. Drusilla Cornell, Michael Rosenfield, and David Gray Carlson (New York: Routledge, 1992), 305–29.

14. See D. A. Miller, *The Novel and the Police* (Berkeley and Los Angeles: University of California Press, 1988); and John Bender, *Imagining the Penitentiary: Fiction and the Architecture of Mind in Eighteenth-Century England* (Chicago: University of Chicago Press, 1987), 165–98.

15. See Michel Foucault, *Discipline and Punish: The Birth of the Prison,* trans. Alan Sheridan (New York: Vintage, 1979), and *The History of Sexuality,* vol. 1, trans. Robert Hurley (New York: Vintage, 1978).

muted, more Foucauldian types of power that Miller describes in the novel, such as the regulation of sexuality, have a place in this study, particularly in my discussion of Dostoevsky, but are not its central focus. Both Dostoevsky and Solzhenitsyn take upon themselves a larger than literary role; their works, I will argue, do not only mirror the forms of power specific to their respective historical worlds, but seek to exercise power and authority there. In general, the gap that I spoke of earlier between the real world and the imaginary literary realm is not at all wide, and in some instances hardly discernible in nineteenth- and twentieth-century Russia. We will explore the specifically Russian literary and political conditions in which writers claim authority not only as the authors of fictive realms, but as lawgivers in the realm of the real, and in which the government turns to the realm of the literary and the aesthetic in order to exercise its power.

The Drama of Power

The work of a diverse body of scholars, including Clifford Geertz, Boris Uspenskii, and Richard Wortman shows that political power constructs itself by displaying itself as something sacred. In ritual and ceremonial displays of power, the ruler as performer seeks to create his or her legitimacy. In sharp contrast to the alleged multivalence and unpredictability of carnival, the spectacle of power is unidirectional. In "Centers, Kings, and Charisma," Clifford Geertz argues that all the trappings of power—"stories, ceremonies, insignia, formalities . . . either inherited or invented" are means not only of identifying centers of power, but ways of making power.[16] Power constructs itself by displaying itself as something sacred. According to Geertz, rulers and politicians everywhere in all types of regimes define a religious aura around themselves. The ruler and the would-be ruler project a sense of the sacred, which Geertz calls a sense of "how the world is made," but for that particular culture and historical period. The concluding line of Geertz's essay is particularly important:

> It is not . . . standing outside the social order in some exalted state of self-regard that makes a political leader numinous but a deep,

16. Clifford Geertz, "Centers, Kings, and Charisma: Symbolics of Power," in *Local Knowledge: Further Essays in Interpretive Anthropology* (New York: Basic Books, 1983), 124.

intimate involvement—affirming or abhorring, defensive or destructive—in the master fictions by which that order lives.[17]

A brief discussion of the history of Russia's political theology helps to set the stage for the fate of these "master fictions," or, legal fictions, in the nineteenth and twentieth centuries. In *Tsar and People*, Michael Cherniavsky shows that the distinction between the "king's two bodies"—the king's natural body and the body politic—that obtained in medieval Western Europe did not hold in Russia in the equivalent time period.[18] The person of the tsar and the office of the tsar were conflated into one sacred body. No secular theology of the state appears in Russian history until the time of Peter the Great, and even then, the emphasis shifts from the image of the tsar as a Christ to the image of the tsar as God the father, creator, and ruler.[19] Cherniavsky finds a countermyth to the ruler as saintly prince or sovereign emperor in the myth of the Russian people as "Holy Russia," which he traces back to the seventeenth century. Lotman and Uspenskii similarly argue that until the eighteenth century the Russian tsar is described and evaluated in religious terms, as a Christ, before whom the individual subject is to give of himself or herself unconditionally.[20] The political space is not neutral, but charged with the elements of a religious drama.

This study examines the reappropriation of these myths of the ruler and the people in the nineteenth and twentieth centuries, that is, the persistence and reaccentuation of the religious model by the state and by the writer. The secularization of the state in Peter's time does not mean that the religious models of evaluation and legitimation disappear. They remain available, but in modified form. Other actors step forward to play the roles already created by the myths. For example, Lotman shows that by the mid-nineteenth century the tsar is no longer the symbolic recipient of the individual's self-giving. He is replaced by

17. Ibid., 146.

18. See Ernst H. Kantorowicz, *The King's Two Bodies: A Study in Medieval Political Theology* (Princeton, N.J.: Princeton University Press, 1957), 7–23.

19. See Michael Cherniavsky, *Tsar and People: Studies in Russian Myths* (New Haven, Conn.: Yale University Press, 1961), 93.

20. See Ju. M. Lotman, "'Agreement' and 'Self-Giving' as Archetypal Models of Culture," and B. A. Uspenskii, "Tsar and Pretender: *Samozvanchestvo* or Royal Imposture in Russia as a Cultural-Historical Phenomenon," in *The Semiotics of Russian Culture*, ed. Ann Shukman (Ann Arbor: University of Michigan Press, 1984), 125–40 and 255–92. See also V. M. Zhivov, "Istoriia russkogo prava kak lingvo-semioticheskaia problema," in *Semiotics and the History of Culture* (Columbus, Ohio: Slavica Publishers, 1988), 46–128.

a mythologized notion of "the people." In chapter 2, we see how this mythologized notion of the people enters into late-nineteenth-century discussions of the Russian jury, the voice of the people in the courtroom, finding its expression in a religious language.

The crucial element of the Russian monarchical scenario, according to Wortman, is the myth of foreignness. The ruler's superiority to and distance from the people enhanced his or her right to autocracy. How Russian writers represent their authority can be traced by looking at where they figure themselves along a scale of proximity to, or distance from, these two mythologized entities: the ruler and the people. As an aristocrat, Sukhovo-Kobylin constructs a drama around himself that emphasizes distance from the people. Dostoevsky constructs a drama that emphasizes closeness. But both are responding to the drama that the tsar creates around himself.

Inasmuch as royal power puts on a play of itself, the ruler being a substitute for God, the play can be performed poorly or well. The posture of power meets its adversarial double in imposture. The history of royal imposture in Russia begins in the late-sixteenth-century dynastic crisis set in motion by the death of Ivan the Terrible's son, Dmitrii, and culminates in the coronation of a series of False Dmitriis in the beginning of the seventeenth century. Episodes of royal imposture continue in the eighteenth century, Pugachev being the most well known example—and continue throughout the nineteenth. As a construct, the significance of imposture continues through the twentieth century; it is an important theme in the 1966 Siniavskii trial. I explore how the accusation of imposture functions as a term of public discourse, where it serves as a means of evaluating various forms of authority—political, literary, and moral.[21]

Bodies

Meaning in law is not enacted by words alone. In "Violence and the Word" (1986) Robert Cover writes: "Legal interpretation takes place in a field of pain and death."[22] He continues: "the interpretive commit-

---

21. For a study of royal imposture as a literary theme, see Caryl Emerson, *Boris Godunov: Transpositions of a Russian Theme* (Bloomington: Indiana University Press, 1986); and my *Holy Foolishness: Dostoevsky's Novels and the Poetics of Cultural Critique* (Stanford, Calif.: Stanford University Press, 1992), 99–123.

22. Robert Cover, "Violence and the Word," *Yale Law Journal* 95 (1986): 1601.

ments of legal officials are realized in the flesh" (1609). A concrete example of the interrelation of writing, law, and violence can be found in the Russian imperial practice of branding the word *thief* on the body of the convict. The state demonstrates its power by inflicting pain on its subjects. We will examine how Sukhovo-Kobylin, Dostoevsky, Solzhenitsyn, and Siniavskii variously respond to forms of corporal punishment, rewriting what the state writes on the body of the prisoner. The process of rewriting serves as part of the writer's own self-fashioning and may also serve as part of his effort to re-create a sense of order and authority for his audience. Order, authority, and law emerge out of the profound disorder of pain and violence. But powerful traces of pain and violence persist and, as we shall see, resurface repeatedly in the very process by which the author seeks to reinvent himself and reestablish his community.

I begin in the mid-nineteenth century with the elusive figure of Aleksandr Sukhovo-Kobylin, the playwright charged with the murder of his mistress. The dead body of Simone Demanche sets in motion Sukhovo-Kobylin's trajectory from aristocratic playboy to writer—a trajectory that ultimately fails. Kobylin's career spans a period in which Russian law and society undergo significant change. We will explore how the system of carefully maintained social distances can be seen as a form of theatricality, which breaks down during Kobylin's lifetime. How does the spectacle of power and its collapse shape his literary production?

The next chapter presents a cultural history of the jury trial in the first decade following the legal reform of 1864. Alexander II's manifesto, which begins by quoting the New Testament "Let justice and mercy reign in your courts"—introduced the jury trial in criminal and civil proceedings, gave the judiciary a greater degree of autonomy, and established the institution of the bar. I examine several aspects of the working of the reform, focusing on the jury and the professionalized bar in particular. In the decades following the reform, the Russian jury became known for its high rate of acquittals. I am interested in some of the ramifications of this perception. How does the jury's "mercy" figure in an emerging national and religious narrative about the Russian people? To what extent does the jury represent a new form of authority in Russian culture? I suggest that the jury represents a transition away from the authority of the father-tsar.

In chapter 3 readers will be introduced to two unfamiliar Russian authors of the late nineteenth century: A. S. Suvorin and N. D. Akhsharumov. In 1866 Suvorin published several installments of his novel *It Takes All Kinds*, which was sympathetic to the political activism of the time. The novel offered readers attractive portraits of young radicals and emancipated women. In the same year, charged with libeling the nobility and shaking society's faith in the government, Suvorin was the defendant in one of Russia's first open literary trials. That year also saw the publication of Akhsharumov's fantastical story about a literary author brought to court by his heroine, who seeks compensation for the fate she suffers in his story—a story of forced emancipation from her traditional marriage. In both fictions, the heavily politicized aesthetic of Russian realism play a crucial role. In reading the two trials, one fictitious and the other real, I trace the law's attitude toward the problem of authorial responsibility. What overlap, if any, can be seen in the law's model of the author and that created by the new aesthetic of realism?

Chapter 4 turns to Dostoevsky. In *A Writer's Diary* Dostoevsky discusses a series of legal cases from 1876, all of which focus on the family, marital and extramarital relations, women, and children. The chapter shows how in the *Diary* Dostoevsky positions himself as a moral legislator, first by constructing a personal narrative of legitimation by suffering, and second, by exerting his authority, sometimes personally, and sometimes symbolically. In reading Dostoevsky's commentaries on these cases, which include child abuse and attempted murder, I ask how he uses his literary skills to move from violence to order. I am interested in an aspect of Dostoevsky's literary art that will perhaps seem surprising to readers accustomed to the dialogism and open-endedness of a Dostoevsky novel. I emphasize instead Dostoevsky's skill in creating a sense of closure, in telling a story that imposes a suspiciously meaningful pattern on meaningless pain.

In chapters 1 through 4 a clear set of configurations of law, narrative, and authority emerge. The figures of the ruler, impostor, father, and son serve as tropes for both political and literary authority. In studying literary texts and legal conflicts of late-nineteenth-century Russia, we encounter the emergent nationalism, political radicalism, and the new scientific ideas about criminality and sexuality of this time. The issues with which the legal and literary cases engage are on the whole consistent. But in turning to Solzhenitsyn and the twentieth century in chapter 5, readers will experience a sense of discontinuity.

The revolution of 1917 destroyed the institutions and the legal culture created by the 1864 reform. As the Russian philosopher Grigorii Pomerants wrote in 1996, "in Russia no one remembers prerevolutionary Russian law." In September 1992 I had a conversation with two members of the Supreme Soviet working on legal reform, in particular, a project to reintroduce trial by jury.[23] I asked what public opinion was about trial by jury and was told that no one knew what it was. I also naively asked whether nineteenth-century debates about the jury's suitability for Russia could prove useful in similar debates in the twentieth century. I received the rather heated answer that seventy years of totalitarianism had completely obliterated consciousness of the legal forms of the past. Particularly culpable in this forced forgetfulness were the ideas of revolutionary justice promulgated in the 1920s and 1930s, during which one could denounce one's own parent as a "class enemy."

The discussion that in chapters 1 through 4 presents a fairly consistent set of themes thus necessarily breaks down when we approach twentieth-century Soviet Russia. Yet the themes and figures on which the analysis turns—the letter and spirit, the father-ruler and the impostor, the significance of the carnival body—reappear in modified form in chapters 5 and 6. The discussion of the spectacle of power in mid-nineteenth-century Russia in chapter 1 introduces readers to a similar discussion in the last two chapters. The spectacle of power is just as important in Stalin's time as it is in imperial Russia. The Stalinist show trial is only one example. The gruesome language of punishment, with its relentless emphasis on the suffering of the body, remains, if not constant, then consistent throughout the entire period discussed in this study. Finally, Siniavskii's 1966 trial, which I discuss in chapter 6, is illegible without at least some familiarity with Russian cultural forms that develop in the nineteenth century and earlier, particularly royal imposture. It is part of my purpose to show that the study of Russian law and literature in the nineteenth century provides a rich context for its study in the twentieth—if we pay attention both to the historical ruptures that take place and to the reemergence and reaccentuation of previous themes.

Chapter 5 traces the development of Dostoevsky's use of the paradigm of legitimation by suffering in Solzhenitsyn's *Gulag Archipelago*. Solzhenitsyn can speak for the Russia that has lost its tongue because he himself was there in the camps and suffered. In analyzing the *Gulag*,

---

23. Margarita Petrosian and Inga Mikhailova, both members of Komissia po pravam cheloveka pri Verkhovnom Sovete Rossiskii Federatsii, Moscow, 1992.

my point of departure has been my own experience of reading the work. It is a massive book, in many ways excruciating to read. I was led to question how this experience might be part of the book's purpose. I examine how the trope of wounding functions as part of the process whereby Solzhenitsyn constructs himself and his reading audience. The overwhelming scale of the book also functions as part of this process. Its scale is a crucial part of its aesthetics and its rhetorical force. Here the work has much in common with the massive architectural works created in the Stalin era. Solzhenitsyn's work reveals how far an author may be constituted by the very authorities he seeks to resist.

The sixth and final chapter is devoted to the trial of Andrei Siniavskii, charged with libeling the Soviet government. I offer a reading of Andrei Siniavskii's trial in light of the works he published abroad under the pseudonym of Abram Terts, which led to his trial and incarceration. His writing seeks to free the literary work from the strictures of the law, cultural norms, and artistic rules. At Siniavskii's trial the Soviet state, the master of play with surface, pretends to a role of virtue seduced and betrayed and by the impostor Terts. The state calls upon a series of already existing cultural narratives from the nineteenth century in order to indict Siniavskii as Terts. Siniavskii's performance at his trial, and the questions he raises in his literary works, present a brilliant series of reflections on the relations between writing, subjectivity, law, and the body.

Siniavskii's model of literary language challenges the concept of individual intentionality crucial to legal judgment. At the same time, he insists on an impenetrable barrier separating his own literary authority from the law's jurisdiction. In examining Siniavskii's argument for complete literary autonomy, we return to the fundamental question about the interpenetration of legal and literary authority. Siniavskii's defense of his own writing at his trial points to a problem that has implications beyond the confines of Soviet law. In order to flesh out those implications, I shift the discussion in two different directions, first, by considering some aspects of the history of American libel law. What does American libel law tell us about the law's understanding of literary authorship? Does American libel law grant literature an exemption from its rule? Second, Siniavskii makes claims about the uniqueness of literary language and its destabilizing effect on meaning. Over the past twenty years, literary criticism, particularly the work of Derrida, has made similar claims, but in far broader terms, about the operation of all language, leading to the conclusion that no text may be said to have a single determinate meaning. At the end of the chapter, I explore how law may respond to these qualities of language.

All the writers in this study, regardless of the quality of their individual voices—serious or playful, authoritative or subversive—are engaged in the problem of authority. The scene of their conflict with the law powerfully shapes the authority they present to the world in their writing. The stories they tell, or, to put it from the law's perspective, their "crimes," do not fall easily into the neat opposition between resistance or accommodation but more often reveal the more unsettling pattern of mimesis, or, imitation, of the law. This pattern emerges with particular clarity in the case of our first author, the playwright Sukhovo-Kobylin. The pattern of imitation has disturbing implications for what may be taken as the fundamental proposition of the law and literature movement, namely, the mutual constitution of authority in law and literature. I will explore these consequences in the conclusion.

Chapter 1

The Theater of Sukhovo-Kobylin

V sudakh cherna nepravdoi chernoi
I igom rabstva kleimena;
Bezbozhnoi lesti, lzhi tletvornoi,
I leni mertvoi i pozornoi,
I vsiakoi merzosti polna!

In the courts you are black with black injustice
And branded with the yoke of slavery;
Full of shameless flattery, foul lies,
Laziness deathly and disgraceful,
Replete with every vileness!
—A. Khomiakov, "Russia," 1854

On November 9, 1850, in the Presnenskii district of Moscow, the police officer Il'inskii reported to his chief, the *ober-politsmeister* of Moscow, that "outside the Presnenskii gate on Khodynskoe field the dead body of a woman of unknown identity had been found."[1] The police report made on the basis of an inspection of the corpse at the place of its discovery included the following points.[2] The woman was about thirty-five years old. The body was found face down, with the arms bent under it. When the body was turned over, "it appeared that the woman had her throat cut." Her braid was undone, and her hair was twisted around her throat near the wound. The body was frozen. The woman was clothed in a dress of green checked material, under which were a white calico skirt; another skirt, quilted, covered in "drap-de-dames" of

1. "List dela 2," quoted in Viktor Grossman, *Delo Sukhovo-Kobylina* (Moscow: Gosudarstvennoe izdatel'stvo khudozhestvennaia literatura, 1936), 7.
2. I have combined here excerpts from the police report as quoted by Grossman, *Delo Sukhovo-Kobylina,* in the body of his text and in the appendix, N. V. Popov, "Sudebno-meditsinskaia ekspertiza po delu A. V. Sukhovo-Kobylina," 295–331.

a dark color; and a third skirt of cotton. Her drawers, of white calico, were down around her shins. On her legs were white silk stockings and warm black velvet half boots. She had a blue satin hat and wore a tortoiseshell comb missing one tooth. There was no cross on her neck. Gold earrings with jewels adorned her ears. On the middle finger of her left hand were two gold rings, one "sprinkled with roses," both with jewels; on the middle finger of her right hand she wore a gold ring. In her pocket was a set of keys. The cursory medical examination, also made on the spot, showed that the woman had been of a "fairly strong constitution." The cut to the throat was below the larynx and was about five inches long. The arteries were completely cut. There was a small quantity of blood on the snow just under the throat. On the upper part of the neck there was a scar approximately the size of a little finger. The left eye was swollen shut, surrounded by a bruise the size of a hand. The left side of the body was of a dark red color, with multiple spots of various sizes. The left arm was bruised from the shoulder to the elbow. Bruises were also found on the waist. An autopsy performed on the eleventh of November showed that four ribs were broken. The medical examiner concluded that the cause of death was the wound to the throat, and that the death did not occur where the body was found.

The next day the body was identified as that of Elizabeth Louisa Simon-Demanche, the mistress of the future playwright, Aleksandr Vasil'evich Sukhovo-Kobylin, a wealthy and brilliant aristocrat, who at the time held the rank of retired titular counselor.

The Case

Over the next seven years Sukhovo-Kobylin and the house serfs in his employ who served Simon-Demanche were prosecuted for the murder. The house serfs were the cook, Efim Egorov; the coachman, Galaktion Koz'min; and two maids, Pelageia Alekseeva and Agrafena Kashkina. At their first interrogation, the servants denied all knowledge of their mistress's death. On November 17, 1850, Kobylin himself and his orderly were arrested. Traces of blood found in his apartment, a suspicious love letter, and the fact that Kobylin himself had reported Demanche's disappearance all played a role in the arrest. The military governor general of Moscow, Count A. A. Zakrevskii, whose house was very near Simon-Demanche's apartment, ordered on November 18 that the "very strictest measures" be used to uncover the guilty party.[3] On November 19, the investigating commission, noting "something troubling the conscience" of the cook Egorov, ordered that he be subjected to "the strictest isolation in a secret room."[4] The next day Egorov confessed to the murder of Simon-Demanche, giving as the reason revenge for the way she treated the servants. He testified that he entered her bedroom while she was sleeping and suffocated and strangled her, while Koz'min beat her with an iron. After Demanche was dead, Egorov and Koz'min ordered the two maids to dress her. The two men took her body to a ravine just outside the city, but it seemed to Egorov that the murdered woman made a sound in her throat, and, "fearing that she would come back to life," he slit her throat.[5] The other serfs made similar confessions, and Kobylin was subsequently released on November 21. In September 1851 the Moscow Aulic Court (*nadvornyi sud*) acquitted Kobylin but sentenced his serfs to public flogging, branding, and hard labor. Because the court was not in complete agreement, the sentence was not carried out and the case was transferred to the next highest judicial level, the Moscow Criminal Chamber (*ugolovnaia palata*), which did not significantly modify the findings of the previous court. In 1852, the case was heard in the Senate, which had received statements from the cook Egorov and the coachman Koz'min recanting their confessions. Koz'min said that he had been tempted into confessing by a promise of money, "eternal freedom" for himself, and a release from service for his entire family, and that in addition, he was told that "soon there would be a general manifesto," presumably giving all serfs their freedom. Egorov stated that he had been tortured. His arms were tied behind his back in such a way that his elbows touched; he was hung from a hook in the wall in this position, struck in the face, and given salted herring to eat and nothing to drink.[6]

The senators could not come to agreement about the case, and it was referred to the Ministry of Justice. The minister of justice, Count Panin, decided to reopen the investigation. The State Council concurred with his decision. As a result, in 1854, Sukhovo-Kobylin spent

---

3. Grossman, *Delo Sukhovo-Kobylina*, 159.
4. Leonid Grossman, *Prestuplenie Sukhovo-Kobylina* (Leningrad: Izdatel'stvo Priboi, 1928), 81.
5. Ibid., 83.
6. Grossman, *Delo Sukhovo-Kobylina*, 167–77.

nearly six months in prison, where he worked on *Krechinskii's Wedding*, the first play of what would become his trilogy. The play was performed for the first time in November 1855. Its debut coincided with the senate's decision to leave Sukhovo-Kobylin "under suspicion."

In the spring of 1856, Sukhovo-Kobylin's mother had a note sent to the empress, asking for her help. In the same year Count Panin personally informed Sukhovo-Kobylin and his mother that he had received an order from the empress to terminate the case. Sukhovo-Kobylin began writing *The Case*, his second play, which he did not complete until 1861. In May 1857, the State Council acquitted the house serfs and sentenced Kobylin to undergo a church penance for conducting a love affair. Kobylin began writing *The Death of Tarelkin*, the final play of his trilogy, and finished it in 1869. The conditions of censorship did not permit *The Case* to be performed until 1881. *The Death of Tarelkin* met with a similar fate. It did not premiere until 1900, three years before the author's death.

A study of Sukhovo-Kobylin's case, in the strictly legal sense of the word, reveals the workings of Russian imperial law in the prereform period. The proceedings I have just described were secret and written. Testimony was not given orally to the judge by the witnesses or the accused, but written down by secretaries who then presented it to judges, who evaluated it by means of formal rules, which were meant to limit the judge's arbitrary power. Evidence was given under oath before two witnesses. Evidence given by a man was superior to that given by a woman; and that given by a learned man was better than that given by an unschooled witness. Evidence given by those who had not been to confession, by criminals and "fornicators," was not acceptable.[7] The best evidence of all, according to Peter the Great, was a personal confession—a line that Sukhovo-Kobylin was to use in *The Death of Tarelkin*. Investigation and trial merged into one long process, fueled, in many cases, Sukhovo-Kobylin's among them, by bribes. *The Case* contains a bitterly satirical treatise on the three different kinds of bribes: the "pastoral, Arcadian bribe," taken in agricultural products, the "industrial bribe," taken out of the victim's inheritance, and finally, the "criminal, or pitfall bribe," which completely exhausts the victim's resources and "strips him naked."[8]

---

7. M. F. Vladimirskii-Budanov, *Obzor istorii russkogo prava*, 6th ed. (St. Petersburg, 1909), 665.

8. A. V. Sukhovo-Kobylin, *Trilogiia* (Moscow: Iskusstvo, 1986), 154–55. Henceforward all citations will be given parenthetically in the body of the text.

Near the end of his life, Sukhovo-Kobylin said, "*The Case* is my revenge."[9] *The Case* is a response not so much to the murder as to the seven-year legal case, as if the real crime were not the murder but the legal proceedings that it occasioned. Even though Sukhovo-Kobylin's critics, in both the nineteenth and twentieth centuries, disagree as to his involvement in the murder of Simon-Demanche, they agree that his play reveals the horrors of Russian legal procedure before the reform.[10] That there is no rule of law, or even a professed ideology of the rule of law, in Russia in 1850 goes without saying. There is no equality before the law, no access to one's accuser, no right to a defense, no principle of innocent until proven guilty. In 1855, as we have seen, Sukhovo-Kobylin is neither innocent nor fully guilty, but "left under suspicion." The judiciary institutions are subordinated to the tsar's autocratic power. Count Panin was ordered to terminate the case against Sukhovo-Kobylin. The police and the courts are one institution. Instead of "procedural norms," which allow for flexibility and predictability in the exercise of the law, there is a forest of specific and particular regulations.[11] The poet Gavriil Derzhavin, who wrote in the late eighteenth and early nineteenth centuries and served as minister of justice under Alexander I, said that "a court is nothing but the act of the criminal compared with the laws, and the decision . . . by written order, as to what is to be done with the criminal."[12] Derzhavin is well known for his poem of 1790, "To Rulers and Judges," a reworking of Psalm 82. In the poem Derzhavin uses the biblical text to criticize the harshness and corruption of Russian law. Law is to be grounded in a larger narrative of justice. But in his description of the court, made many years later, he abandons the link between nomos and narrative. In the prereform inquisitorial court there is no contest about what happened, no evaluation of the individual circumstances of the case, no interpretation and no *story*, but a grid of matching crimes and punishments: "the act of the criminal compared with the laws."

---

9. Iu. Belaiev, Mel'pomena, quoted in Leonid Grossman, *Teatr Sukhovo-Kobylina* (Moscow: Izdanie V. T. O., 1940), 27.

10. For example, Leonid Grossman, *Prestuplenie Sukhovo-Kobylina*, argues for Sukhovo-Kobylin's guilt; Viktor Grossman, *Delo Sukhovo-Kobylina*, relying on a medical reassessment of the nineteenth-century case documents, argues for his innocence. Maia Bessarab, *Sukhovo-Kobylin* (Moscow: Sovremennik, 1981), agrees with Viktor Grossman, arguing that Demanche's servants killed her on their own initiative (115–30, 184–85).

11. For the concept of "procedural norms," see Richard Wortman, *The Development of a Russian Legal Consciousness* (Chicago: University of Chicago Press, 1976), 245.

12. Quoted by Wortman, *Russian Legal Consciousness*, 106.

The formal rules governing the status of evidence generated scenarios of justice that had little to do with reality.[13] The best example of this can be seen in the minister of justice himself, Count Panin, who was notorious for his adherence to the letter of the law. One of his biographers described him as having no worldview of his own. Panin memorized whole volumes of legal codes. He was a gifted speaker but seemed to have no internal connection to what he was saying. Count Panin believed that he was not empowered to undo any decision he had made, especially if it were in writing. This resulted in absurd consequences for his subordinates: the wrong man had to go on leave, for example, because the count had already signed a document containing his name.[14]

Kastor Nikiforovich Lebedev served as chief procurator in the Sixth Department of the Senate during the time Kobylin's case was heard there. He was the object of parody in Kobylin's plays. Lebedev's memoirs shed further light on the operation of the law. Lebedev remarks that he quickly learned the forms and "conventional expressions" but could not readily master the suspension of the personal so necessary for legal work: "I would lose my way and, thinking of a case as a person, a state matter as a private one, allowed myself to imagine a person, with feelings, a heart able to become angry and participate in a case."[15] Lebedev, looking for the emotions and the stories behind the law, found instead the law's conventionality.

This overview of prereform Russian law provides the groundwork for understanding Sukhovo-Kobylin's literary "revenge." But the legal case does not simply lead to the literary *Case*. In order to see how Kobylin's entanglement with the law figures in his self-fashioning as a writer, we must look beyond the details of the literary and legal "cases" to the larger cultural forces that shape both. I will argue for a thematic unity shared by Kobylin's literary work, the case, the murder, and the love affair in the context of the Russian aristocracy and autocracy under the rule of Nicholas I. It is true that the writing of the plays and the effort to get them produced extends into the late 1850s and beyond,

---

13. See for example, M. Maikov, *Vtoroe otdelenie ego imperatorskogo velichestva kantseliarii 1826–1882* (St. Petersburg, 1906), 1:340.

14. See Nikolai Semenov, "Graf Viktor Nikitich Panin," *Russkii arkhiv* 12 (1887): 538–66.

15. Cited by Wortman, *Russian Legal Consciousness*, 202. It is from Wortman's study that I became aware of Lebedev's memoirs.

when Alexander II had already ascended the throne and when new attitudes and models of behavior, authorship, and authority were emerging. *The Case* and *The Death of Tarelkin* were not performed until the end of the nineteenth century, when Russian legal and social institutions had undergone significant change. Count Panin, who terminates the case against the author, oversees the legislation that will emancipate the serfs. But, as we will see, there is a certain archaism about Sukhovo-Kobylin.

Theatricality and Power

The dominant metaphor shaping the cultural and the literary texts, that is, Sukhovo-Kobylin's plays, comes from the theater itself. Theatricality is a broad term and is used by nineteenth-century observers and present-day historians to describe Russian public life both before and after the reform in 1864. Richard Wortman writes about the "ongoing theater of power" in the Russian imperial court, and Laura Engelstein analyzes Russian political life in theatrical terms in her essay "Revolution and the Theater of Public Life in Imperial Russia."[16] Engelstein shows that the revolutionaries of the 1860s and 1870s took full advantage of the public stage that the jury trial afforded them. As we will see in chapter 2, nineteenth-century Russian writers complain about the excessive theatricality of the jury courts.

In what sense then is prereform law specifically theatrical? Criminal proceedings were conducted in secret, without the public, and therefore without the possibility of theatricality given by the public jury trial, with its oral contest between the prosecution and the defense.[17] Nonetheless, the execution of punishments and the operation of the law in general in the prereform period are theatrical in the sense that they are spectacular; that is, the exercise of the law is a demonstration

---

16. See Laura Engelstein, "Revolution and the Theater of Public Life in Imperial Russia," in *Revolution and the Meanings of Freedom in the Nineteenth Century,* ed. Isser Wolloch (Stanford, Calif.: Stanford University Press, 1996). I thank Laura Engelstein for sharing her manuscript with me before publication.

17. Lotman writes about "the Decembrists' total inability to cope with their interrogation and trial; in this tragic situation of behavior they had no witnesses to whom they could address heroic acts, counting on their understanding, and there were no literary models, since death without monologues, in the vacuum of military-bureaucratic life, had not yet become a topic for the art of that time." See Ju. M. Lotman, "The Decembrist in Everyday Life: Everyday Behavior as a Historical-Psychological Category," *Semiotics of Russian Culture,* 96.

of the tsar's own personal power.[18] These demonstrations are spectacular whether they take place in the privacy of "the secret room," to use the language of the Demanche case, where the audience and the spectacle are one and the same, combined in the person of the torture victim, or whether they take place in public, before an audience of many.[19] In the mid-eighteenth century, Empress Elizabeth replaced the death penalty with beating with the knout and branding. These punishments were also executed publicly. The suspension of capital punishment was only temporary, and the beatings that replaced it often resulted in the death of the prisoner.[20] The death penalty was reinstated in the latter part of the eighteenth century and carried out in public until 1881.

The same argument that Foucault has made for European law in the classical age applies to Russia in the middle of the nineteenth century.[21] Law retains features of the archaic trial by combat. In the highly ritualized contest between ruler and criminal, the ruler must always win. The procedures and mechanisms for the production of the truth are part and parcel of the demonstration of the tsar's power. The closed inquisitorial proceeding, the secrecy, the use of torture in order to obtain a confession, the public and physical punishment of a criminal— all of these are theatrical devices that display the superior power of the tsar over his subjects. The ability to punish is part of the theater of power.

One of the most vivid examples of law's theatricality in this period is the mock execution of the Petrashevskii circle on December 22, 1849, in Semenovskii Square in St. Petersburg. Nicholas ordered that the sentence of death be read aloud to the prisoners and the assembled public (which one account numbers at three thousand people), and that upon the completion of all the ceremonies usually performed before execu-

18. For a study of public punishments critical of the use of theatrical metaphors, see Steven Wilf, "Imagining Justice: Aesthetics and Public Executions in Late Eighteenth-Century England," *Yale Journal of Law and the Humanities* 5 (1993): 51–78. Wilf's attention to aesthetic theory in relation to theory of punishment is important. According to Wilf, Burke's argument that obscurity is a crucial part of the effect of terror contributed to a shift in the way public punishments were carried out. I discuss aesthetic theory and punishment in the Soviet era in chapter 5.

19. I take this analysis of torture from Elaine Scarry, *The Body in Pain: The Making and Unmaking of the World* (New York: Oxford University Press, 1985), 28. For a more detailed discussion of torture, see chapter 5 of the present study.

20. See N. S. Taganstev, *Russkoe ugolovnoe pravo*, vol. 2 (St. Petersburg, 1902), 967–81.

21. See Foucault, *Discipline and Punish*, 32–69.

tion the tsar's mercy be declared: "the Emperor gives them life."[22] Nicholas demonstrates his godlike power not only to end life, but to restore it. The mimesis of capital punishment was itself a terrible form of punishment. It led to the insanity of one of the prisoners. Dostoevsky would write about it for years to come.[23] The practice of theatricalized mock-execution did not end with the death of Nicholas in 1855, but continued into the reign of Alexander II, as we shall see in a later chapter.

The Spectacle of Power at Home

The spectacle of power at court was imitated by the spectacle of power at the noble estate. The noble estate was the site not only of grand theatricals, but in general, according to historian Priscilla Roosevelt, was characterized by a theatricalized pattern of life, which "encompassed serf performances, elaborate displays of hospitality, theatricality in the material culture of the estate, and the theatricalization or ritualization of private life."[24] Domestic amateur theater had been a part of Sukhovo-Kobylin's childhood, as it was for many others of his class. On holidays, matinees were staged in the Kobylin home. The most popular of these were domestic "vaudevilles."[25] Scenes from plays were performed or read, often by the author's mother, Mariia Ivanovna. Sukhovo-Kobylin's grandfather, Ivan Dmitrievich Shepelev, ran a magnificent serf theater at the family's estate at Vyksa (the site of the family's iron foundry). Shepelev's theater rivaled the Marinsky Theater in St. Petersburg in size.[26] Comedies, dramas, operas, and ballets were performed; the ballet master was the famous Petr Andreevich Iogel', mentioned by Tolstoy in *War and Peace*. The settings and the costumes were luxurious and abundant: Shepelev himself directed the performances and rehearsed his actors daily. He saw to every detail, super-

---

22. For more on the execution, see *Politicheskie protsessy Nikolaevskoi epokhi: Petra-shevtsy* (Moscow, 1907), 4.

23. For a detailed description of the episode and Dostoevsky's role, see Joseph Frank, *Dostoevsky: The Years of Ordeal, 1850–1859* (Princeton, N.J.: Princeton University Press, 1983), 49–66.

24. Priscilla Roosevelt, *Life on the Russian Country Estate: A Social and Cultural History* (New Haven, Conn.: Yale University Press, 1995), 130.

25. Bessarab, *Sukhovo-Kobylin*, 11.

26. See Roosevelt, *Russian Country Estate*, 138.

vising how the actors should "make faces" *(grimasnichat')* and what wigs should be worn.[27] The grandfather's concern for the composition of the actors' faces is shared by the grandson, as we will see. In the serf theater, a striking example of the serf owner's power manifests itself. The serf is compelled to put on a costume, move his or her body in a particular fashion, declaim certain lines, and "make faces"—all according to the master's wish. Errors in performance were corrected by the administration of corporal punishment. The pleasure of the spectacle is enhanced by, or perhaps corresponds to, the power that is exercised in its performance.[28] The serf theater, together with imitations of court ritual and military routine, are part of the nobleman's mimesis of the tsar's theater of power.[29]

Theatricality, Pleasure, and Distance

Wortman stresses the importance of the creation and maintenance of social distance in the Russian autocracy and aristocracy. The cultivation of foreignness is one example. Social distance is also a crucial aspect of the forms of pleasure favored by Kobylin and his milieu. Jean Starobinski's *The Invention of Liberty*, a study of eighteenth-century aristocratic culture in France, provides insights about social distance that also apply to Kobylin. The aristocratic "staging" of life, as Starobinski puts it, creates pleasure. Even those pleasures in which individuals gathered together nonetheless maintained the principle of separation. Starobinski writes that "each participant, intent on his own pleasure, isolated himself yet again . . . and the revelry around him was simply a living picture of the pleasures he could himself lay claim to."[30]

The masquerade ball was one of the preeminent forms of aristocratic pleasure in nineteenth century Russia. As Lotman shows, mas-

27. E. M. Feoktistov, "Glava iz vospominanii," in *Atenei* 3, ed. B. L. Modzalevskii and Iu. G. Oksman (Leningrad, 1926), 103 and 107.

28. Lotman argues for a connection between the parade and the ballet. The parade, favored by Alexander I, is, according to Lotman, "a grandiose performance that every single day reaffirmed the principle of autocracy." He goes on to say that both "the parade aesthetic and the ballet aesthetic had a deep common root—the serf-owning structure of Russian life." Ju. M. Lotman, "The Theater and Theatricality as Components of Early Nineteenth Century Culture," trans. G. S. Smith, in *Semiotics of Russian Culture*, 155.

29. Roosevelt gives examples in *Russian Country Estate*, 146–47.

30. Jean Starobinski, *The Invention of Liberty: 1700–1789* (New York: Rizzoli, 1987), 87. I am grateful to Bruce Rosenstock for bringing this work to my attention.

querades were extremely popular in Russia among the nobility from the time of Catherine. Catherine herself proposed a ball at the Hermitage in which the men would dress as women, and the women as men.[31] In his memoirs for 1849, Senator Lebedev writes that among the episodes that attracted the attention of Moscow society were the "pranks of the social lionesses Princess Iusupova, Urusova, and Countess Orlova-Denisova. Having gotten bored at a masquerade, they wanted to have supper at Deusseau's; here the noise attracted the police."[32]

In *Masquerade and Civilization* Terry Castle writes that the "goal" of the masquerade was "liberty from every social, erotic, and psychological constraint."[33] The author draws attention to the significance of masquerade costume, which not only provides anonymity and hence a sense of freedom, but also "bespoke the possibility of astonishing transfigurations" (55). Because the masquerade costume suspends the normal sartorial code—by which identity is made legible—and in so doing suspends the distinctions between persons that normally prevail, it "makes magically available the body of the other" (76). Several aspects of Castle's argument can be seen in Lermontov's *Masquerade*, published in 1842, and, in all likelihood, known by Sukhovo-Kobylin.[34] The gambler Arbenin says:

> Under the mask all ranks are equal,
> A mask has neither soul, nor name, but a body
> And if the features are masked
> Then the feelings are boldly unmasked.[35]

Because of the disguise, the body and its feelings and sensations are more, and not less, pronounced. The body in question is a female body, the masquerade being a site of female promiscuity. Arbenin, pointing to a woman in Turkish fancy dress, says:

---

31. Lotman, "Agreement and Self-Giving," 140 n. 24.

32. Lebedev, "Iz Zapisok Senatora K. N. Lebedeva 1849-i god," *Russkii arkhiv* 7 (1910): 353–54.

33. Terry Castle, *Masquerade and Civilization: The Carnivalesque in Eighteenth Century English Culture and Fiction* (Stanford, Calif.: Stanford University Press, 1986), 53.

34. See Grossman, *Teatr Sukhovo-Kobylina*, 13.

35. M. Iu. Lermontov, *Izbrannye proizvedeniia v dvukh tomakh* (Moscow: Gosudarstvennoe izdatel'stvo khudozhestvennoi literatury, 1963), 2:84.

Do you know who she is?
Perhaps a proud countess or a princess,
Diana in society . . . Venus at the masquerade,
And perhaps this very same beauty
Will come to you tomorrow for half an hour.

(86–87)

The pair Diana/Venus signals the opposition between chastity and erotic license. A woman of high rank, normally unavailable, makes herself sexually available at the masquerade. However, her temporary freedom from constraint does not signal any real social power. "Woman on top" is part of the pleasurable illusion of the masquerade.

The freedom and transformation of the masquerade ball are ephemeral, strictly limited in time and place. Furthermore, the freedom from social constraint pertains only to those who can gain entry to the ball, that is, the aristocracy. The urban non-noble classes had their own form of dress-up entertainment, which took place in booths and tents on the street.[36] Senator Lebedev points out that a former police chief of Moscow, Bering, issued memoranda against the *balaganshchiki* (street buffoons) who disguised themselves as animals and other figures (365). Civil and church authorities had always prosecuted these and other forms of popular entertainment.

A fascination with the transformation of identity can also be seen in Kobylin's interest in French theater of a specific type. While traveling abroad, he was drawn to light comedy, vaudeville, and the actors Bouffe and Pierre Levassor.[37] The special virtuosity of these two actors was their ability to transform themselves into several different characters in the course of a single performance. In the last play of his trilogy, Kobylin's hero Tarelkin transforms himself into another character, named Kopylov. Tarelkin announces that he will die "in violation of the law and of nature" (273). In order to carry out the change, Tarelkin removes his wig and false teeth, declaring "Long live nature!" But nature is assumed here as a disguise. The distinction between nature and artifice is confused. In notes to the play, Sukhovo-Kobylin emphasizes that the transformation takes place on the stage, that is, before the public:

36. For more on popular entertainment in Russia, see Malcom Burgess, "Fairs and Entertainers in Eighteenth-Century Russia," *Slavonic Review* 38 (1959): 95–113.
37. See Grossman, *Teatr Sukhovo-Kobylina*, 62–67.

The transformation must be accomplished quickly, suddenly and accompanied by a change in the expression of the face and its features. This is a matter of mimicry and a task for an artist. Here, for example, one can point to the French comic actor Levassor. . . . He developed the play of his facial muscles to such a degree of mobility that he could change the form of his nose as he wished and, with the help of a wig, beard, and mustache, almost instantaneously assumed the form of the most varied characters. (349)

What impresses Sukhovo-Kobylin is not the subtlety or profundity of the actor's emotional register, but his ability to assume a variety of identities by means of the manipulation of the physiognomy, as if the actor's own features and habitual expression belonged to a mask that could be removed at will—his own or someone else's. Kobylin's stage instructions reveal his fascination with the plasticity of the actor's face and his own desire to sculpt it according to his will.

Lotman gives an example of an amateur social gathering in elite society at which "certain people acted themselves; A. A. Bashilov played Bashilov, B. K. Danzas played Danzas."[38] Lotman comments that in the theater, people and things are transformed into signs; the special pleasure of this performance was that the individual transformed himself into a sign of himself. The episode is also significant for understanding the relation between the everyday life of the nobility and the official world of the government. Boris Karlovich Danzas, a landless nobleman, worked in the Ministry of Justice for sixteen years before becoming a senator in 1851.[39] The kind of person who will be Sukhovo-Kobylin's adversary in the Demanche case is one whose tastes and pleasures he himself shares.

It was important for the aristocrat to show the ease and pleasure with which he could manipulate and transform the surfaces of his life—his own personal appearance and that of those around him, the furniture and paintings in his estates—and just as easily manipulate his outward behavior, cultivating the appearance of passion and boredom in his love affairs. Sukhovo-Kobylin wrote to a friend that he had "tasted all the pleasures," and on another occasions wrote that he "felt nothing."

However, the aristocrat's freedom to fashion himself and his sur-

---

38. Cited by Lotman, "The Theater and Theatricality," 162 n. 22.
39. See Wortman, *Russian Legal Consciousness*, 60, 188–89.

roundings according to his own taste is illusory. His capacity to do so depends on the serf laborer below him and the tsar above, dispensing favor and wealth. As Wortman shows, the Russian nobility was more dependent on the ruler than their counterparts in Europe. The play with appearance depends on a rigidly controlled social structure. Lotman argues that life under Nicholas I was "realized as a hierarchy of social norms: the Europeanized, post-Petrine state system of the bureaucratic type, the semiotics of rank and official gradations, the rules of behavior, determining one's activity as a nobleman, a merchant, a government bureaucrat or an officer."[40] Although they were introduced well before Nicholas I, the so-called formal rules of evidence discussed earlier that rank evidence according to the status of the person giving it are another manifestation of the "rule of roles." Russian society in the first half of the nineteenth century is characterized by a highly stratified social order in which set codes of behavior for each layer of society are carefully maintained and in which mobility is extremely limited. In the second play of the trilogy, *The Case*, Kobylin ironically reduces the social hierarchy to its essential components: those who have power and those who do not. The fourteen classes created by Peter the Great are replaced in the dramatis personae by a mere five: "Superiors, Forces, Subordinates, Nonentities, or private persons, and A non-person," that is, Tishka, the house servant. The Superiors include "A Very Important Person," about whom "the author remains silent" and "An Important Person, by birth a prince, a pleasant person at the club, a beast at work." Notably absent from the play is the figure at the apex, the tsar. In mid-nineteenth-century Russia, the structure was beginning to show its cracks.

Starobinski describes the cultivation of the aristocratic façade as an effort to suspend the reality of the larger social forces that lay beyond it:

> Here the theatrical role of the façade takes on its full significance. Facing the outside world, on the side opposite the prompter, the façade marks the limit of a privileged universe, with an elegant display of signs imposing *an illusion of authority*. Within, on the prompt-side, or behind closed doors, there are for those who live in this domain the mirrors and wainscotting which establish, conversely, *the authority of illusion*.[41]

---

40. Ju. M. Lotman, "Gogol's Chlestakov: The Pragmatics of a Literary Character," trans. Ruth Sobel, in *The Semiotics of Russian Culture*, 178.

41. Starobinski, *The Invention of Liberty*, 74.

A similar play of forces is at work in Kobylin's Russia. His social world depends on the illusion of authority, and his theater exposes the authority of illusion.

Dangerous Games

How Russian aristocratic society amuses itself in this period—with masquerades and theatrical performances, in other words, play with the violation of the rule of roles—provides a mirror image of what it fears—the actual violation of the social hierarchy. The dominant issue facing Russian society in the middle of the nineteenth century was unrest at home and abroad, the perception of fundamental change threatening the existing order. In his Manifesto of March 1848 Nicholas I describes a Europe "shaken by rebellions, threatening the overthrow of lawful powers and all social structures." The "insolence," which originated in France, "now knows no borders, and in its madness threatens Russia, entrusted to us by God."[42] As we will see, social upheaval with a French connection appears as a major theme in the Sukhovo-Kobylin case.

Senator Lebedev's memoirs for 1849 help to provide a more detailed and concrete picture of the issues that we have introduced thus far: masquerade, imposture, crime, and anxieties about the stability of the social order. Lebedev describes Count Zakrevskii's decree in 1849 against beards "worn in imitation of foreign conspiracies." There was no need to imitate foreign conspiracies in 1849, the year the Petrashevskii circle was arrested. Lebedev comments that the affair reveals the influence of foreign propagandists, particularly the Poles, and furthermore the lack of activity on the part of the government, which provokes "ardent young men to take part in social affairs" (361). Lebedev writes: "They say the tsar wants to conduct the case strictly according to the law—with a trial." He dismisses this as extremely unlikely. Lebedev describes the rumors surrounding the circle's activities: blaspheming church rites, attacks against the tsar's family, and taking "for themselves the roles of rulers and representatives" (362). The language of the rumors is significant. We know that the primary activity of the circle consisted in discussions—of the conditions of the peasantry, of Fourier's utopian socialism, of Belinsky's broad-ranging critique of Russian society. There was some possible involvement with the print-

---

42. "Manifest 14 Marta 1848," *Epokha Nikolaia I*, ed. M. O. Gershenzon (Moscow: Obrazovanie, 1910), 9.

ing of revolutionary pamphlets. Lebedev's account of the rumors about the Petrashevtsy suggests that criticism of the nature of the government and the social order are perceived as an attack against the person of the tsar and against religion. The assumption of political roles outside those given by the tsar is read as imposture.

Count Zakrevskii's order about beards prompted Countess Rostopchina to write a lampooning verse. Rostopchina, who also wrote novels and comedies, was well known in Petersburg elite society. Rostopchina compares Zakrevskii to "a Russian pasha" and asks why he bothers to make such a fuss, since after all, the inhabitants of Moscow are not building barricades (a reference to the upheavals in Europe):

Why all this noise
All the strange use of force?
Without an outcry your active mind
Could spare neither paper nor ink.
What law will you think to institute,
What new orders will you establish?[43]

The episodes of Moscow life in 1849, the year before Demanche was killed, suggest that to whatever extent the social hierarchy was suspended at the masquerade ball, the suspension was extremely limited and temporary. Outside the ballroom, the wearing of clothing inappropriate for the time and place incurred the wrath of the authorities, for whom it signaled political conspiracy or, at the very least, the disruption of public order. The play with identity made possible by masquerade costume, when lifted out of the context of masquerade, feels like a threat to the government.

Imposture

Outside the masquerade ball, the assumption of another's identity is imposture—a dominant theme in Kobylin's trilogy. In the first play, the hero Krechinskii tricks a pawnbroker by substituting a paste diamond for a real one. He creates a new identity for himself using a few props. According to Leonid Grossman, a possible source for *Krechinskii's Wedding* was an episode involving a certain "Polish dandy Krysinskii . . . who

---

43. Lebedev, "Iz zapisok Senatora Lebedeva," 364.

gave himself out as a count" and was involved in the false substitution of a valuable brooch belonging to a Petersburg lady of high society. The "count" turned out to be a servant.[44] The Krysinskii episode is not the only one of its kind in Russian society at this time. Senator Lebedev's memoirs for 1848 describe his prosecution of a case of imposture perpetrated by a Pavel Petrovich Popov, who gave himself out as a Polish landowner. The son of a petty bureaucrat, Popov apparently had an affair with a Golitsyn princess, the wife of a landowner, Cherepov. According to Lebedev, he helped her steal from her husband and hide a runaway convict from the police. Upon Cherepov's death, Popov married the widow, with whom he had three daughters. In 1827 Popov, by means of petitions, received the Order of Vladimir for saving someone from a fire, and from that point on "gave himself out as a nobleman." Popov ended up working in the Ministry of Justice under Count Troshchinskii. According to Lebedev, what motivated Popov's imposture of nearly twenty years, ultimately, was his desire to legitimize his daughters.[45]

In the Petersburg premiere of *Krechinskii's Wedding* in 1856, the actor Samoilov performed the part of Krechinskii with a Polish accent. The two cases of imposture that I have just described also involve a false Polish identity. Historically, the first impostor, false-Dmitrii, a runaway Russian monk, came via Poland to Moscow. In the mid-nineteenth century Poland was one of Russia's chief adversaries. Having been reconquered in 1830, and subject to an aggressive policy of Russification, Poland was seen as a source for rebellion in Russia, as Senator Lebedev's remarks on the Polish influence over the Petrashevtsy reveal. Imposture, a form of social climbing in the Popov case, has more serious political implications. It is a threat to lawful rule, a threat to the social order, and a threat to Russia's national identity. Imposture invades the center of authority, as the example of Popov and the Ministry of Justice shows, hollowing it out from within. Other impostors and liars in the tsar's government, particularly in the notorious Third Section, have been discussed by Lotman and others.

Absent Authority

Lebedev's comments about the Petrashevskii case and the general state of affairs at home and abroad reveal his sense of what disorder is. He

---

44. See Grossman, *Teatr Sukhovo-Kobylina*, 8–9.
45. Lebedev, "Iz Zapisok Senatora Lebedeva," *Russkii arkhiv* 1910, vol. 10: 233–34.

describes the remarks of his colleague, S. P. Poludenskii, who had just
returned from a three-year trip abroad: "Everything there breathes the
overthrow of the existing order, hatred for Russia. . . . Servants and
coachmen reject kings and threaten upheaval" (363). Lebedev's sense of
disorder is mirrored by his sense of what constitutes order. He is critical of anything that he perceives to be an excessive display, even if it is
generated by the tsar. In describing the expectations surrounding the
tsar's trip to Moscow, Lebedev quotes Panin's disapproval of any
unnecessary public appearance, which is either "a trial or vainglory,
and therefore harmful, because it weakens trust" (360). The tsar must
never be seen to be seeking public approval. His power simply is. It
inheres in his person. This definition of the tsar's power helps to
explain Lebedev's reaction to a trip the tsar takes to Warsaw in light of
the disorder at home. The disciplinary measures—such as Zakrevskii's
edict about beards—"especially taken in the tsar's absence are weak
and somehow not fully legal and arbitrary and therefore produce dis-
content" (362). What gives the law force and legitimacy is the presence
of the person of the tsar. Laws made in his absence lose these qualities,
and the legal officials who make them, while not exactly pretenders
who seek to usurp power that is not theirs, cannot help but overreach
themselves; their measures are "arbitrary." Lebedev's sensitivity about
what makes the law lawful reveals attitudes about the tsar's status that
might at first seem obsolete in mid-nineteenth-century Russia, a trace
of the sacralization of the tsar.[46] Legal officials cannot act on their own
initiative because there are no general legal principles out of which
their rulings could be derived or justified. The source of law is the tsar,
and yet the tsar, not only on occasion, but in a fundamental sense, is
absent. The dynamic of an absent, dreaded, and yearned-for source of
authority is crucial to an understanding of Sukhovo-Kobylin's model of
authorship, as we will later see.

A Savage in Parisian Dress

Lebedev's characterization of Russian life in 1849, which, as we have
seen, emphasizes excesses on the part of the social elite, insolence on

---

46. For a history of the tsar's sacralization and a discussion of the persistence of the
association between the tsar and Christ, see V. M. Zhivov and B. A. Uspenskii, "Tsar' i
bog: Semioticheskie aspekty sakralizatsii monarkha v Rossii," in *Iazyki kul'tury i problemy
perevodimosti,* ed. B. A. Uspenskii (Moscow: Nauka, 1987), 47–152.

the part of social inferiors, and baleful foreign influence, can help us understand the way that Sukhovo-Kobylin and the events that made him notorious were perceived. E. M. Feoktistov, who knew the Kobylin family, particularly Elizaveta (whose journal he helped to edit), and who in 1883 became the government's chief censor, characterizes Kobylin as having a

> coarse, brazen nature, not in the least softened by education; this gentleman, who spoke French magnificently and possessed the manners of a gentleman, who tried to seem a true Parisian, was, in essence, in his instincts, a cruel savage, who was not stopped by any abuses of his rights as a serf owner; his household trembled. I have had the occasion to observe more than once that such people, distinguished by a masculine beauty, self-confident to the point of insolence, with a brilliant wit, but at the same time, completely heartless, produce an enchanting effect on women. Alexander Kobylin could boast of a whole series of love affairs, but they destroyed him.[47]

Feoktistov's portrait emphasizes physical beauty and seeming refinement, a façade of French sophistication and culture masking the cruelty of a Russian serf owner, whose very insolence and heartlessness attracts women.

In Paris in the spring of 1842 Sukhovo-Kobylin met Louise Simon-Demanche. By autumn of the same year, Demanche had moved to Russia. An emphasis on aesthetics, the element of masquerade disguise, play with social hierarchy, a certain blurring of the social boundaries, but always within limits—these are the dominant motifs of their love affair. Kobylin's diary for winter 1842 notes their first sexual encounter, which he calls somewhat euphemistically the first "pleasurable encounter" (sladostnoe svidanie). According to the diary, the couple spent two hours together in a small hotel. In a diary entry for May 1, 1843, Kobylin writes, "I am organizing an attelage à la Domino," that is, a procession in masquerade costume. He remarks on Louisa's "tender and elegant figure."[48] Simon-Demanche worked as a model in a store on Kuznetskii Most, a fashionable shopping area in Moscow. She also managed a wine shop that Kobylin had provided the capital for.

---

47. Feoktistov, "Glava iz vospominanii," 110.
48. Cited by Bessarab, Sukhovo-Kobylin, 68.

In one sense, Demanche is dressed up and put on display, but in another sense, she must be kept inside the house, she cannot appear in society with Kobylin. From his perspective, marriage between the two was undesirable, given Demanche's inferior social status. The same problem had ruined the marriage plans of Kobylin's sister, Elizaveta (the writer Evgeniia Tur), who fell in love with her older tutor, then Professor Nadezhdin. The mother, who may have been in love with Nadezhdin herself, made the marriage impossible. Kobylin, the aristocrat, took sides with the mother against his sister.

Demanche came to take on a role somewhere above a servant, but below the lady of the house. She shopped for food and ordered meals that Kobylin shared. She was asked to help find a governess for Kobylin's sister. Mariia Ivanovna requested that the governess be of a modest and humble character, and that she be able to carry out instructions given her and not take her own initiative. The theme of service, and knowing one's place, as Maia Bessarab points out, is part of the affair between Kobylin and Demanche.[49] In a diary entry written in 1856, after the murder, Kobylin describes a fond memory of Demanche preparing tea for him at a picnic at Voskresenskoe, a Kobylin estate outside Moscow. It is haymaking time. He goes to see to the hay, she goes to gather mushrooms. He finds her later between two birch trees, fussing over a samovar, which she has placed on a rug. The sound of the mowing proceeds "quietly and regularly"; the sun is low in the sky. Kobylin describes himself "breathing in the tranquillity of this picture" and noting the happiness he feels, in contrast to the happiness that others will seek in Moscow, Petersburg, or California.[50] Kobylin unwittingly quotes his own parodic character, Krechinskii, who woos the provincial landowner Muromskii with his profession of love—not for Muromskii's daughter, Lidochka, but for the countryside: "Yes, I adore the country. The country in summer is paradise: the air, the tranquillity, the peace." Muromskii asks his opinion of the threshing floor. There, Krechinskii answers, "Everything is alive; everywhere there is work, quiet, regular work." Krechinskii's lines and the language of Sukhovo-Kobylin's diary are strikingly similar.

In writing the entry in his diary, Kobylin may seek in some way to Russify himself and his French mistress retroactively. The beauty of the

---

49. Ibid., 12–13.
50. Sukhovo-Kobylin, "Iz dnevnika A. V. Sukhovo-Kobylina," *Russkii arkhiv* 5 (1910): 287.

Russian countryside—the birch trees, the setting sun, and the hay—combined with the labor that is performed—both by the mowers and by Demanche—contribute to the appeal of the "picture." We might note that in *Anna Karenina* Tolstoy's hero participates in the mowing and finds pleasure in forgetting himself in the work. Kobylin's pleasure lies in beholding the scene and the service others perform for him. In a letter of 1849 Elizaveta Kobylin writes that her brother lives "happily . . . he arranged his life according to his taste," but that when he became angry, because a dish did not come out well, he broke plates and slapped people.[51]

The Demanche-Kobylin affair is the social hierarchy writ small. In the superior position is Sukhovo-Kobylin and his family, below him is Demanche, and below her are the house serfs, the cook, the coachman, and the maids. Demanche treated her servants poorly. She ordered that the sister of the cook, Egorov, be married off to a serf in one of the Kobylin country estates. One of the maids complained to the authorities about a beating she received from Demanche, who was ordered to pay ten silver rubles in compensation.

The social world constituted by the Kobylins, Simon-Demanche, and the serfs, like its larger counterpart, is unstable. Kobylin, for one thing, has other affairs. His alibi for the night of the murder is in fact that he was at an evening given by Nadezhda Naryshkina, with whom he later had a daughter. After the murder, Naryshkina left Russia for Paris, where she had an affair with and then married Alexandre Dumas *fils*. The aristocratic set in which Sukhovo-Kobylin moves is surrounded by rumors of scandal and sexual excess, on the part of men and women.[52] The suggestion of female sexual impropriety will appear in Kobylin's play *The Case*.

Rivalry between Demanche and Naryshkina is a central theme in several of the society versions of the murder. In a letter to a relative describing the affair and the crime, Tolstoy wrote:

> A certain Mr. Kobylin was keeping a certain Madame Simon, and he supplied her the services of two men and a maidservant. Now, Mr. Kobylin, before keeping this Madame Simon, formed a liaison with Madame Naryshkina, nee Knorring, a lady from the best

---

51. Cited by Bessarab, *Sukhovo-Kobylin,* 108.
52. See Richard Fortune, *Alexander Sukhovo-Kobylin* (Boston: Twayne Publishers, 1982), 13.

Moscow society and a lady very much in vogue, and he had not stopped corresponding with her, although he was keeping Madame Simon. On top of all this, one fine morning Simon is found murdered, and certain evidence indicates that she was killed by her own servants. This might not have amounted to anything much, were it not for the fact that the police, when arresting Kobylin, found among his papers some letters from Madame Naryshkina, in which she reproaches him for abandoning her and threatens Madame Simon, which only adds to the many other reasons for concluding that the murderers were but the instruments of Madame Naryshkina.[53]

Implicit in Tolstoy's characterization of the affair is a distinction between an acceptable rivalry between men, on the one hand, and an unacceptable, comic, and grotesque rivalry between women. We will return to the problem of rivalry between women in chapter 4.

Another variant of the story casts Sukhovo-Kobylin himself as the murderer. According to this version, Sukhovo-Kobylin wanted to break off relations with Demanche for the sake of Naryshkina. When Demanche came unexpectedly to Kobylin's apartment, she found him and Naryshkina together. She struck Naryshkina in the face, and Kobylin, "beside himself, grabbed the first thing he could find, a heavy candelabra from the fireplace, and hurled it at the Frenchwoman, and killed her on the spot." Kobylin then bribed and threatened his serfs to remove the body and take the blame on themselves.[54]

Senator Lebedev's reading of the crime distributes blame more evenly:

The involvement of persons of the highest circle, but also the guilt of the cook Egorov and the coachman Kuzmin [*sic*], are without doubt, in my opinion. The correspondence . . . attached to the investigation is extraordinarily curious; especially curious are the letters of Demanche herself . . . then the letter of Countess S——s [a reference to Elizaveta Kobylin]. These letters are a course in the rules of French depravity [*kurs Frantsuzskikh razvratnykh pravil*]. . . . It is sad to see this Frenchwoman, who flew to Moscow, end in a

---

53. Quoted in ibid., 15.
54. Pavel Rossiev, "A. V. i Frantsuzhenka Simon," *Russkii arkhiv* 6 (1910): 317.

terrible death, and these ladies and lords violating the rights of the family, and this gifted S-K swallowed by intrigues, and finally, these peasants, given by their master in slavery to his French lover. There is no doubt that the murder was completely calculated, deliberate, and in cold blood.[55]

Lebedev's remarks reveal his concerns about the erosion of the boundaries of nationality and class, and the disruption of tradition. The Kobylin correspondence is a textbook of the decadent practices of a foreign culture, which replaces and usurps Russian law and the institution of the Russian family; the same social practices and the same intrusion of the foreign element upset Russian class relations. The Russian serfs are made to serve a woman who has no business being their mistress, as she is not Kobylin's wife, nor is she Russian, but "his French lover."

According to Sukhovo-Kobylin, the house servants committed the crime in order to rob Demanche. Mariia Ivanovna, Kobylin's mother, supports this claim. She writes to her daughter Evdokiia that Egorov, the cook, tried to sell Demanche's gold watch to another cook in service to one Polivanov, but that the police never interrogated the prospective buyer because, they claimed, he was dead. Mariia Ivanovna claims to have met the buyer alive and well in 1854: "When the living are shown publicly to be dead, and it all comes to nothing, what can you expect after this? Polivanov's cook is registered as dead in the case and in the reports to the minister, but he cooked for me yesterday."[56] Mariia Ivanovna's version of events suggests that the police fail to protect the aristocracy from the lower classes. This bizarre death and resurrection will be a feature of Sukhovo-Kobylin's third play, *The Death of Tarelkin*.

The rumors about Sukhovo-Kobylin's love life, and the fact that Demanche's body was discovered with her earrings and rings left undisturbed, made robbery an unconvincing motive for the murder to Kobylin's contemporaries. In a letter of 1850 to his sister Evdokiia, Kobylin asks her and her husband not to believe the "slander" about Demanche's ill-treatment of her servants: "She irritated her servants, but she did not treat them poorly, and besides which, I am certain, and

---

55. "Delo ob ubiistve Frantsuzhenki Luizy Simon-Demansh," quoted in Rossiev, "Sukhovo-Kobylin," 316.

56. Quoted by E. N. Konshina in "Vstupitel'nye zamechaniia," in "Pis'ma A. V. Sukhovo-Kobylina k rodnym," ed. E. N. Konshina, *Trudy Publichnoi biblioteki SSSR imeni Lenina* 3 (1934): 203.

everything indicates, that her murderer could be the murderer of one of us."[57] In a diary entry for 1858, Kobylin describes his horror at the news that Demanche's former servants, now acquitted, as he was, had arrived at Chern', where one of the Kobylin estates was located. "This news put me in a dreadful position: it seemed to me that I breathe the same air that was in their lungs."[58] The illusion of distance separating his body from those of his servants has been erased. Kobylin writes that he is inclined to leave Russia and resettle abroad, no doubt in an effort to regain that distance.

The Violation of the Aristocratic Façade: Branding

As Kobylin's mistress, Louise Simon-Demanche was one of the many beautiful objects with which he surrounded himself, part of the accoutrement of his private pleasure. The tea-making scene discussed earlier is one example of the beautiful and idyllic tableaux that Kobylin was able to create for himself in the closed-off world of his estate. Simon-Demanche could dress up and deck herself out—she worked as a model, as we have seen—but she could not appear in society. The police report lingers over the details of the murdered woman's luxurious clothing, jewels, and the size and shape of her fatal wounds. The crime and the investigation forcibly remove her from the world in which she was enclosed and place her before the public eye. The crime that killed Demanche also shattered the beautiful aristocratic façade of Sukhovo-Kobylin's self-fashioning.

We gain an appreciation of Kobylin's sense of violation from his response to two significant events. As I noted earlier, the Senate's decision to leave Sukhovo-Kobylin "under suspicion" and the premiere performance of *Krechinskii's Wedding* coincide. In his diary entry for November 1855 Kobylin writes:

> What a strange fate that at the same time that my play little by little enters the ranks of noted works of literature, attracting general attention, the lowest rabble of our country, the shameless scribblers of judicial trash, gather in a horde to brand my name with legally protected slander.[59]

---

57. Ibid., 234.
58. Sukhovo-Kobylin, "Iz dvnevnika A. V. Sukhovo-Kobylina," 287.
59. Ibid., 284–85.

The nobility are not subject to branding. It is a punishment reserved for serfs. As we have seen, Kobylin's own serfs were to have been branded, according to the sentence of the Moscow Aulic Court in 1851, but the execution was postponed. A branded criminal is made to declare his criminality and to bear witness to the ruler's power over his person. The letters spelling the word *thief (vor)* were branded on the criminal's face, *V* on the forehead, *O* on the right cheek, and *R* on the left.[60] Branding is the absolute antithesis of the play with roles enacted in masquerade and theatrical transformation. The identity of the criminal is forcibly, painfully, and permanently fixed on his person. He is forever marked as a social outcast.

Kobylin sees being left under suspicion as a kind of branding. His serfs are not branded, but his name is. The personal name, a fundamental projection of the person in the world, is mutilated by slander. Furthermore, the distinction between master and servant is blurred, because the master is punished—even if only symbolically—with the servant's punishment.[61] Significantly, Sukhovo-Kobylin's interpretation of his sentence reveals his understanding of the law not as a set of rules or general concepts but as a contest between persons. It is not his rights as a citizen that are violated but the integrity of his person.

In December 1855 Sukhovo-Kobylin continues in the same vein:

> Fate is either strange or blind. . . . through the door of a damp jail, through the gates of Voskresenskoe, she led me to the stage of the Moscow theater, and, dragging me through the dirt, she has suddenly placed me upright and triumphant before that very person who cursed me and, like Pilate, tied my arms behind my back and beat me on the face. Now fate takes me further—submitting me to public shame and subjecting my honest name to branding.[62]

Voskresenskoe, as we have seen, is a Kobylin family estate. In May 1855 the author read the text of his play *Krechinskii's Wedding* to a group of actors he had invited to Voskresenskoe. But the author seems to be punning on the meaning of the word. Voskresenskoe was named after a

---

60. Ia. Barshev, *Osnovaniia ugolovnogo sudoproizvodstva*, cited by Grossman, *Prestuplenie Sukhovo-Kobylina*, 84–85 n. 1.

61. For the significance of corporal punishment in the self-consciousness of the Russian nobility, see Irina Reyfman, "The Emergence of the Duel in Russia: Corporal Punishment and the Honor Code," *Russian Review* 54 (1995): 28.

62. Sukhovo-Kobylin, "Iz Dnevnika A. V. Sukhovo-Kobylina," 284–85.

church of the resurrection *(voskresenie)* of Christ located at the edge of the park.[63] The references to Pilate and other biblical imagery suggests that Sukhovo-Kobylin sees his theatrical debut as an opportunity for personal resurrection.

In a later diary entry Sukhovo-Kobylin writes that by means of his theater he transforms himself from "villain" *(zlodei)* into "author."[64] Once his façade was destroyed, Kobylin attempts to resurrect it in his writing for the theater, in order to regain what the murder and the larger social forces at work at the time had wrecked. His theater is a means of reinventing himself, of putting before the public a restored version of himself. The choice of media is significant. The publication of a written work creates an audience, but not in the immediate sense produced by the performance of a play. The title of Sukhovo-Kobylin's first play, *Krechinskii's Wedding,* in Russian *Svad'ba Krechinskogo,* contains his own initials, S-K, as do the name and patronymic of Tarelkin's alter ego, Sila Kopylov, in his last play, *The Death of Tarelkin.*[65] In the contest between the writer and the law, the writer attempts to rewrite what has been inscribed upon him by the state. But the attempt is risky, as the marks of punishment leave their trace and powerfully shape the next layer of text. In Kobylin's case, the public display, that is, the performance of his play, may become a public flogging, a repetition of the personal humiliation the author had already suffered. This is how Sukhovo-Kobylin describes his experience of the first performance of *Krechinskii's Wedding:* "sitting next to my sister, I counted the number of blows that I received from the executioner."[66] In this moment of anxiety, the artistic theater and the theater of punishment have merged into one.

Krechinskii and Kobylin

In the eponymous hero of *Krechinskii's Wedding* we can see certain features of Kobylin himself, but negatively transformed. In a sense Krechinskii may be Kobylin's way of having his cake and eating it too. He puts himself before the public, but in a deliberately distorted form. We learn about Krechinskii's background from his servant Fedor. While at the university Krechinskii "carried on." Afterward, he spent his time

---

63. See Bessarab, *Sukhovo-Kobylin,* 76.
64. Ibid., 148.
65. The latter point has been made by Richard Fortune in *Alexander Sukhovo-Kobylin.*
66. See Bessarab, *Sukhovo-Kobylin,* 149.

in drinking bouts and card games, with "counts and princes" for company (86–87). In Fedor's words, Krechinskii had a slew of women
(otboiu net), and with the love affairs, there were "letters, notes, all kinds
of scribbles . . . what a mess [i takaia idet kasha]: they ask, and love, and
get jealous, and get spiteful." We recall the personal correspondence
attached to Sukhovo-Kobylin's case, the love letters that Senator Lebedev found so distasteful, "a course in the rules of French depravity."
The correspondence includes notes from Simon-Demanche, announc-
ing that she will leave Kobylin: "I would not go if I knew that you are
sad and upset, but you, it seems, are happier than ever";[67] a letter from
an unknown woman, proclaiming, "I am yours forever"; and a letter
from another who describes how she loves Kobylin "in spite of everyone: I struggled with my family, with my rules, my religion."[68] The
kasha Fedor refers to in the play finds a direct parallel in the kasha in
Kobylin's love life. Fedor describes one particular lover over whom
Krechinskii had particular power. She would remain on her knees
before him for hours and kiss his hands like a slave. In Fedor's words,
she would have pawned her body for him three times over, but
Krechinskii refuses, saying that he did not want a woman's money. In
the course of the play he will have no such qualms. Krechinskii may be
seen as a crude and ugly exaggeration of Kobylin, an embodiment of
everything that the public would want to say about him, of course,
according to Kobylin himself. Kobylin's reinvention of himself as
Krechinskii both displays and conceals Kobylin from the public, pre-
serving his distance from it. The fact that we hear about Krechinskii's
love life from someone else reinforces the sense of quotation.

Krechinskii has squandered his estate, his horses, and his silver; he
has few clothes, and his rooms are unheated. His only companion is the
disreputable Raspliuev (whose name suggests "spitting"), who assists
him in his shady dealings. To save himself, he decides to marry the
wealthy and naive Lidochka Muromskaia, whom he describes as "a
steamed turnip, a nothing" (93). Her dowry will provide the capital for
a new round of gambling. Krechinskii plans on winning two million
rubles and settling down into a respectable old age. Having conquered
the daughter, Krechinskii must gain the father's approval. He must
refashion himself as a worthy suitor, wealthy, and with the appropriate
family background. But first, he has to pay off his gambling debts and

---

67. From "Pis'ma" in Grossman, Delo Sukhovo-Kobylina, 337.
68. Quoted in Bessarab, Sukhovo-Kobylin, 109.

thus avoid the public scandal that would destroy his plans. He asks Lidochka to send him her diamond solitaire pin, for which he has in his possession a paste copy. Krechinskii struggles mightily to compose the request in the necessary language of a love letter, and his first effort results in a parody, as the stage directions indicate:

> My quiet angel! Send me one of your wings, your pin with the solitaire *(parodying)* [Kobylin's stage direction], reflecting the brilliance of your heavenly fatherland. We must provision the ship upon which we will be carried under the four winds: the diamonds, the clubs, the spades, and hearts. I will stand at the helm, Raspliuev at the sails, and you will be our ballast. (102)

Krechinskii manages to convince a pawnbroker that the paste solitaire is the original and returns home with the necessary cash and Lidochka's diamond. At the last minute, the pawnbroker realizes his mistake, and the police arrive to arrest Krechinskii and Raspliuev.

The Power of Invention

Near the end of the play, Krechinskii cleans and redecorates his apartment. He gives Raspliuev a new identity as a landowner and dresses him in his own frock coat, remarking "a whole person has appeared" *(tselaia persona stala)* (121). According to the stage instructions, Krechinskii then turns the new person Raspliuev before the audience. The use of the term "persona" instead of the more standard *litso* for "person" is significant. With it, Kobylin suggests the link between the person and the "persona," that is, the dramatic role. There may also be another dimension to the use of the term. *Persona* was used in Russian legal language. By the end of the play, Raspliuev wants to undo his new identity and refuses to give the police his last name. As a final touch to his preparations, Krechinskii hangs a picture of a Catherine-era general in a prominent position, "for genealogy," he says (121). Personal history and identity are created out of the exigencies of the moment. Krechinskii plays the part of stage director and author, so to speak, by redesigning the set, the costumes, and the identities of the characters, including his own. In so doing he creates a play within the play, a structure that, according to Lotman, draws attention to the spectators' sense of the performance as such, as theater.

Raspliuev is awed by Krechinskii's ability to manipulate appearances and transform people and things. Raspliuev compares him to Napoleon and calls him a "great hero, magician, and wizard" (118). Raspliuev's praise of Krechinskii, however, is double-edged. Raspliuev tells Krechinskii: "You wind everyone around your little finger, you simply have power! But if you crawled into my skin, it would be another matter" (113). In Raspliuev's estimation, Krechinskii's ability to manipulate appearances is not only a matter of artistic inventiveness, but also the power to compel others to do as he wishes. The spectacle of power at the center of Russian society, at the court of the tsar, mimed by the serf owner at his estate, is mimed in Kobylin's theater, which emphasizes the power of the spectacle to create illusions in the minds of the spectators.

The process of creating new personae ungrounded in noble birth or connection to the center is dangerous. The inauthentic inventions take on a life of their own in the next play of the trilogy, *The Case*. Maxim Kuz'mich Varravin is in charge of the investigation. As Richard Fortune writes, "the name Varravin suggests Barabbas (in Russian, Varavva)."[69] Barabbas was imprisoned for murder and sedition but released by Pilate in place of Christ. Varravin's immediate underling is Kandid Kastorovich Tarelkin. Richard Wortman and Leonid Grossman have identified the prototype for Tarelkin as Senator Kastor Nikiforovich Lebedev (note that Lebedev's first name and Tarelkin's patronymic correspond).[70] Kobylin takes specific revenge on Lebedev in the character of Tarelkin. The author notes that Tarelkin "speaks like Demosthenes, especially when the latter put stones in his mouth" (150). Nel'kin, an admirer of Lidochka, describes Tarelkin as a "rag, a crumpled piece of chancellery stationery" (162).

Varravin and Tarelkin prosecute the case, which has now metastasized into a case against Lidochka Muromskaia, accused of collusion with Krechinskii, in spite of the fact that the pawnbroker has been paid off by Muromskii. The play opens with a letter from Krechinskii to Muromskii, urging him to pay whatever bribe he is asked, for Lidochka's sake. The power of invention previously displayed by Krechinskii is now wielded by Varravin and Tarelkin. They have, as it

69. Richard Fortune, *Alexander Sukhovo-Kobylin* (Boston: Twayne Publishers, 1982), 81.

70. See Wortman, *Russian Legal Consciousness*, 65; and Grossman, *Teatr Sukhovo-Kobylina*, 35–36.

were, rewritten *Krechinskii's Wedding*, replacing fraud with conspiracy, illicit sex, and other crimes. As one of the characters remarks, "a Case can be made out of anything"—the punning reference to the title of the play underscoring Sukhovo-Kobylin's claim about the law's use of fiction in his own case (153). Raspliuev testifies that he was the go-between for Krechinskii and Lidochka, that he brought Krechinskii "a woman all wrapped up" (156). In the play, Lidochka's nurse is questioned as to whether a baby was born. Tarelkin proposes to Varravin that a medical commission be invited to examine Lidochka—as a means of extracting one final, enormous sum of money, twenty-five thousand rubles, from Muromskii. The prince suggests the possibility of charging Lidochka with infanticide: "However, if there was a baby, then we must discover where it is. . . . Here, perhaps, another crime lies concealed" (230). The scene in which Tarelkin and Varravin discuss the medical examination was one of the grounds given for the play's repeated censorship. Sukhovo-Kobylin emphasizes the salacious pleasure the two "Superiors" derive from contemplating their plan and instructs the actors to leer and laugh. The officials of the law, in charge of maintaining sexual propriety among their subjects, contemplate using the law in what amounts to a sexual violation of one of their subjects.

The Embodied Metaphor

Raspliuev's false testimony can help shed some light on the poetics of Sukhovo-Kobylin's theater as a whole. In *Krechinskii's Wedding* Raspliuev brings Krechinskii not "a woman all wrapped up," but her diamond solitaire pin, that is, not the woman herself, but the sign of her value, her jewel. In *The Case* the metaphor is realized. The sign is embodied retroactively as the woman who owns it. To give another example, in *The Case*, Tarelkin says, "okh, okho, okh" as an expression of misery. He is pursued by his creditors everywhere he goes. In *The Death of Tarelkin* "okh" the expletive has become Antiokh Elpidiforovich Okh, a policeman. The transformation of things and people into signs of themselves marks out the space of theater. In Sukhovo-Kobylin's plays, however, the reverse process, the transformation of signs into people, indicates a kind of devolution, a reduction of play on the part of individuals, and an increase in the power of the police, which is in part realized in their power to play and to invent. Not only is Lidochka's sign, her pin, retroactively embodied as Lidochka herself, it manages to give birth to a baby, whom she may be accused of murdering! The embodiment or literalization of signs is a crucial component of the language of punishment, as in the example of branding, in which the process of naming of the criminal as such—by imprinting the letters of the word *thief* on his face—inflicts pain and humiliation.

Play, in the nightmarish world of the law, is realized as play with language. Varravin and the prince display a particular sensitivity to nuance and ambiguity in language. The case against Lidochka rests on a single word: whether, at the moment Krechinskii was arrested, she said, "it was a mistake" or "it's my mistake," suggesting, according to the police, her knowledge of, and willing participation in, the fraud. Two witnesses testify that they heard the personal pronoun, and according to the rules of formal evidence, two pieces of matching evidence constitute "perfect," or, "complete" evidence, as Varravin points out. When Muromskii pleads his case before Varravin, the latter concludes that the case is "on one hand, perfectly simple and natural, and on the other, completely unnatural" (195). The simple fact of Lidochka's age—she is nineteen, and, to her father, still a child—is, for Varravin, evidence of possible criminal wrongdoing, inasmuch as it is the age of legal maturity, which he terms "criminal maturity" *(ugolovnoe sovershennoletie)* (196). This exchange may have a basis in the Simon-Demanche case. The coachman Koz'min recanted his testimony in part because he was underage at the time that he gave it.[71] Muromskii tries to defend his daughter on the grounds of her love for and devotion to Krechinskii. Varravin responds: "We now wish to determine the degree of this love in accordance with the law." Muromskii lamely protests: "I didn't mean in that way" (197). Varravin waxes poetic about the slippery nature of the truth: "Where is the truth, I ask you? Where is she? Where? What darkness! . . . What night! . . . and in this night what ambiguity!" (197–98). Varravin takes the "ambiguity" one step farther—to multivalence. He remarks to the prince that when young women such as Lidochka, who have read French novels, use the word *mistake* *(oshibka)* they mean the French term *une faute*, that is, a sin, or moral fall. The prince says that Muromskii caught his daughter "en flagrant delit," at the scene of the crime, hinting that she was caught, not in a criminal act, but in a sexual one.

---

71. See Grossman, *Delo Sukhovo-Kobylina*, 107.

This passage may in some sense correspond to Kobylin's experience at the hands of the Moscow police. Among the evidence against him was a love letter written to Demanche. To paraphrase, Kobylin requests Demanche to return to Moscow from the country, saying that since she prefers to listen to a voice of passion that pronounces a name not his own (suggesting a flirtation on her part, perhaps, with another), he prefers that she, "an ungrateful and perfidious woman," should remain under his eyes and under the point of his Castillian dagger: "Return and trrr . . . emble."[72] The police interpret the erotic play as a murder threat. As in the real-life case, in Sukhovo-Kobylin's play *The Case* the police resolve ambiguity in language by criminalizing it.

The criminalization of language and the literalization of the sign continue in the last play of the trilogy, *The Death of Tarelkin*. Raspliuev, now a policeman, interrogates Liudmila Brandakhlystova (another borrowing from Gogol, the name suggests "abuse and beatings"), Tarelkin's common-law wife. He asks, "What did he turn to?" When Liudmila answers that Tarelkin would turn to face the wall whenever she got into bed with him, Raspliuev takes this as evidence that Tarelkin is something akin to a werewolf, because he could change himself into other things, in this case, a wall. According to Raspliuev, Tarelkin would turn *into* a wall. Brandakhlystova is arrested for living with a criminal.

The Religious Theme

Muromskii's estate manager, Ivan Sidorov, describes the legal bureaucracy as a world ruled by Antichrist:

> Antichrist has lived for a long time. . . . he's an elderly, solid person. . . . You see, he's in the service and was recently promoted to acting state councilor—and has a buckle for thirty years of blameless service. He himself has given birth to a tribe that is plentiful and predatory—it is all the great and minor officials, and this tribe has covered our entire Christian country; and all our sorrows, labors, and ills are from this Antichrist. . . . the end of the world is near. (173)

---

72. Ibid., 70.

According to the stage instructions, Ivan Sidorov is to look around, lower his voice, and add: "now is just the rehearsal." A noise is heard in the background, and Tarelkin enters, having just escaped his creditors. This comic anticlimax resonates significantly with the religious subtext of the passage. In the Revelation of John, two beasts appear, one from the sea and one from the earth. The first is given power over all nations on earth; the second compels all to worship the first; without the mark of the second, no one may buy or sell. The scene that we have just quoted occurs early in *The Case*, before Varravin is introduced. Later in the play, Muromskii directly labels Varravin "Antichrist." Tarelkin is the lesser and Varravin the greater "beast." Sidorov's line—"now is just the rehearsal"—the cue for Tarelkin's entrance, suggests the same structure of a play within a play that we have already encountered in *Krechinskii's Wedding*. The "rehearsal" can be seen in the context of the plays themselves: *The Case* as a rehearsal for *The Death of Tarelkin*, the relatively benign opening of the play as a rehearsal for the horrific ending, in which Muromskii, tricked, betrayed, and bullied by Varravin, collapses. In terms of the religious context, the appearance of Antichrist heralds the appearance of Christ. The present order, in which Antichrist masquerades as a civil servant, signals the end of time.

Sukhovo-Kobylin himself did not profess such a worldview; instead he uses its characteristic language and images in order to curse the legal bureaucracy.[73] In the plays, Ivan Sidorov is a member of a religious group known as the Old Believers, who originate in the seventeenth century. One Old Believer text from mid-nineteenth-century Russia reads in part: "Jesus Christ forgave sins, but Antichrist established the courts."[74] This religious evaluation of the courts is profoundly significant in the prereform era and after. Religious discourse already present in Russian culture resonates with the new legal discourse made possible by the reforms of 1864. Debates about the new jury courts are articulated by means of a series of New Testament tropes.

---

73. For more on the language of the plays in general and on Ivan Sidorov in particular, see Grossman, *Teatr Sukhovo-Kobylina*, 85–95. Grossman points out that Kobylin's father was extremely pious, and that the author grew up hearing the type of expression that he gives to his character Sidorov.

74. Quoted in Zhivov, "Istoriia russkogo prava kak lingvo-semoticheskaia problema," 84.

In *The Case,* the legal world constitutes a hellish inversion of the church. In both, all distinctions are erased. Lidochka comes home from church and says: "There there are neither poor nor rich" (165). In both the legal and religious world, all are guilty of something, and all stand in need of redemption. In the realm of the law, the accused must literally buy themselves out with cash. At the head of the church is Christ; at the head of the legal department is Varravin, whom Pilate released instead of Christ. The law is figured, at one point in the play, as an "old buffoon," who carries Judas's wallet around his neck, the buffoon and the church being old adversaries. Indeed, the inversions multiply. The prince decides to resubmit the entire Muromskii case for reinvestigation, threatening to deprive Varravin of the "pitfall bribe" he and Tarelkin have worked so hard to extract from Muromskii. Varravin ironically echoes Sidorov's Biblical diction: "It's simply chaos, a confusion of languages; the end of time has begun" (231). The inverted order is itself inverted.

A Nation of Werewolves

The antiworld of *The Case* anticipates the supernatural, demonic world of *The Death of Tarelkin,* in which no identity is stable and all boundaries are erased. Characters proliferate and undergo fantastic transformations: Tarelkin becomes Sila Silich Kopylov, Varravin appears for a few scenes as Captain Polutatarinov, and Raspliuev becomes a police investigator. At the end of *The Case* Varravin, having accepted Muromskii's "pitfall bribe," makes a great show of indignantly returning his money, but the wallet is empty. Tarelkin, tricked out of his share, ends the play by cursing society: "there is no justice on earth nor compassion: the strong oppress the weak, the sated consume the hungry, the wealthy rob the poor" (266). In *Death of Tarelkin* the eponymous hero carries out a scheme both to evade his creditors and take revenge on Varravin. Tarelkin stages his own death and comes back to life in the guise of Kopylov.

Blasphemy and the supernatural dominate the last play of the trilogy. Tarelkin, having made off with Varravin's correspondence, and planning to use it to extract money from him, describes the letters as "my body and blood" and blasphemously suggests a parallel between the packet of papers and the Holy Trinity. Tarelkin says that the letters are "indivisible, not subject to doubt, and incorruptible" (284). Peering closely at Kopylov, Varravin, disguised as Captain Polutatarinov, recognizes his adversary. He concocts a bizarre story for the gullible Raspliuev, now a policeman, that Tarelkin/Kopylov is a vampire, with a proboscis and a sting like a scorpion's, who sucks human blood. In the scene, Varravin comically generates a whole list of Russian terms for *vampire:* "Do you know what a vampire is? . . . a hag? . . . a wraith? . . . a werewolf?" *(Znaete li vy, chto takoe vuidalak? . . . vudkoglak? . . . upyr'? . . . Mtsyr'?)* (308–9). The list, with its internal rhymes and literary references to Pushkin and Lermontov, emphasizes play with language.

Varravin/Polutatarinov assures Raspliuev that he is sure to win a reward for this unique prisoner and instructs him not to give the "vampire" any water. Raspliuev reports back to Okh, his superior, that "not since the creation of the world have the police caught a werewolf" (316). He informs Varravin, no longer disguised, that both Tarelkin and Kopylov were "sucked to death." Varravin puts Raspliuev in charge of the investigation. Amazed at the change in his fortunes, Raspliuev vows to turn every mouse hole inside out—the very same mouse holes in which he himself used to hide. *The Death of Tarelkin* ends with Tarelkin returning Varravin's letters. Varravin consigns Tarelkin to hell: "Go straight to hell; they won't refuse you—they'll take you!" (347).

Sukhovo-Kobylin gives the newly exalted Raspliuev one of the most remarkable passages in the entire play:

> Everything is ours! We will call in all of Russia. . . . I now am of the opinion that our whole fatherland is a pack of wolves, snakes, and rabbits, who have suddenly turned into people, and I suspect everyone; and therefore it follows that a law must be enacted—everyone must be arrested. . . .everyone in our fatherland must be subjected to verification: who are they? From where? Have they turned into something? Do they possess stings or poison? Are there those who live who have in fact already died, or those that have died but, in violation of the law, live? (325)

The principle articulated in *The Case*—"a case can be made out of anything"—is here carried to its ultimate conclusion. All of Russia is guilty of a crime; every Russian is an impostor, an animal in human guise. A connection can be drawn between this comic and macabre image and the masquerade ball. As we have seen, the violation of natural boundaries, and the temporary transformation of personal identity—what

Bakhtin calls the nonidentity of the self with the self—may be experienced as pleasure within the limits of the masquerade. Raspliuev transforms the aristocratic masquerade into an accusation of criminality directed at the entire social body. The temporary and playful suspension of identities has become real—within the world of the play.

In his plays, Kobylin projects the accusations made against him outward, against Russian society, and particularly, against the legal bureaucracy. He was not the first to represent the bureaucrat as a vampire. Before *The Death of Tarelkin* was written, Countess Rostopchina published a set of verses commenting on the indifference on the part of the Petersburg aristocracy to the Crimean War. She compared the nobility to "a dirty vampire, / Which day and night sucks / All the best juices from the Russian people."[75]

Senator Lebedev cites the verse in his memoirs of 1854. In a diary entry noting the occasion of the ascension of Alexander II, Sukhovo-Kobylin uses very similar imagery to describe the aristocracy. In *The Death of Tarelkin* Sukhovo-Kobylin uses the image of the vampire bureaucracy in the era in which that bureaucracy was proclaimed to be obsolete. *The Death of Tarelkin* was written over the period 1857–69, which saw the emancipation of the serfs and the transformation of the old courts.

Kobylin's Theater and the Theater of Public Life

The value that Kobylin places in the plasticity of the actor's face in his stage directions for *The Death of Tarelkin* echoes the emphasis on the improvisation of identity and the theater within the theater in *Krechinskii's Wedding*. For Kobylin the theater opens up the space of transformation and play with appearances that had been closed by the figurative branding of his name. That privileged world of order and beauty has been shattered. The aristocratic world, as we have seen, with its masquerade balls and amateur theatricals, marks out a delimited space in which individuals, surrounded by members of their own class, reveled in the pleasures of the flesh and the play with appearances. To some extent Kobylin's theater attempts to transfer the free space of the aristocratic world to the public stage. But something is lost in the trans-

---

75. Senator Lebedev quotes the verse in his memoirs for 1854. See "Iz zapisok Senatora Lebedeva," *Russkii arkhiv* 1910, vol. 7: 346.

lation. The good taste, ease, and refinement of the aristocratic tableaux are lacking. The social hierarchy has collapsed, and anyone may become anything. In *The Case* and *The Death of Tarelkin* the theatrical stage, the magical space of transformation, is illuminated with images that are both comic and darkly horrifying.

As for the other theater, the ongoing theater of public political life, Kobylin was thoroughly negative. His response to the reforms can best be seen from a speech given by Tarelkin, disguised as Kopylov, which parodies the ideas of progress and reform so important to the 1860s:

> Always and everywhere Tarelkin was in front. No sooner would he hear the noise of a reform that was taking place . . . than he would shout right then and there: forward! When they hung out the banner, Tarelkin always walked in front of the banner; when progress was declared, then he would go in front of progress—so that Tarelkin was in front, and progress behind! When the emancipation of women was taking place, Tarelkin cried because he was not a woman and could not remove his petticoat before the public and show it . . . how emancipation ought to be carried out [ellipsis in original]. When Tarelkin was no more, those in front were left without a face, and those behind got a kick in the behind! (288)

Reform is Tarelkin dressed in drag (another boundary crossing), performing a striptease before the public. Humanism, progress, and emancipation are empty slogans mouthed by the likes of Tarelkin. Tarelkin's response to the new humanism is to declare a personal moratorium on the eating of chicks ("our little brothers") and a strict commitment to the consumption of larger birds, such as turkey and geese.

In the diary entry for November 1855 that we have already discussed, Kobylin recalls that when Simon-Demanche would see him in a black frock coat, she would remark that he had the air of "un homme de lettres." We note in passing the significance of the language of clothes. With the performance of his plays, Sukhovo-Kobylin had actually become what his costume had previously suggested. But to become "a man of letters" in Russia in the latter part of the nineteenth century does not mean the recovery of aristocratic distance so necessary to the functioning of Sukhovo-Kobylin's sense of individuality. It meant instead rubbing shoulders with the people. For example, in "The Peasant Marei" (1876), Dostoevsky describes how his prison experience of the 1850s forced him into close contact with ordinary convicts, in whose *branded* faces he learned to see the tender and compassionate Marei of his childhood. This experience is a source of his own authorial legitimacy and inner rebirth. Kobylin cannot bear the thought that he has breathed the same air as his serfs. He cannot adopt the model of writer that begins to emerge in the late 1850s. In his plays change and transformation are external, false, and demonic. In *Krechinskii's Wedding* lies and false substitutions are perpetrated by the eponymous hero, a scoundrel. But in *The Case* and *The Death of Tarelkin* they are perpetrated by the law itself. The "center does not hold." The law corrodes identity and the social hierarchy.

In diary entries written during the early years of the reform period, Sukhovo-Kobylin describes the emancipation of the serfs as "a dreadful mix-up in relations" and expresses concerns about possible uprisings on the part of the peasantry, who expect to receive not only the land they till, but all of Russia. The nobility are to give up their land in exchange for legal guarantees, but there is no law and no justice in Russia. At a name day celebration and feast given for his own peasants, Kobylin fears for his life. We can see the phantasmagoric exchange of identity in *The Death of Tarelkin* as an image of what was to Kobylin a terrifying and misguided "mix-up" in social relations dictated by the tsar himself. The tsar, who stands at the very apex of the social hierarchy, presides over its destruction. For Kobylin, the tsar has lost all his aura, grace, and power. In *The Case,* the beleaguered Muromskii pleads to be taken to his "lord," but his request is denied. Symbolically, the tsar is dead, and there is nothing to replace him with. The "people" for Kobylin, remain the *chern'*, the rabble, fearful and loathsome. They never become the transcendent signifier of Russia's greatness, as they do for Dostoevsky and others. The emancipation of the serfs is like the murder of Louise Simon-Demanche writ large. Sukhovo-Kobylin's attack on unjust laws and unjust legal institutions does not translate into the imaginative re-creation of an alternative civility and community guided by just laws and a just legislator. In Tarelkin's speech, the social and individual transformation expected of the reforms turns out to be a circus trick, another form of imposture.

Conclusion

The sickening sense of flux and change that Sukhovo-Kobylin describes in his diary can be related to the loss of relations of power and subordination that made possible the expression of his individuality. In the much-quoted excerpt from Khomiakov's poem, with which this chapter opens, the poet addresses Russia: it is Russia who is black with the blackness of the injustice of her law courts, Russia who is "branded with the yoke of slavery." But Sukhovo-Kobylin does not write in the name of Russia. He deploys the metaphor of branding about himself. It is his name that is branded.

The trilogy reveals another dimension to the loss of individuality. It is not only political, but economic, forces that make possible what to the author are disastrous upheavals in social status. Krechinskii, Raspliuev, Tarelkin, and Varravin all are driven by the desire for money. Money makes possible a terrifying flux of identity. Money destroys the unique irreplaceable identity of the noble individual, because it destroys stable boundaries between groups of individuals. The vampire/werewolf images of *The Death of Tarelkin* capture the infinite exchange of identity that money produces. Who holds this money? Jewish pawnbrokers, called "Christ betrayers" by the characters in *Krechinskii's Wedding* and "vampire" bureaucrats. The image of the legal scribe as accursed Jew originates in the New Testament, which refers to the Pharisees, those who adhered most strictly to the letter of the law, as "lawyers." The biblical Barabbas, the murderer and seditionist whom the Jews ask Pilate to release instead of Christ, is the prototypical false substitute. Christ dies so that others may live, but Barabbas lives so that another—Christ—may die. The pawnbrokers and rapacious bureaucrats like Varravin who control the circulation of cash also regulate the circulation of identity. To abandon Russia to their care is to leave the proverbial fox to guard the chicken coop. Russia is left bled dry, drunk in the taverns, fleeced in the law courts—to use the language of Ivan Sidorov in *The Case*. The project of self-reinvention that lies behind the theater of Sukhovo-Kobylin cannot succeed because the cultural context in which such a self could thrive is irretrievably lost.

In the reform era, the social hierarchy so important to Kobylin is undermined. The reforms created new forms of justice: hearings before justices of the peace, and trial by jury in major criminal cases. The people replace the tsar as the source of justice—within limits that we will discuss in the next chapter. I will argue that these new forms of justice *carnivalize* the carefully articulated social distinctions that I have discussed in this chapter. The dominant metaphor for Kobylin and his case is theatricality; the dominant metaphor for the reform era is carnival. Carnival and theatricality are both forms of pleasure that involve play with roles. What distinguishes the two are the principles of individuation and distance, emphasized in aristocratic theatricality, and muted in carnival. Bakhtin argues that in carnival, as a popular festive form, individuality is lost, and the collectivity of the social body dominates. Bakhtin makes the further distinction between the closed-off individuated classical body and the opened multiple body of carnival. Kobylin characterizes the Russian people, embodied in his servants, as a source of pollution from which he must escape. Judgment before the public eye, of his theater and his person, represents a horrifying violation of his individuality. In contrast, positive rhetoric about the new courts in the 1860s and 1870s celebrates the Russian jury trial as a form of carnival, in which the harshness of the old law is overcome, and a new form of collective Russian national justice emerges.

Chapter 2

Trial by Jury and Trials of the Jury

In Russia practically no one remembers prerevolutionary Russian law. Certain fragments from novels: the jury court *(The Brothers Karamazov, Resurrection)*, the difficulties of divorce *(Anna Karenina)*.[1]

The legal reform of 1864 initiated by the government of Alexander II transformed the trial from a secret, written proceeding based on the "inquisitorial" principle into an open, public, oral proceeding organized to a far greater degree by the adversarial principle. Pretrial criminal investigations retained some features of the inquisitorial principle. An examining magistrate interrogated suspects without the presence of an attorney. Porfirii Petrovich, from Dostoevsky's *Crime and Punishment,* who uses sophisticated psychological methods to track down Raskolnikov, is a literary example of such a magistrate.[2] The reform simplified the structure of the court system and established the institution of the bar, justices of the peace, and the system of trial by jury for major criminal offenses.[3] The reform contained special provisions for ecclesiastical, military, commercial, and peasant courts, as well as for

---

1. Grigorii Pomerants, "The Reality of Fiction," *Znamia* 7 (1996): 235. The awareness of prerevolutionary Russian justice may be growing. For a comparison of current judicial procedure with the past, see Sergei Pashin, "Rossiskii sud prisiazhnykh vchera i segodnia," *Znamia* 6 (1996): 177–88.

2. For a study of Porfirii Petrovich in the context of the reform, see Richard H. Weisberg, *The Failure of the Word: The Protagonist as Lawyer in Modern Fiction* (New Haven, Conn.: Yale University Press, 1984), 45–54. Weisberg also suggests a link between the figures of the lawyer and the novelist, a point that I will take up later.

3. For a history of the reform, see Samuel Kucherov, *Courts, Lawyers, and Trials under the Last Three Tsars* (Westport, Conn.: Greenwood Press, 1953), 21–106. There are remarkably few studies of the Russian jury system. One of the best is Girish Bhat's recent dissertation, "Trial by Jury in the Reign of Alexander II: A Study in the Legal Culture of Late Imperial Russia, 1864–1881," University of California at Berkeley, 1995. I rely on Bhat for details of the operation of the courts in this period.

non-Russian residents. Male Russian citizens between the ages of twenty-five and seventy who satisfied certain property, income, and residence requirements could serve on juries. The insane, blind, deaf, and dumb, convicted criminals, and those employed as servants could not. There was no literacy requirement.

The Russian judicial reform borrowed elements from the English, French, and German legal systems, but the ultimate product was unique. The decision of the Russian jury was counted by a simple majority, and not unanimity. The jury answered "yes" or "no" to the questions put to it, but could find that a suspect was guilty but deserved indulgence. Like the juries of continental Europe, the Russian jury was not bound by law to pronounce a guilty verdict even if it found that the accused did commit the crime. The law outlining the procedure for jury trials states that after completing his instructions to the jury, the chairman of the court was to remind the jurors to determine the guilt or innocence of the accused according to their "inner conviction, based on the aggregate of all the circumstances of the case."[4] Unlike England, if a suspect confessed a crime, the case could still go before the jury. Cases involving "sacrilege" and crimes of a sexual nature were heard before juries, but not before the public. The *Juridical Gazette,* the organ of the Moscow Juridical Society, reported that during 1864, that is, before the reforms were instituted, 160 cases of sacrilege were prosecuted in Russia, out of which 71 individuals were sentenced to hard labor. In the same year, 1,912 cases of murder were prosecuted; out of these, 438 were sentenced to hard labor.[5] In the 1870s the tsarist government began to remove political cases from public jury trials. The 1917 revolution abolished the institutions created by the reforms.

The ideology guiding the tsarist legal reform, including earlier efforts made by Alexander I and Nicholas I, fall under the category of statist legalism. The law is an extension of the state, and legal institu-

---

4. Two decrees of the 1864 reform detailed the procedure for trial by jury, decree 41475, on judicial institutions, *Uchrezhdenie sudebnykh sudoproizvodstva,* and decree 41476, on criminal procedure, *Ustav ugolovnogo sudoproizvodstva.* They were published in *Polnoe sobranie zakonov Rossiiskoi Imperii* (The Complete Collection of Laws of the Russian Empire), series 2, 1825—81, vol. 39 (St. Petersburg, 1867). Henceforward I will refer to this collection as *PSZ* and give decree and article number in the body of the text. For the chairman's instruction to the jury, see *PSZ* 4176:804.

5. S. Shaikevich, "O polozhenii ugolovnogo pravosudiia v Rossii v techeniia 1864 goda," *Iuridicheskaia gazeta,* no. 6, September 15, 1866, 3–4.

tions that operate efficiently serve the state's interest. For example, Nicholas I, upon discovering a case involving the debts of one Ivan Balashev that had dragged on for twenty years, demanded that proposals be made to reform Russian legal procedure.[6] The reforms initiated by Alexander II in 1864 can also be seen in part as the state's effort to legitimate itself as nonautocratic, as "rational" and "enlightened." Alexander's Manifesto of November 1864 contains language about a "swift, just, and merciful court, possessed of an appropriate independence," but also stresses the need "to strengthen in the people that respect for law, without which public prosperity is impossible."[7]

The government of Alexander II initiated its reforms not for the purpose of instilling a legal culture in the population at large, but in order to increase the effectiveness of the law as a force of social control. In *The Development of a Russian Legal Consciousness* Richard Wortman shows that economic factors and the need to prevent social upheaval after the emancipation of the serfs were the arguments that persuaded Alexander II of the necessity for legal reform. The old system was not equal to the task of protecting private property. According to Wortman, the paradox of the state's efforts at reform throughout the nineteenth century was that the state's interest in developing more efficient legal mechanisms ultimately led the challenges to its autocratic power. The need for a better legal system created a need for legal expertise, which grew among a specialized body of reformers. Wortman argues that these reformers were distinguished by a legal ethos that stood in opposition to the interests of the autocratic state. The reformers emphasized the importance of an independent judiciary, which could operate without extralegal administrative constraints.

My emphasis is not on those who made the reform, but on those who received it, and especially, those members of the educated reading public who wrote about it. The new public jury trials, the justices of the peace, and the new professionalized bar generated, in the press, an explosion of interest. Several new publications appeared devoted entirely to the courts: for example, Moscow and St. Petersburg each had its own *Juridical Gazette*. The *Court Gazette*, another St. Petersburg publication, was a daily. The *Jurist*, a newspaper edited by two attorneys, began publication in the early part of the twentieth century and stated explicitly that its purpose was to acquaint readers with the "ongoing

---

6. See Wortman, *Russian Legal Consciousness*, 160.
7. Quoted in Wortman, *Russian Legal Consciousness*, 61–62.

phenomenon of our judicial life."[8] Court reporting became a regular feature of the daily newspapers. The reportage spanned the spectrum from dry accounts that approximated transcripts to sensationalistic docudramas. Readers could learn about the jury trials of the day and follow cases heard before justices of the peace both in their own and in other cities. For example, the *St. Petersburg News* for August 28, 1866, reported that "a certain important person" (a Gogolian phrase) refused to pay a small bill, and that upon being ordered to do so by a justice of the peace, he "threw" his money on the table and said: "better to pay up than to have dealings with this vulgar court."[9] He was sentenced to seven days of house arrest for this comment. The term I have translated as "vulgar"—*kholopskii*—is significant. It means what pertains to a *kholop*, a slave or serf, and hence, "base, servile." The new institution of the justice of the peace, according to the defendant in this case, breached the boundaries of class.[10] Like Sukhovo-Kobylin, this unnamed "important person" would prefer to retain his uniqueness before the law. The hearing before the justice of the peace and the public jury trial entered Russian literature, appearing in the works of Dostoevsky, Tolstoy, Chekhov, and many other less well known authors.

Many scholars see a negative attitude toward law and legal institutions, a rejection of the "juridical worldview," to use Weber's term, as part of the backdrop against which the impact of the reforms must be measured, and most identify the Slavophilism of the 1840s as crucial to subsequent Russian antilegalism in the latter part of the nineteenth century.[11] B. Kistiakovskii's essay "In Defense of Law," published in the first decade of the twentieth century, castigates the Russian intelligentsia for its neglect of legal culture. Kistiakovskii's essay appeared in *Landmarks (Vekhi)*, a controversial antirevolutionary anthology premised on the notion that social change must be based on change within the individual. Kistiakovskii quotes B. N. Almazov's caricature of the Slavophile Konstantin Aksakov:

---

8. *Iurist 1902*, no. 1, November 3, 1902, 5.

9. "Skromnyi chelovek," *St. Peterburgskie vedomosti*, August 28, 1866, 2.

10. For a study of the justices of the peace, see Joan Neuberger, "Popular Legal Cultures," *Russia's Great Reforms, 1855–1881*, ed. Ben Eklof, John Bushnell, and Larissa Zakharova (Bloomington: Indiana University Press, 1994), 231–46.

11. Andrzej Walicki's study of the history of Russian legal philosophy succeeds in combating this stereotype. For a discussion of the Slavophile position, see his *Legal Philosophies of Russian Liberalism* (London: Oxford University Press, 1987), 9–104.

For organic reasons
We are completely unequipped
With a healthy juridical sense,
With this child of Satan.
Russian nature is broad,
Our ideal of justice
Cannot fit into the narrow forms
Of juridical principles.[12]

My purpose is not to enter the debate about "Russian nature" and its capacity to absorb a Western legal system. Such an approach obscures what is specifically Russian in the new legal system and how it relates to already existing elements in Russian culture. The question about the Russianness of the new system was very much on the minds of late-nineteenth-century Russians. I am interested in how the new legal system, in particular the jury, was necessarily involved in the broader problem of Russian culture and national identity. In this chapter, and in chapter 4, on Dostoevsky and the new courts, the examination of particular jury trials and of debates in the press about the jury and the institution of the bar takes us directly to questions of "us and them," Russia and the West, and to questions about the internal dynamic of Russian society, relations between high and low, between the Russian Orthodox and the Jew, and between men and women. The emergence of the Russian jury provides another perspective on the self-imagination of the Russian body politic in the late nineteenth and early twentieth centuries.

Carnival

We can see in the reception of the jury an orientation toward multiplicity and open-endedness, the celebration of a breakdown in the hierarchy of judgment, and the emergence of a new form of judicial heteroglossia in the public space. I will argue that the changes brought by the reform—from secret to public hearings, from judge-centered administrative proceedings to jury trials—can best be characterized by

---

12. B. Kistiakovskii, "V zashchitu prava," *Vekhi: Sbornik statei o russkoi intelligentsii,* 2d ed. (Frankfurt am Main: Possev, 1967), 131. For a discussion, see L. Schapiro, "The *Vekhi* Group and the Mystique of Revolution," *Slavic and East European Review* 34, no. 82 (December 1955): 56–76.

the term *carnivalization*. Bakhtin distinguishes between the operation of the law, the state, all of its organs and apparatus, and everything related to the state and the dominant cultural hierarchy, what he calls "official culture," and everything that on the other side, dislodges and unsettles the language, procedure, hierarchy, law, and categories of "official culture." The antithesis of official culture is carnival. In carnival, all distinctions are made relative, all that is fixed and permanent, particularly judgment, is subject to decay, death, and rebirth; all decorum, propriety, and distinction is suspended. Unlike official pageantry and ceremonial, what predominates in carnival is not the display of power and rank, but laughter that destroys all distinctions, even that between the spectator and the spectacle. The participants in carnival laugh at themselves.

The public square, as a "chronotope," a particular way of organizing time and space, has a crucial relation to carnival. Bakhtin describes the public square as "the whole of science, the whole of art," and "the highest court . . . in which all the most elevated categories, from that of the state to that of revealed truth, were realized concretely and fully incarnated, made visible and given a face" ("Forms of Time," 132). In the space of the public square, "the laying bare and examination of a citizen's whole life was accomplished" (132). The clown and the fool have an intimate link with the chronotope of the public square; one of the main functions of the fool was "the making public of specifically nonpublic spheres of life" (161).

The potential similarity between the jury trial, the public square, and certain aspects of carnival was alarming to some. Count Kankrin, the former finance minister, in memoirs published in 1865, the year between the promulgation of the reform and its introduction into practice, characterizes the jury trial as an institution that leads to "spectacle" and "scandal," in which "justice takes the form of a theatrical performance, whose influence on the morality of the people and, in particular, on the morality of the young is obvious."[13] The jury is a throwback to "barbaric times" before the development of positive law, when there was no distinction between "precise legal proof and simple personal conviction."[14] The reformers had argued that the jury system

---

13. Quoted in "Vzgliady russkogo ministra pervoi polovinoi XIX stoletiia," *Otech-estvennye zapiski* 164 (February 1866): 276.

14. Ibid.

would spread legal knowledge and respect for law, and this emphasis is evident, as we have seen, in Alexander II's Manifesto of 1864. But according to Kankrin, the public jury trial spreads vice, not virtue. What the press glorifies as the jury's life experience and attentiveness to individuality Kankrin vilifies as primitive ignorance of the law. What transpires in the court is not the evaluation of evidence, but the play of emotions and the arousal of passions.

At a jury trial, a reincarnation of the public square, the line separating the private and the public is blurred. The defense and the prosecution, in order to unmask and discredit each other's witnesses, may, like Bakhtin's fool, "betray to the public a personal life down to its most private and prurient little secrets." This possibility, and the possibility of a general breach of decorum, is reflected in the provisions of the 1864 reform:

> The defense may neither expatiate on matters not having a relation to the case, nor permit himself to violate the necessary respect for religion, the law, and the established powers, nor to use expressions offensive to any person. (*PSZ* 267)

We may observe that the warning applies only to the defense. The government is leery of creating a public forum in which law, religion, and the established powers would come under attack. The anxiety about irrelevant and irreverent discussion in the courts was not new in 1864. Previous efforts at court reform had addressed similar concerns. Peter the Great eliminated oral testimony from the courts in part out of this fear. A line that appears in his decree of 1723 reads: "in the courts people talk too much," or, "say too many extraneous things" (*v sudakh mnogo daiut lishnego govorit'*).[15]

As in carnival, the central actor at a jury trial may be said to be the people. The power of judgment, which had formerly inhered in the tsar or his officials, is now dispersed to a corporate body that mingles social classes: merchants, civil servants of all ranks, nobles, and peasants sat together and were sequestered together. The radical journal the *Contemporary* noted the significance of the mixed composition of the jury, which consisted of "persons belonging to various classes of society and

---

15. *Reformy Petra pervogo: Sbornik dokumentov*, ed. V. I. Lebedev (Moscow: Gos. sotsial'no-ekon. izd-vo, 1937), 136.

differing in their manner of thinking and level of education.[16] The Russian historian Alexander Afanas'ev, relying on late-nineteenth-century official registrars of jurors, has concluded that the great preponderance of jurors outside St. Petersburg and Moscow "were peasants, while nobles, civil servants, and merchants made up only one-fourth of the jurors." In the capital districts, nobles and high-ranking civil servants made up the greatest numbers of jurors, but these districts represent only a twentieth of the total population of jurors.[17]

In a jury trial, languages are mixed: the official language of the law with its specialized terminology, the language of medical experts, the sometimes illiterate language of witnesses, and what was often the high literary style of the defense and prosecution are all heard together. The result is a judicial heteroglossia, and the text of the trial may be said to read like the text of a novel, which, for Bakhtin, is the primary literary form to inherit features of carnival.

It is not only the linguistic epiphenomena of the jury trial that are carnivalesque. The research of nineteenth- and twentieth-century Russian and Western scholars has shown that in comparison to their Western counterparts, and in comparison to prereform courts, Russian juries acquitted higher numbers of defendants.[18] The Russian jury's pattern of convictions and acquittals can be considered carnivalesque to the extent that its higher rate of acquittals shows a suspension of prevailing norms. The jury's finding in particular cases effectively undermined the severity of the law. For example, the code of 1866 defined "theft with breaking" (krazha so vzlomom) so broadly as to include the simple removal of an object from a trunk or chest "by means of tearing the seal attached to it."[19] In order to avoid the severity of the punishment for this crime, Russian juries often acquitted confessed suspects, which lead to a reform of the law in 1882. Afanas'ev correlates an increase in the number of acquittals with peasant holidays, which suggests that the carnival of the peasant holiday spilled over into the decisions of the jury.

The jury's freedom to acquit a confessed defendant meant that the

---

16. A. Unkovskii, "Novye osnovaniia sudoproizvodstva," Sovremennik 95 (April 1863): 546.

17. Alesander K. Afanas'ev, "Jurors and Jury Trials in Imperial Russia, 1866–1885," in Eklof, Bushnell, and Zakharova, Russia's Great Reforms, 220.

18. See Bhat, "Trial by Jury," 188.

19. Istoricheskii ocherk 1866, quoted in I. V. Gessen, Sudebnaia reforma (St. Petersburg, 1905), 165.

link between crime and punishment, while not severed, could be and was imagined differently. Previous methods for the determination of judicial truth, such as the confession, and the match in testimony between two witnesses, were suspended. As the example of the nobleman before the justice of the peace shows, distinctions of rank also lost some of their significance. These changes were not complete. The Russian jury did not, of course, acquit all defendants. Rules and norms were not abandoned, but to a certain extent reinvented. The tsar still retained a very significant degree of power.[20] As we will see, the persistence of religious norms limits the carnival of the new justice. The carnival of the Russian jury trial, in several senses, was an ephemeral phenomenon.

Acquittals

The acquittal rate became a subject of controversy in the reform era, both for the government and for the press. In order to give a sense of what these cases were like, I will provide several examples, beginning with two cases that were very ordinary, without sensationalistic features, and without political implications. Both cases are taken from accounts published in the *Juridical Herald* in 1873 under the heading "Juridical Practice."

The first is a summation. In June 1873 the Tula Circuit Court heard the case of Agaf'ia Trifonova, a peasant woman accused of theft with breaking. Tula, located south of Moscow, was an industrial area in imperial Russia. Nastas'ia Gormysheva, a former house serf, made out a declaration to the police that Trifonova had been her guest on December 26, 1872. While Gormysheva took a nap, Trifonova allegedly removed several items from a locked trunk and took a women's padded coat that was hanging on the wall. None of the property except the coat was found on the defendant. This evidence, contradictions between her testimony and that of several witnesses, and a previous arrest for theft led to the institution of criminal proceedings against Trifonova. The source does not specify, but it seems that Trifonova was

---

20. Laura Engelstein writes that "the tsar appropriated the institutional appurtenances of a rule-of-law state (legal codes, independent judiciary, trial by jury), while continuing to exercise absolute sovereignty through the mechanisms of a virtually unimpeded administrative state." "Combined Underdevelopment: Discipline and the Law in Imperial and Soviet Russia," *American Historical Review* 98, no. 2 (April 1993): 343.

taken into custody very close to the time that Gormysheva made out
the complaint against her.

During the trial, the jury was informed about Trifonova's previous
arrest, and that she had been released from prison only four days before
her alleged involvement in the present crime. The first witness to be
questioned was the alleged victim, who said that Trifonova took the
coat and left her own jacket behind. The trunk from which the items
were taken was under the bed on which the victim slept while the crime
took place. The lock was not in good repair and could be opened with a
nail. The prosecution for the most part pointed to the contradictions in
the defendant's testimony. The defense argued that there was no evidence for theft with breaking, inasmuch as no one saw the defendant
remove the property and the property was not subsequently found.
There was no evidence of "breaking," since according to the victim's
testimony, the lock on the trunk was poor. As far as the coat was concerned, there was no evidence of theft, because the defendant left her
own garment in its place. To the question as to whether Trifonova had
"stolen various property" and unlocked the trunk, the jury answered in
the negative.

We may speculate as to the reasons. The interval of time between
arrest and trial—approximately six months—may have been significant. For her previous theft of a dress, a justice of the peace sentenced
her to a jail term of three months. The jury may have wanted to avoid
the harsh penalty for "breaking," which involved hard labor. Or they
may have thought that "stealing" was an inappropriate description of
the substitution of one garment for another. According to this jury, the
involuntary trade that Gormysheva was forced to participate in was
not a serious criminal offense. The jury in the Trifonova case did not
come to a determination of the facts, but reinvented the law according
to its own rationale.

The next example of a questionable acquittal is a murder case in
the Iaroslav district, north of Moscow. The victim was an elderly
woman, Ul'iana Agafonova, a member of the Anabaptist sect, who
lived in her own house with two other people, Varvara Zherekhova,
age seventy-seven, and Varvara's brother Karp Zherekhov, age sixty-
six. Maxim Zherekhov, age twenty-one, was accused of the murder, and
his aunt and uncle, Varvara and Karp, were accused of concealing the
crime. Maxim spent one and a half years in prison awaiting trial. The
victim's nephew, Andrian, told the police that upon being informed of

his aunt's death, he went to her house, where he found her body prepared for burial, with a kerchief tied in such a way that her face was almost entirely covered. He noticed marks on her chin and cheeks. It was two months after the burial that rumors began to circulate that Ul'iana had been murdered for her money by her other nephew Maxim. The corpse was exhumed, and an autopsy revealed signs of violence.

The jury panel of fourteen (twelve members and two alternates) consisted of four noblemen, a retired private, three merchants, two teachers, two peasants, and two members of the *meshchane* (burger class).[21] All of the defendants denied that they were guilty. A lengthy and detailed act of indictment was read aloud to the jury. The indictment included changes in testimony given by Karp to the pretrial investigator. Karp, like the other defendants, initially denied his guilt but then confessed after several interrogations. He said that on the night of Ul'iana's death, his sister Varvara was out, and that Ul'iana sat spinning. His nephew Maxim entered the house, complaining of cold, and Ul'iana gave him warm water to drink. Maxim joined his uncle at the stove for a short time, complained of cold again, and received more water from Ul'iana. The light went out; he heard Ul'iana fall on the floor and cry out, when he lit the light again, he found his nephew on his knees at Ul'iana's head. His nephew told him to be quiet and that nothing would happen. According to the indictment, it had to be assumed that Maxim strangled his aunt, since he did not typically carry a weapon. Varvara returned home shortly after the murder. She went to get another woman to wash the body for burial.

One of the witnesses who assisted in the preparation of the body was asked by the defense attorney for Varvara whether it was perhaps a custom to cover the face. The witness answered that it was customary to tie a kerchief around the head, and when the chair of the court asked in what fashion, the witness answered that "it's known that you are going to the Day of Judgment." The answer is unclear. Is it women in particular who must not look into the face of divine judgment? The note of religious awe is significant.

During the trial, the results of the autopsy were read aloud. Details of the wounds to the face and jaw, the condition of the vessels of the brain, fractures in the ribs, and the condition of the lungs were all spec-

---

21. I use Afanas'ev's definition of this term.

ified. The conclusion was that the victim died by strangulation and that her ribs were broken while she was alive. The specialized medical language contrasts sharply with the monosyllabic answers of most of the witnesses and the defendants. When the prosecutor pointed a contradiction between pretrial and courtroom testimony as to whether Varvara paid gold to the women who washed the body, the witness said, "Forgive me, for Christ's sake." At various moments when witnesses gave incriminating testimony, the defendants were asked whether they had anything to say. Karp answered, "It's all untrue," but when pressed for detail, said, "I don't know what to say, your honor." For the defendants the whole procedure is a terrible judgment, which they are powerless to alter.

The main point of the prosecutor's speech was the contradictory testimony given by the suspects, particularly Karp, and by Maxim's father, who testified in court that he gave his son money but had previously denied doing so. The secretary of the court read aloud the father's previous testimony. Maxim was found with gold after the murder, but no clear account of how he got the gold could be produced. The defense argued that the medical evidence was not compelling, that no clear account of how much money Ul'iana possessed was forthcoming, and that Maxim's character—a country boy who liked to drink every now and then—was incompatible with murder. The second defense attorney argued that since it was unclear how much money Ul'iana had, and since it was unclear whether or how much money Varvara gave to the women who washed the body, there was no case against Varvara. As far as Karp was concerned, the defense raised a question as to how his confession was obtained and said that it was sufficient to look at him to realize that he could not have participated in such a terrible crime. Although the jury found that Ul'iana was indeed murdered, they found all the defendants not guilty.

Karp's confession to the pretrial investigator, which incriminated Maxim, Varvara, and Karp himself, was set aside by the jury. We can speculate as to what may have induced the jury to respond to the confession in this way—suspicions about the repeated interrogations that led to the confession, Karp's character, consideration for his and his sister's advanced age, the lack of corroborating evidence, or the reminder from the witness that everyone faces divine judgment. In the prereform era confession was the "best evidence"; in the postreform era, juries evaluated confessions according to a variety of criteria. The meaning of legal truth had changed.

The Trial of Vera Zasulich

From these relatively obscure but revealing acquittals I turn to cases that were well known and much written about in their time and beyond, beginning with the trial of Vera Zasulich in 1878.[22] Zasulich shot and severely wounded the governor-general of St. Petersburg, V. V. Trepov, because he had a political prisoner, Bogoliubov, beaten for not removing his cap upon seeing him. The beating caused an uproar in the house of preliminary detention where it took place and in the press. A. F. Koni, one of nineteenth-century Russia's foremost jurists, served as chairman of the court. In his memoirs, Koni writes that Count Palen, the minister of justice, was outraged that he would not guarantee a conviction in the Zasulich case.[23] Zasulich said that she shot Trepov as an act of revenge and was charged with premeditated attempted murder. The defense, P. A. Alexandrov, was a former prosecutor who went on to become a renowned liberal lawyer. He emphasized Zasulich's previous suffering, her own previous imprisonments—"prison was her alma mater"—and suggested that she could not have planned the attack in cold blood, but in a state resembling temporary insanity. He described the scene of Bogoliubov's beating as the creation of a sacrificial victim: "the sacrament was performed. . . . the victim was carried away."[24] The public responded with applause and cries of "Bravo!" Koni at this point reminded the public that the court was not a theater. This breach of decorum, however, was mild compared to the commotion that was to come at the end of the trial. Koni's instructions to the jury emphasized the possibility of mercy:

> Perhaps her sorrowful, nomadic youth will provide an explanation to you for the bitterness that accumulated in her, which made her

---

22. Other famous political trials of the time were the Trial of the Fifty (1877) and the Trial of the 193 (1877 to 1878). For a discussion of these trials see Engelstein, "Revolution."

23. A. F. Koni, *Izbrannye proizvedeniia* (Moscow: Gosudarstvennoe izdatel'stvo iuridicheskoi literatury, 1956), 539.

24. "Delo Very Zasulich," in *Sud prisiazhnykh v Rossii: Gromkie ugolovnye protsessy 1864–1917gg*, ed. S. M. Kazantsev (Leningrad: Lenizdat, 1991), 296.

less calm, more impressionable, and more vulnerable to the effects of the life that surrounded her, and you will find a basis for mercy.[25]

The jury returned a verdict of not guilty. Koni describes what followed: "shrieks of joy, hysterical sobbing, applause, foot stomping, the cries 'Vera! Verochka!'" One of the judges, G. A. Baranstov, also applauded "with fervor." Koni writes that he was afraid the joy would turn into something dangerous and warned the other judges not to take any steps.

Several elements of carnival can be traced in this trial: the reversal of judgment, the formation of a joyous crowd in which at least some hierarchy is overcome (Baranstov's applause), and the crowning of the carnival king—the defense was lifted on the shoulders of the crowd and carried into the street. The courtroom and the street merge into one. The Zasulich trial presents a symmetrical contrast to the staged spectacle of Bogoliubov's beating. Everyone was overcome by "a feeling of joy," Koni writes, while he and the other judges sat "like Roman senators during the attack of the Gauls on Rome."[26] The barbarians had stormed the gates, and the guardians were powerless to stop them. The Zasulich trial became a spontaneous public festival with serious overtones of political subversion. There were, however, several limitations to the carnivalesque in the Zasulich trial. The first has to do with the defense strategy. Bogoliubov, as a gentleman, ought to have been immune from corporal punishment. The defense stressed the illegality of his beating. The attempt to overturn the expected judgment against Zasulich, who confessed to the shooting, depended on the articulation of the traditional hierarchal distinctions between classes. Second, the Senate, Russia's highest judicial authority, subsequently overturned the jury's acquittal.[27]

---

25. Ibid., 316. For another discussion of the trial and Koni's speech, see Bhat, "Trial by Jury," 240–45.

26. Koni, *Izbrannye proizvedeniia*, 569.

27. For a comparison of the Zasulich trial to the fate of Fannia Kaplan, who attempted to assassinate Lenin, see Evgenii Danilov, "Tri vystrela v Lenina, ili za chto kaznili Fanni Kaplan," *Neva* 5–6 (1992): 307–24.

The Wrath of God

The Mel'nitskii case of 1884 reveals to what degree the jury trial had become troubling to the autocracy. The jury as carnivalizer of tsarist judgment became politically threatening, even when the case is not political. A son was found innocent of acting as his father's accomplice in the embezzlement of a large sum of money from a state orphanage. F. I. Mel'nitskii, the father, was found guilty of embezzling 307,000 rubles from a state-run orphanage, but a large part of the stolen money was not found. In December of the same year, bonds and cash totaling 234,000 rubles were found in the apartment of Mel'nitskii's relatives, including his son, Boris. In the subsequent trial, the jury was asked: was it proven that Boris "by prior arrangement with his father, was his accomplice in the theft and acted with a selfish purpose, but upon receipt of the money concealed it and spent it according to his own will?" The jury found that Boris did not act with a selfish purpose and was not guilty of the theft.

The defense argued in part that the careless procedures with regard to money were responsible for the fact that so much of it ended up in the Mel'nitskii's hands. The public prosecutor of the Moscow Circuit Court appealed the case, and the appeal was heard in the Criminal Department of the Senate in March 1884. The hearing became a trial of the institution of the jury itself. The prosecution was lead by the well-known criminologist N. A. Nekliudov, who made his first appearance in Russian public life with a stint in prison for antigovernment activity, and now was the chief procurator. In the 1860s Nekliudov was known to the liberal-progressive elements of Russian society as the author of the first statistical study of crime in Russia. The study provided ammunition for the liberal-progressive argument about climactic and physiological factors that contributed to criminality.

But Nekliudov changed. In his speech, Nekliudov said that the legal reform, "the glory and pride of the previous administration," had more recently been subject to public censure, which was completely justified in his view. The present climate was reminiscent of that terrible page of the Bible which reads:

And God repented that he created man on earth. . . . And God said, "I will destroy men from the face of the earth." Justice demands

that we acknowledge that a significant part of the reproach falls
deservedly to the account of the defense, who does not wish to distinguish the innocent from the guilty and turns the same means of
defense for both an obvious malefactor and for an individual who
accidentally stumbles into crime and insists no matter what that its
Barabbas be released to it, to this end crucifying the witnesses and
even the law itself. . . . I firmly believe that the . . . strict control on
the part of the Ruling Senate over the activities of the chairmen of
the court and over the defense will place criminal justice on that
height on which it ought to stand. I also firmly believe under the
influence of this control will come that day, finally, when the judicial flood will pass, and we, having turned that gloomy page of the
Bible, will hear, like Noah, the ringing out of a new and better life:
"I will not curse the court of man." An example that our sovereign
would not be ashamed to follow.[28]

Invoking the stereotypical wrathful God of Genesis, Nekliudov reminds
his audience of the awesome punitive power of the state, its quasi-
divine status, and its capacity to destroy its own creation. One commen-
tator remarked that the "expression of the idea of mercy of the New Testament . . . let justice and mercy reign in your courts . . . turned out to be
unsuitable for the Senate orator."[29] The quote from the New Testament
opens the section of the legal code establishing the new jury system. The
conflict between the government and the new judiciary played itself out
rhetorically as a conflict between God the Father and God the Son.

The Old Testament references in Nekliudov's speech are highly
suggestive, especially in the context of the New Testament language
used to characterize the new jury system by the government and members of the Russian public. For Nekliudov and the ruling Senate in 1884,
the New Testament of justice and mercy proclaimed by the previous
tsar, Alexander II, and embodied in the new court system does not
replace the Old. In this particular rewriting of Christian history, the Old
Testament God can at any moment revoke the New Testament. The
God of the New Testament, the God of love, exists only at the pleasure
of the God of the Old Testament, the God of wrath. What God gives he
can take away. Nekliudov seeks to remind all the participants in the

---

28. "Sudebnye ustavy i zakliuchenie ober-prokuratora po delam Mel'nitskikh i
Sviridova," *Zhurnal ugolovnogo i grazhdanskogo prava* 5 (May 1884): 160–61.

29. V. Volodimirov, introduction to "Sudebnye ustavy i zakliuchenie ober-prokuratora po delam Mel'nitskikh i Sviridova," 91.

new courts, most importantly the lawyers and chairmen, but also the Russian educated public at large, that the new jurists seem to have forgotten their status as creatures of the tsar's will. The "carnival" was out of control. The father-tsar sought to reassert his control over his rebellious creation.

National Narratives: The Holy Russian Jury

The carnivalization of the old legal procedure and the possibility of reinventing Russian justice—within certain fixed limits—also meant the possibility of rewriting the Russian national narrative so as to incorporate the new legal culture. For example, the first issue of the *Juridical Gazette,* published in 1866, the year the new courts went into operation, proclaimed that the jury system was a "restoration of ancient Russian justice." The new legal system resonated powerfully with existing narratives of Russia's national history, and with elements of Russian religious culture. We will see that the New Testament opposition between the letter and the spirit is an important feature of the rhetoric surrounding the new jury. The Russian people emerge as the collective hero of the story, embodying the new law of the spirit.

In characterizing the reception of the jury court, we are dealing with constructions of the Russian jury produced by newspaper reporters, prominent members of the bar, government officials, and literary authors. In 1896 the lawyer K. K. Arsen'ev lamented that Russian jurors were "mysterious strangers."[30] These mysterious strangers had been the object of veneration and praise in the press.

In April 1876 the *Week (Nedelia)* ran a lengthy article about the Russian jury trial in response to a recent ethnographic study of folk courts. Taking the example of a property dispute, the article distinguishes two tendencies. The first, Roman law, "will weigh the arguments of both sides and try to find something that will give greater weight to one side, even if this addition is a sheer formality." The other, the jurist, the "country jurist," will divide the disputed property between the two, relying on his instinct that "both are to blame" *(grekh po polam).* The *Week* goes on to say that the principle of distributing responsibility is "applied in all cases in which the feeling of natural justice does not permit the unconditional recognition of the right of one side."[31] Russian national justice is supremely attuned to the individual,

---

30. Arsen'ev, quoted in Afanas'ev, "Jurors and Jury Trials," 217.
31. *Nedelia,* April 15, 1876, 119.

to individual circumstances such as personality and financial obligations. The article concludes by suggesting that the individualization of
criminal law is something that the West is moving to. "Isn't trial by jury
(which would have been more natural for us to invent and give to the
West rather than the other way around) evidence of this?" Trial by jury
is understood to be an extension of "Russian national justice," not alien
to it, so much a part of that characteristically Russian attentiveness to
individuality that the jury should have been a Russian, and not a Western, invention. "Natural justice" and "national justice" merge in the
Russian jury. Rome, the West, and the formalism of the law of the officials are on one side, and the Russian people, nature, and justice on the
other.

M. P. Timofeev's *The Jury in Russia,* published in 1881, makes a similar point about the feeling for justice inherent in the ordinary Russian,
especially the peasant. Timofeev recounts an episode in the early years
of the jury trial when a group of peasant jurors refused to sit with a
peasant who had been found guilty of bribe taking in his previous
capacity as a judge in a peasant court. For Timofeev, this collective self-
purification is extremely significant. It reveals the peasants' own attitude about their legal duties: "only pure, unstained elements should be
a part of the court of conscience."[32] This feel for justice is linked to the
Russian peasant's religious sensibility. The very act of sitting on the
jury transforms the Russian peasant:

> The coarse, uneducated peasant is in court made into a person in
> the full sense of the word; the atmosphere of the court, the fear of
> answering before his conscience, and the oath before God, better
> than any Western-European training, influence our simple people,
> bringing forth in the service of justice their pure instincts, their
> good relations with their fellow man. (12)

The procedure of the judicial oath causes a remarkable transformation
in the peasant, bringing forward his "pure instincts," and presumably,
suppressing his impure ones. The inherent but dormant goodness and
purity of the Russian peasant is resurrected in court, when the peasant
sits on a jury. The metaphorical angelic state of the ordinary Russian
juror has a literal side. Timofeev includes diary entries from a Russian

---

32. M. P. Timofeev, *Sud prisiazhnykh v Rossii: Sudebnye ocherki* (Moscow, 1881), 9.

juror who observes that some of his fellow jurymen were so poor that they could not buy food during a lengthy court session and were obliged to fast (331).

Timofeev's contrast between "Western" legal training and what is implied to be the uniquely Russian religious sense is also important. The lists specifying prospective jurors for each province and city had to note who was an Orthodox Christian (*PSZ* 41475:103). In taking the oath, Orthodox jurors swore to "almighty God, his sacred Gospels, and his life-giving cross . . . to apply all the strength of [their] reason to a careful examination of the circumstances . . . in accordance with the truth and the conviction of [their] conscience," remembering that they were answerable in everything "before the law and before God on the Day of Judgment" (*PSZ* 41476:666). As Girish Bhat shows, the Russian oath was far more religious in character than the oath used by the French. The ceremony of kissing the cross and the Gospels, and the reminder that the juror would ultimately face divine judgment, had a powerful religious impact on the juror.[33] According to Timofeev, the jury's main task as "representatives of the public conscience" is safeguarded by the "oath before the face of Almighty God" (32). In terms of the generational conflict that we have been tracing, the jury, the "sons," freeing themselves from the harsh law of the father, making their judgments according to their conscience alone, are reminded that ultimately they face the judgment of their divine Father.

A more playful attitude toward the duties of the juror can be seen in an article from the *Stock Market News (Birzhevye vedomosti)* in February 1876. The jury is not the embodiment of the Russian people's timeless natural justice but is subject to the "curse of the given environment, its vices, doubtful virtues, prejudices."[34] Nonetheless, "all of this is better than what we have invented so far." Of all the members of the court, the jury is the highest. The jury consists of the

> people's judges—they are taken directly from life . . . and each one of them is higher in position than the lawyers with their badges, and the prosecutor with his cross, and the judges in their sparkling uniforms. . . . Everyone turns to them, everyone quarrels, lies, demonstrates truth or falsehood, streams of eloquence pour fourth, they wear out their tongues with social mores, laws, and

---

33. See Bhat, "Trial by Jury," 97–136.
34. *Birzhevye vedomosti*, no. 31, February 1, 1876.

the human soul, and the latest discoveries and inventions. Keep
clear of all this, be as wise as snakes and as innocent as doves. . . .
Alas, Darwin confirms that the dove is an extremely vicious bird.

We can hear a disparaging note in this and other characterizations of
the courtroom oratory of the time. The *Stock Market News* finds the jury
is "higher" than those who pour forth streams of eloquence at it. The
New Testament reference to snakes and doves suggests a similarity
between the difficulty of the task facing the jury and that facing the
apostles of Jesus, but the references to the environment and to Darwin
undercut any association between the jury and some notion of the
Russian jury's apostolic mission. In his description of the first jury trial
in a provincial area, V. N. Leshkov, the chairman of the Moscow Juridical Society and one of the editors of its *Juridical Gazette,* makes a similar
distinction between the excesses of the defense lawyer and the self-
restraint of the jury, guided by its conscience and by common sense.

Tolstoy's novel *Resurrection* (1899) contains a passage very close to
the critique of courtroom oratory from the *Stock Market News*. Here is
the narrator's description of the prosecutor's speech:

> His speech contained everything that was the very latest then in
> fashion in his circle and that was taken and is still taken even now
> for the last word in scientific wisdom. There was inheritance, and
> innate criminality, and Lombroso, and Tarde, and evolution, and
> the struggle for existence, and hypnotism, and inspiration, and
> Charcot, and decadence.

Unlike other commentators, Tolstoy also attacks the jury. In the novel,
the jury members at first sense the artificiality of their position and then
come to a decision based on incidental factors, such as the overbearing
tone of one of their members, their boredom, and weariness. One
columnist for the *Jurist,* writing for the newspaper in 1902, responded
to Tolstoy by defending the jury. He wrote that for the Russian juror, the
summons to appear in court is like a sacred icon. "The simple Russian
person, who makes up the main contingent of jurors, brings a profound
religious sense to his activities."[35]

A. A. Kvachevskii, who participated in the formulation of the

35. M. Orshanskii, "L. N. Tolstoi i pravosudie," *Iurist,* 1902, no. 6, 235.

reform of 1864, wrote a handbook on the jury, designed to aid trial lawyers. Kvachevskii emphasizes the positive link between the jury and the concrete social environment:

> The law has in mind to provide in the jury judges who are more familiar with life than the learned judges, who stand closer to life than they, and who therefore will be guided in their verdicts not only by general rules, but also by life experience, which illuminates these general rules. . . . The jury will not bend everything to fit the letter of the law alone, but will consider the law with its lived meaning.[36]

Kvachevskii makes a distinction between the abstract knowledge of judges and the "life experience" of juries. The law without the jury is the letter without the spirit. The law and the jury thus complement one another.

V. Nikitin, a reporter who wrote frequently on the new justices of the peace, and about the jury courts, does not find a balance, but a tension between the law and the jury.[37] The law, according to Nikitin, seeks to classify crimes and intentions, but the jury is interested in motivation. The jury considers an act to be a crime not simply in virtue of factual guilt,

> but only when the characteristics determining the intention indicate base . . . instincts. . . . They are not satisfied by analysis of the mental provocation and attempt to reach the causes and conditions that could lead to unnatural instincts.[38]

Nikitin gives the example of a defendant who has murdered a lover out of jealousy. The jury considers this equivalent to suicide because it means "delivering yourself to the arms of the law at the very scene of the crime" (138). According to the jury's reasoning, such a crime testifies to the profound attachment the murderer had for the victim, and to the murderer's lack of understanding about the consequences of the

---

36. A. Kvachevskii, *Sud prisiazhnykh po russkim zakonam: Rukovodtsvo dlia prisiazhnykh zasedatelei* (St. Petersburg, 1873), 480–81.

37. For more on Nikitin and the justices of the peace, see Neuberger, "Popular Legal Cultures," 231–46.

38. V. Nikitin, "Neestestvennyi dualizm," *Molva*, 1876, no. 7, 38.

crime. Therefore a jury will find the defendant guilty, but without premeditation. According to Nikitin, the jury defines murder out of jealousy very nearly as an act of self-sacrifice. The focus of the jury's attention is on the internal drama of the murderer's emotions, and not on the
fate of the victim. In a later chapter, we will examine a case of jealousy
that fits this model: a woman who confesses to the attempted murder of
her lover's wife is found innocent.

As Kistiakovskii points out, most of the praise for the jury in late-
nineteenth-century Russia has to do with its conscience and feeling for
the accused, and not its knowledge of the law or impartiality.[39] Some of
the more ardent supporters of the jury begin to suggest a link between
these qualities and the New Testament concept of the spirit as opposed
to the letter. M. Iur'in, writing for the newspaper *Day (Den')* in 1863,
uses the metaphor of the dead letter to characterize law in general:
"Without the living influence of the demands of conscience on positive
law, the latter remains the deadest of letters and the most immoral of
despotisms."[40] The opposition between the letter and the spirit, the Old
Testament and the New, became the dominant metaphor used to distinguish the old legal system and the new jury trial. In his memoir, I. S.
Aksakov, who served in the old system, uses the metaphor of the dead
letter to characterize the hopelessness of the judge's task. The judge

> reads carefully from cover to cover, examines the handwriting,
> persistently interrogates the paper, searches for some living hint in
> a living human sense that could be liable to his judgment: the
> paper is silent—the official account of the testimony of the criminal
> is lifeless and dead.[41]

In Aksakov's memoir, the dead letter signifies the limitations of the prereform system. In the reform era, Russian jurors come to symbolize the

---

39. See Kistiakovskii, "V zashchitu prava." Marianne Constable's history of the
"mixed jury" argues that the standard of impartiality is a relatively recent development
in the Anglo-American legal tradition. From the twelfth to the nineteenth centuries,
aliens had the right to have members of their own communities serve on juries, hence
"mixed juries." Persons and the law of their communities were understood to have a vital
connection to one another. The rise of positivism and the growth of sociology and behav-
ioral science contributed to the acceptance of impartiality and other related understand-
ings of what law is. See Constable, *The Law of the Other: The Mixed Jury and Changing Conceptions of Citizenship, Law, and Knowledge* (Chicago: University of Chicago Press, 1994).

40. M. Iur'in, "O novom sude," *Den'*, no. 7, February 16, 1863, 8.

41. Quoted in Gessen, *Sudebnaia reforma*, 30

"able ministers of the New Testament; not of the letter, but of the spirit: for the letter killeth, but the spirit giveth life" (2 Cor. 3:6).

Law and Literature

The defenders of the new courts glorify the jury at the expense of other members of the court, particularly defense attorneys. Juries are "higher" than lawyers, who pour forth streams of eloquence, as we have just seen. The nature of courtroom oratory was a subject of great controversy in the reform era. In a series of articles published in the late nineteenth and early twentieth century, A. F. Koni addresses this question at some length. For Koni, all aspects of the trial, including the pretrial investigation, the interrogation of witnesses, the speeches of the prosecution and the defense, and the chairman's instructions to the jury, require skill at public speaking. All of these procedures require clear, forceful, effective speech. Koni gives advice on gesture, tone, dress, and diction. For example, he urges members of the bar to avoid foreign words such as *alibi,* which are incomprehensible to the jury. If the attorney finds it necessary to engage in psychological analysis, he would do better to avoid Dostoevsky and imitate Tolstoy instead. Discussing a recent handbook on courtroom oratory, Koni finds that the tasks of the lawyer and the creative artist have much in common. Koni writes that both literature and law refract reality through the prism of the creative imagination. The main difference is that the courtroom orator will ultimately formulate conclusions for the defense or the prosecution, whereas the artist will develop the impressions he has received into "poetic images." However, the difference between the two is not as great as it may first appear, since the courtroom orator, in order to communicate his conclusions to his audience, must learn "both to think and consequently to speak in images."[42] In speaking of his own early years as a prosecutor, Koni remarks that there were few examples of courtroom oratory that he could follow. He used religious writings, such as the *Lives of the Saints,* as sources for pithy expressions and vivid images. For Koni there is a clear and explicit relation between literary art and the art of courtroom oratory. However, this self-consciously literary creativity is only one dimension of legal oratory. The members of the court have an

---

42. A. F. Koni, "Iskusstvo rechi na sude," in *Izbrannye proizvedeniia,* 100.

obligation before the law, before society, morality, and before the living person standing before them.

Filthy Lawyers

What models, not only of oratory, but general behavior, the new generation of Russian attorneys should follow presented a problem. Within a decade after the introduction of a professional bar, public dissatisfaction with it was high. In 1875 the *Week,* a passionate advocate of the new jury system, published an extremely negative article about the bar. The author was M. Gromnitskii, a legal official under the old system who became the procurator of the Moscow Circuit Court after the reform. Gromnitskii characterizes lawyers as follows: "there is no moral indecency which could not appear in print if the hero of this indecency is a lawyer."[43] The word Gromnitskii uses for "indecency" is *bezobrazie,* that which has no form or shape, that which disfigures and pollutes.[44] The "coarse and uneducated [*neobrazovannyi*] peasant becomes a person" in the courtroom, takes on his human image, but the lawyer, in perpetrating his "moral indecencies" both in the courtroom and in his chambers, loses his human image and causes others to lose theirs. In describing legal circles in Moscow, Gromnitskii emphasizes the lack of discrimination in accepting cases, the use of unscrupulous agents to get cases, the competition among lawyers, the envy, the slander, and the dissemination of false rumors to besmirch another's reputation. Gromnitskii says that even the "purest lawyer" who enters into relations with other lawyers ends up covered in "a pile of dirt."[45]

Criticism of lawyers is extremely widespread. Koni also takes his fellow members of the bar to task for their behavior in the courtroom. In an article published in 1914 on the jury Koni cites I. P. Zakrevskii (the procurator for the Kazan and Kharkov provincial court, later a senator), who initially supported the jury system and then later turned against it. Zakrevskii writes:

> I protest against the transformation of the court in which juries sit into an arena for the utterance of sophistry, for the arousal of every

---

43. M. Gromnitskii, "Advokat ob advokatakh," *Nedelia,* 1875, no. 52, 1759.

44. As Robert Louis Jackson points out in his analysis of this term in *The Brothers Karamazov;* see *Dostoevsky's Quest for Form—a Study of His Philosophy of Art* (New Haven, Conn.: Yale University Press, 1966).

45. Gromnitskii, "Advokat ob advokatakh," 1759.

kind of emotion, for the drawing of unnecessary psychological studies, for the performance of spectacles that would be pleasing to women.[46]

Women could not serve as jurors, but they could sit in the audience, and somehow their tastes invidiously control the proceedings that exclude them.

Koni elaborates at length on the danger of the court as spectacle. He writes that defense lawyers permit themselves the use of "ironic tricks" and "mocking nicknames" that have no relation to the matter at hand but "arouse in the public, who come to the session out of idle curiosity, a cheerful mood and indecent giggling."[47] Koni cites with approval a Senate proclamation of 1892: "the conditions of contemporary legal proceedings ought not to permit the witnesses to leave the court morally trampled upon, for the court is supposed to be a sanctuary of truth and justice, and not a shameful spectacle for the unbridling of morals."[48] Koni describes a case heard in the Moscow Circuit Court of a husband accused of the premeditated murder of his wife. According to Koni, the improper questions of the defense lawyer transformed the proceedings in a "peremptory trial" of the dead victim. For example, one witness was asked what prevented him from having a love affair with the dead woman—his own lack of desire or her virtue. The chairman of the court declared that he did not know what motivated the witnesses "to throw clods of dirt at the grave of the deceased."[49] The distinction between the innocent and the guilty, victim and perpetrator, is blurred when everyone is subject to abuse. The loss of distinctiveness is characteristic of carnival laughter, which, Bakhtin writes, "is directed at all and everyone, including the carnival's participants" (*Rabelais,* 11). To enter the courtroom is to run the risk of being smeared with filth. The grotesque body in question, the source of the filth, is not the body of the people in its festive celebration, but the guild of lawyers.

Theater in the Courtroom: Pro and Contra

One of the most important attacks mounted against this body was Evgenii Markov's feuilleton "Sophists of the Nineteenth Century,"

---

46. Cited by A. F. Koni, "Prisiazhnye zasedatelei" (1914), quoted in Kazantsev, *Sud prisiazhnykh v rossii,* 70.

47. Ibid., 45.

48. Ibid., 47.

49. Ibid.

published in the liberal newspaper *Voice (Golos)*. Markov was a well-known publicist in his time, who authored works on pedagogy, several novels, and a series of travelogues. The epigraph to his feuilleton is a modified quote from Matthew: "Woe unto you, scribes and Pharisees, hypocrites! for ye make clean the outside of the cup, but your inside is full of extortion and guile" (Matt. 23:25). Markov imagines a scene inside the court building. The clients are "women with tearful faces. . . . with their documents in their hands, helpless, they lean against the walls, whole crowds of peasants, sitting on the staircase, yawn and sigh heavily. . . . in every face there is anxiety." The attorneys are

> another sort altogether: their coats are of the latest cut, their linen impeccable. . . . They will do all they can, but they can't guarantee the outcome. In any case, they must be paid immediately after the proceedings. The black fashionable waistcoats are the masters of the court. The judges are their comrades and friends. . . . They stroll through the halls, chatting with one another about the latest dinner, looking insolently through their pince-nez at the sad, aimless public: of what concern are they? . . . They are resting now, like actors before a long performance. For how long can they be expected to pull out their masks and declaim their roles? No matter what the ending of the courtroom drama, it won't be tragic for them.[50]

Markov's scenario presents a striking contrast to the image of the jury trial as carnival. In carnival the boundaries separating individuals blur; the jury is the collective body of the people, in which distinctions of rank are suspended. According to Markov, the boundaries separating the public from the officials of the court are heightened, and the artifice of the lawyer's role is both unwelcome and exaggerated. Markov's chronotope of the court is not carnival, but a negatively valued theater. The lawyer is all gesture, all convention, he is the black fashionable waistcoat, reduced to a sign of himself. Whether the lawyer is onstage or off, "resting," he is an actor. Markov writes: "He uses science, reli-

---

50. E. Markov, "Sofisty XIX veka," quoted in I. V. Gessen, *Istoria russkoi advokatury*, vol. 1, *Advokatura, obshchestvo i gosudarstvo 1864–1914* (Moscow: Izdanie sovetov prisiazhnykh, 1914), 210–11.

gion, and morality as an actor uses props, solely for the public."[51] The institution of the bar is an example of the "cynical adultery of thought":

> Is there any sense in judging some unfortunate camellia, who sells her body according to a fixed rate, in light of these camellias of the law, who sell, almost from the auction block, their convictions and talent? The adultery of thought is reflected not only in the specialized sphere of the law. If it is cultivated in society, in time it will destroy the whole world of thought, all of science.[52]

The term "camellia" is a euphemism for courtesan, derived from the popular Dumas play *La Dame aux Camellias*.[53] What the courtesan does—selling her body—and what the lawyer does—selling his convictions and talent—are similar, but the evil that the lawyer perpetrates is far more threatening. The lawyer pretends to convictions, emotions, and knowledge, but these are all devices aimed at persuading the jury of his client's innocence. In reality, the lawyer has none.

Many observers at the time commented on the theatricality of the courtroom. For example, the court reporter for the *Stock Market News*, whose impressions of the jury we have already commented on, describes the hearing of a criminal case as "a drama, a repetition of truly dramatic events, with all their petty details, not from the first act, but from the last." Reading about a trial is not the same as being there, just as reading a review of a theatrical performance is not the same as attending it.[54] For this observer, the entire presentation of the case, the testimony of the witnesses, leads to a rapid succession of emotions and impressions, and in this respect, the trial is like a "drama." N. P. Karabchevskii, a Russian attorney, describes in his memoirs what he calls the Romantic phase in French legal oratory:

> The attorney declaimed before the judges and the public in his theatrical garb, with the task of the most pitiful buffoon: to grow

---

51. Ibid., 217.
52. Ibid., 216.
53. First performed in 1848 in France, translated into Russian in 1873, and performed under the title *Kak pozhivesh', tak i proslyvesh'* beginning in 1879. See *Istoriia russkogo dramaticheskogo teatra v semi tomkah* (Moscow: Iskusstovo, 1980), 5:459.
54. "Neznakomets," *Birzhevye vedomosti*, no. 31, February 1, 1876.

indignant, without feeling any strong emotion, to beat himself in the chest, where absolutely no feeling stirred, to squeeze tears from eyes that did not want to cry. . . . And all of this was obligatory, it all entered the program of generally accepted oratorical devices.[55]

For Karabchevskii and for the *Stock Market News* reporter, courtroom drama is normal and acceptable. Katherine Fischer Taylor's recent study of nineteenth-century French criminal justice argues that theatrical behavior on the part of defense lawyers was seen as an effort to overcome an imbalance that lay at the heart of the criminal trial: the single defendant pitted against a "vast social body." Taylor writes according to the norms of the time, the defense lawyer "must become his client, speaking for him better than the defendant could do himself, expressing his case with all the dramatic resources he could conjure."[56]

But for Markov, the theatricality of the lawyer's oratory corrupts his very being. In his essence, the lawyer is an actor, not himself. This particular form of theatricality is dangerous, because it can neither be detected nor contained. It seems to be what it is not and spills over its boundaries. By masking himself in science, morality, and religion, the attorney corrodes science, morality, and religion—"all of thought"—from within. Richard Weisberg characterizes modern literature's lawyer-protagonists in similar terms. Dostoevsky in particular, according to Weisberg, reveals the way that "the legal recreation of events sometimes serves more to fulfill the psychological and artistic goals of the lawyer than to achieve justice in the individual case."[57]

Vladimir Spasovich, one of late-nineteenth-century Russia's best-known defense lawyers, describes the role of attorney as a persona that must be carefully contained:

> Each one of us must be above all a sincere person, and an attorney only when he is before the judge in the fulfillment of his duty. . . . when he speaks like an attorney, he acts a role [*litsedeistvuet*], presenting himself not in his own persona, but another, into which he has entered for a certain time. He dares not forget for a moment

---

55. N. P. Karabchevskii, *Okolo pravosudiia: Sta'ti, soobshcheniia i sudebnye ocherki* (St. Petersburg, 1908), 87.

56. See Katherine Fischer Taylor, *In the Theater of Criminal Justice: The Palais de Justice in Second Empire Paris* (Princeton, N.J.: Princeton University Press, 1993), 53.

57. Weisberg, *Failure of the Word*, 54.

that what is permitted him in the courtroom as an attorney is not permitted him as a person, and he makes a . . . profound mistake if he permits himself to act the attorney [*advokatstvovat'*] outside the natural boundaries of his profession, if he carries his lawyerly devices into an area that does not belong to him, where they appear as elements either of demoralization or of destruction.[58]

The lawyer must play the straight man outside the courtroom; otherwise his techniques of legal argumentation may have a corrosive effect. For Spasovich, the lawyer may mistakenly forget to step out of his courtroom persona, with its conventions and devices; for Markov, he must necessarily forget. The copy overtakes the original. In reserving the right not to be himself in the chronotope of the courtroom, the lawyer destroys himself. The persona consumes the person from within. The "lawyer" is nothing more than surface, lacking the interiority of belief, self, and conscience characteristic of the jury.

In the series of oppositions we have been examining between the spirit and the letter, the New and the Old Testament, the oral and the written procedure, there is an odd skewing. The letter of the law, the Old Testament, and the written procedure are all negatively valued, and the spirit, the New Testament, the "inner conviction," and the oral court are all positively valued. Along the positive pole of values, the jury occupies all the available places. The jury is the spirit, the conscience, the voice of the people. In the New Testament, lawyers are the hated Pharisees, hypocrites. The jury bases its judgments on pure inner conviction, but the lawyer's convictions are modified at will and exchanged for money. This is not to say that the behavior of the Russian attorney was beyond reproach. Jane Burbank's recent study of professional self-discipline in the Moscow bar in the reform period points to a number of violations, including inappropriate behavior in the courtroom, incessant demands made to clients for payment, and failure to carry out necessary legal work.[59] The point is not whether Russian lawyers deserved the reproach of the press, but the characteristic form in which the reproach was made. The lawyer operates in a zone of play, improvisation, negotiation, and appearance and in so doing, is vilified.

---

58. V. D. Spasovich, quoted in Gessen, *Istoriia russkoi advokatury. Vol. 1. Advokatura, obshchestvo i gosudarstvo 1864–1914*, 224.

59. Jane Burbank, "Discipline and Punish in the Moscow Bar Association," *Russian Review* 54 (1995): 44–64.

As adulterer and impostor, he has no positive role in either the Testament of the Father or of the Son.

The Other

Praise for the Russian jury is by no means universal. In a series of articles published in 1895 and 1896, Zakrevskii attacked the jury system, this time focusing specifically on the Russian jury panel. "No matter what you write in the law books, the mob thinks and feels in its own way."[60] Zakrevskii describes the high number of acquittals he saw in his own courts in cases of crimes of violence against women, children, and other dependents, in cases of sexual abuse and battery, including a husband whose cruel treatment and torture of his wife (he beat her and threw her into a river in late October) led to her suicide. In one rape case, Zakrevskii says that the reason the jury acquitted the rapist was that they felt "sorry" for him (zhal' cheloveka) ("Sud," 105). Zakrevskii emphasizes the oppressive aspects of acquittals in cases such as these, noting that "living justice, as it is understood by some, says 'beat as hard as you can, if you are a man, a master, or a boss.'"[61] In contrast to these acquittals, Zakrevskii notes the convictions handed down in cases involving the charge of religious sectarianism, and "blasphemy," which he defines as "the pronunciation of meaningless words, construed as blasphemy (even in an intoxicated state)" ("Sud," 106). Afanas'ev also finds that "merciless cruelty was shown toward horse thieves and persons convicted of sacrilegious offenses, while excessive tolerance was shown in cases involving crimes against women and official corruption."[62] According to Zakrevskii, this type of verdict could not possibly come from people who had some understanding of "freedom of conscience." These acquittals cannot be blamed on the court-appointed investigators and judges: these verdicts are "flesh of the flesh and bone of the bones of the people who issued them" (106). The metaphor is not the jury as the spirit in distinction from the letter of the law. The jury's convictions, both their beliefs and the sentences they hand down, are of the flesh. Zakrevskii turns the tables on the rhetoric surrounding the Russian jury's transcendent justice. In the examples he provides, we see

---

60. I. P. Zakrevskii, "Sud prisiazhnykh i vozmozhnaia reforma ego," quoted in Kazantsev, Sud prisiazhnykh v rossii, 108.

61. Zakrevskii, "Eshche o sude," quoted in Kazantsev, Sud prisiazhnykh v rossii, 139.

62. Afanas'ev, "Jurors and Jury Trials," 227.

the negative side of the jury as carnival. Instead of suspending distinctions, the jury reenacts the traditional exclusions. In these cases, the jury can be compared to what Allon Stallybrass and Peter White have described as the carnival mob that "demonizes *weaker*, not stronger, social groups—women, ethnic and religious minorities, those who 'don't belong.'"[63]

The celebration of the jury as a projection of the Russian folk depends on a series of exclusions, the production of a series of "Others." The mythological enterprise of identifying the Russian jury as the embodiment of the Russian people's transcendent justice excludes other groups as necessarily unjust. An example of this exclusion can be seen in the provisions of the reform of 1864. Jews and sectarians could not be sworn in as witnesses in cases in which their coreligionists who had converted to Russian Orthodoxy were on trial. In showing how witnesses may be influenced in their testimony by unconscious prejudice, Kvachevskii, whose handbook on juries we have already discussed, provides an example of such prejudice not from contemporary legal practice, but from the Jewish response to Jesus described in John 1:46: "Can anything good come out of Nazareth?"[64] The New Testament description of Jewish "prejudice" serves as Kvachevskii's textbook example for late-nineteenth-century Russian jurors. The historical Jew of late imperial Russia, at the very height of the reform period, even before the reaction and anti-Semitic campaigns promulgated by the governments of Alexander III and Nicholas II, remains bound by his New Testament role as the accuser of Jesus. The Jew, not having accepted the New Testament of Jesus, cannot participate in the New Testament of Russia.

Nekliudov's use of New Testament imagery is striking in this regard. Nekliudov says that the defense insists on its Barabbas, "to this end crucifying the witnesses and even the law itself." The defense attorney and his client are like the Jewish mob of the New Testament, who demand from Pilate the release of the murderer and insurrectionist Barabbas instead of Jesus. The sacred suffering victim, crucified by the defense, is nothing other than the law itself. Elsewhere, as we will see, it is the Russian people, or Russia, or the Russian writer that will play

---

63. Peter Stallybrass and Allon White, *The Politics and Poetics of Transgression* (Ithaca, N.Y.: Cornell University Press, 1986), 19. The two authors are extremely critical of what they consider Bakhtin's naive folkloristic approach to carnival. They emphasize the way that the carnival crowd is complicit with official culture.

64. Kvachevskii, *Sud prisiazhnykh po russkim zakonam*, 434.

this role. Whether we turn to the defenders or the accusers of the new court, we encounter the same set of metaphors. No matter on which side the metaphor is deployed—the jury as the ministers of the spirit and not the letter, the defense as the mob demanding its Barabbas—the Jew is always on the wrong side. Vladimir Spasovich, who acted as the defense in the Mel'nitskii case, defended his fellow attorneys with a reference to the New Testament. Attorneys were attacked because they acted without thought for their own well-being; they did not sit well with "the entire Pharisean synagogue."[65] The Pharisees are the chief target of Jesus' speeches—"Woe to the scribes and Pharisees." As we have seen, Markov calls Russian lawyers "Pharisees." In chapter 4, as we will see, Dostoevsky will have recourse to similar New Testament passages to vilify Spasovich in particular, who defends in the Kronenberg case.

In *Billy Budd,* the narrator laments the faded popularity of the Bible and its replacement by other authoritative texts: "one must turn to some authority not liable to the charge of being tinctured by the biblical element."[66] In contrast, the Russian body politic cannot imagine itself without "the biblical element." The drama and spectacle of the New Testament, of Jesus' confrontation with the Pharisees, and of the Passion, are never very far from view. Questions about what is and is not legitimate court procedure, as in the Mel'nitskii case, are "tinctured" with its coloration. Nekliudov's conclusion does not even address questions of legal procedure and their possible violation by the defense. Instead, the more important questions in both the Mel'nitskii case and the debates in the press are who is being crucified, who is responsible, who is on the side of the letter and who the spirit.

These allegorical problems play themselves out not only in the realm of polemical debates. They are enacted in the flesh; they unfold in the day-to-day operation of the new courts. Afanas'ev finds that whereas by law, the percentage of Jews on juries could not exceed the percentage in the population, in fact, the percentage on juries was far lower. For example, Jews accounted for half of the population of Kiev Province but only 10 percent of the jurors.[67]

The oath that jurors swore upon taking up their duties presented a

65. V. D. Spasovich, "Zastol'nye rechi," quoted in Gessen, *Istoriia russkoi advokatury. Vol. 1. Advokatura, obshchestvo i gosudarstvo 1864–1914,* 236.

66. Herman Melville, *Billy Budd* (New York: Tom Doherty Associates, 1988), 42.

67. Afanas'ev, "Jurors and Jury Trials," 223.

special problem. As we have seen, Russian Orthodox jurors swore by "God, his sacred Gospels, and his life-giving cross." The oath is the gate of entry into that privileged space of Russian national justice and compassion. According to the provisions of the reform in 1864, Jews and other non-Russian Orthodox jurors were to swear according to the dictates of their own religious law. Where religion did not specify, or expressly forbade oath taking, the juror could give his solemn promise before the chairman of the court. But in practice, the oath that Jews were required to take was hedged round with peculiar and bizarre requirements. In his study of Russian law pertaining to Jews published in 1877, I. G. Orshanskii describes complaints in the press about the inadequacy of the Jewish oath. Orshanskii received a traditional Jewish education, went on to write broadly about questions of Russian law, and advocated the full integration of Jews into Russian society. Orshanskii includes the demand of one writer to the effect that the judicial oath for Jews be performed in a synagogue and that candles be lit and extinguished during the swearing-in. This procedure, the writer believed, was consistent with Jewish law. In his study of the Russian jury, M. P. Timofeev remarks that "in order for the oath of the Jews to have real meaning, it must be surrounded by many Talmudic complexities that cannot always be fulfilled in the courtroom."[68] As Orshanskii points out, Jewish religious law makes no provisions for the swearing of oaths. Witnesses, according to Jewish law, do not take oaths. Orshanskii concludes that the special concern with regard to the Jewish oath belied the spirit of the new courts, which eschewed the formalism of the old, and furthermore, revealed a mistrust of Jewish testimony and judgment.[69]

The Carnival Body

Another example of the way that the Jew's allegorical role gets enacted in practice is a case reported by the *Voice*, in May 1876. The report comes via another publication, *The Son of the Fatherland (Syn otechestva)*. A wealthy Jew in the city of Gadiach in Poltava Province (in the Ukraine) employed a servant infected with syphilis. According to the story, the Jew "tormented the unfortunate woman so, that she decided to drown herself"—in the town's Jewish well. All that winter and spring the Jews used the water from the well for their cooking, and in

---

68. Timofeev, *Sud prisiazhnykh v Rossii*, 47.
69. I. G. Orshanskii, *Russkoe zakonodatel'stvo o evreiakh* (St. Petersburg, 1877), 436–45.

the spring, they used it in the preparation of their "wafers," that is, matzo. However, a few days before Passover, someone informed the police that there was a drowned body in the "Jewish well" (*v zhidovskom kolodtse*). The Jews raised a hue and cry. One of the Jewish "lawyers" (the term used in the newspaper account is *ablakat*, a misspelling of *advokat*) advised the mistress of the house in which the drowned woman had been employed to crumble up the matzo and mix it with the flour sold to Christians in preparation for their special Easter food, the cheese pastry known as *paskha*. But when customers began to sift through the flour, they found pieces of the "Jewish wafers." The police were informed, and "experts proved that the pieces were from Jewish wafers." What sort of experts these might be remains obscure. The term used throughout the article for "Jewish" is the disparaging *zhidovskii*, that is, "what pertains to Yids." The story concludes that "those responsible for the poisoning and the profanation have been taken into the arms of justice."[70]

This bizarre little news item provides a new twist on the old ritual murder libel, the charge that Jews required the blood of a Christian child to make their matzo. A book published in 1876 in Russia by a Jew who had converted to Catholicism and then to Russian Orthodoxy alleged that a small percentage of fanatical Jews did adhere to the practice of ritual murder.[71] Jews were prosecuted for ritual murder in the Veilizh case of 1823, the Saratov case of 1853, and the Kutais case of 1879. In the case we have just described, Jews unwittingly use the infected body of a Christian to make matzo. The Christian servant woman, "tormented" by her Jewish master, takes posthumous revenge. The Jewish master then perpetuates the contamination by adulterating flour sold to Christians with the contaminated matzo. Like the flour, the story has no clear demarcations. All three *paskhas*—the same word refers to Passover, Easter, and the traditional Easter cheese cake—have been contaminated and profaned. Both Christian and Jew are implicated.

The case reveals a dimension of the carnivalesque that is neither liberating nor subversive. Stallybrass and White argue that "the 'carnivalesque' mediates between a classical/classificatory body and its negations, its Others, what it excludes to create its identity as such" (26). The matzo case depends on a set of classifications crucial to the

---

70. *Golos*, no. 118, May 11, 1876 .
71. See Karabchevskii, *Okolo pravosudiia*, 23–24. The author is Liutostanskii.

self-imagination of the Russian body politic in the late nineteenth century: master and servant, man and woman, Russian Orthodox and Jew,
and the diseased and the healthy. In the newspaper story, the lines separating all these oppositions were crossed. According to the medical
knowledge of the time, syphilis was not exclusively a venereal disease,
especially in rural areas, but in the cities and towns, and especially
among servants, it was associated with sexual immorality.[72] When the
Jews recognized the body of the servant woman, and when they found
out that she had been infected with "such a disgusting disease," according to the newspaper article, they were outraged. A corpse in the well,
let alone a syphilitic corpse, would have been sufficient to contaminate
the water, according to Jewish laws regarding purity. The master then
perpetuates the cycle of contamination presumably by seeking to infect
the Christian population. The classical/classificatory body was transformed into the grotesque body, in which all clear demarcations were
confuted. A corpse became the source of the food symbolizing resurrection. The newspaper story makes clear that each of the participants
wishes to reestablish the boundaries delimiting one group and class
from the other.

This case, like the ritual murder cases of the time, the special provisions regarding the Jewish oath, and a host of other regulations,
including, for example, those proscribing Jewish prayer as a form of
public disorder punishable by the same fines handed down for "unli-
censed games and entertainments," and the concern about converted
Jews who were later revealed as false converts—all point to an anxiety
about the purity of the Russian body politic. The possibility of a new
corporate Russian body in the form of the jury, which suspended distinctions of class, rank, income, and education, has to be balanced
against this darker picture.

Conclusion

In this chapter we have traced several aspects of what I have called the
jury as carnival. The introduction of the jury trial carnivalizes the old,
prereform justice by transforming a secret, written proceeding into an
open public trial. Russian juries, known for their acquittals in particu-

---

72. For a detailed study of the problem, see Laura Engelstein, *The Keys to Happiness:
Sex and the Search for Modernity in Fin-de-Siècle Russia* (Ithaca, N.Y.: Cornell University
Press, 1992), 165–211.

lar kinds of cases, reinvent the law and redefine norms for determining guilt. Religious and national elements come to play a significant role in the debates surrounding the new juries. The jury became the focal point of a national narrative that emphasized the Russianness of the jury system. The same rhetoric castigated the profession of the bar as sophistry. Finally, the construction of the Russian jury as the site of special spiritual and Russian qualities in part depends on certain exclusions. The two main targets of opprobrium—the lawyer and the Jew—correspond in several ways. In 1905 new laws restricting the number of Jews who could enter the bar were put in place.

Reform-era debates about the new courts make use of several competing models of authority. Some writers compare the written formal law of prereform court procedure to the Old Testament law of God the Father. The role of the Old Testament God, who creates and destroys his creatures at his word, was one that the tsarist government was quite willing to embrace. The new courts are figured in language of the New Testament, and the Russian people as ministers of the spirit, the collective voice of conscience in distinction from the letter of the law. In a later chapter, we will see how Dostoevsky draws upon the image of the jury of the people, which has cast off the old law and has cast off the father, in order to fashion a role for himself as father to a new Russia.

In the contest between the two Testaments, the lawyer has no fixed role. He is figured as an adulterer and imposter, who pretends to morality, science, and religion only in order to make his case. The lawyer, like the novelist in Bakhtin's poetics, reserves the right not to be himself. The link between the lawyer and the novelist suggests another dimension to the discussion of models of authority that we have developed thus far. A host of nineteenth-century writers, including the Russian reform-era jurists, literary authors such as Dostoevsky, and the contemporary critic Richard Weisberg, are extremely critical of the lawyer's reliance on artistic and specifically novelistic devices. Verbose legal eloquence, according to Weisberg, undermines individual heroism and Christian values. The great nineteenth-century authors understood that law, "as bound up in narrative form as their own enterprise, was beginning to substitute wit for judgment, elegance for substance, words for values."[73]

In subsequent chapters, I will look at another aspect of this relation

---

73. Weisberg, *Failure of the Word*, 178.

between law and literature, examining not how courtroom oratory is novelistic, but how models of literary authorship are political, and how they relate to the models of political authority discussed thus far. To give an example, we have seen an implicit opposition between a true, legitimate, divine or divinely sanctioned authority, such as that of the tsar or the people, and a false, illegitimate, and temporary authority, that of the impostor, or those who resemble impostors. In subsequent chapters, we will translate this political opposition into literary terms, examining the model of the author as God the Father and the model of the author as imposter. What are the evaluations attached to these models, and what are their ramifications, both in the realm of law and in literature?

The next chapter makes this transition with the Suvorin case, one of the first literary censorship cases to be judged in the new public courts. This trial provides a test of the author's "right" not be himself. The prosecution found itself enmeshed in what at first might seem to be purely literary questions about the author's intention, the problem of interpretation, and the implications of irony. In tracing the prosecution's case against Suvorin, we will flesh out its assumptions about the writer's authority over his or her text. My reading of the trial will emphasize the underlying debate it stages between competing models of literary authorship. In judging the written text, the law is compelled to distance itself from the operations of writing, to deny its own status as written text.

Chapter 3

Crimes of Fiction/Fictitious Crimes: A. S. Suvorin and N. D. Akhsharumov

The "great reforms" of Alexander II, which brought radical change to Russia's courts, also changed the way the Russian press was regulated. A law of 1865 suspended most of the harsh preliminary censorship that had been in place since the early part of the century. Under Nicholas I, for example, there were at least two governmental bodies responsible for censorship, one of which watched over the other. The new law, which remained in effect until 1905, contained two major provisions. Books published in the major cities were released from preliminary censorship. Their authors became subject instead to the judicial procedures created by the reform of 1864: trials in open court. Trials involving the press were conducted without juries. For a fee, editors of journals could take the responsibility formerly held by the censorship committee. In "extraordinary cases," where the potential harm to Russian society was so great that no delay could be tolerated, the censorship committee could immediately ban a book or journal issue before the case went to court.[1] A long delay between the banning and the trial could effectively remove a work from circulation.

In 1866, the year that the judicial reforms went into operation, Aleksei Suvorin's novel *It Takes All Kinds: Scenes from Contemporary Life* was the subject of one of Russia's first literary trials. The novel portrays the aftermath of the political and social upheaval of the early 1860s. Suvorin was charged with committing crimes against the Russian government and society because of statements made by the narrator and the protagonists of his novel.

In the same year, the Russian critic and fiction writer N. D.

---

1. K. K. Arsen'ev, *Zakonodatel'stvo o pechati* (St. Petersburg, 1903), 233.

Akhsharumov published a novella called *The Model: A Juridical Fiction*. The novella is about an author who writes a novel and is put on trial for what takes place in it. The fictitious author has a name that sounds odd both in English and in Russian: Chuikin. Chuikin's novel is about a married woman who embarks on a course of personal emancipation typical for a heroine of the 1860s. At the trial, the defense and the prosecution debate whether the author Chuikin and his novel are responsible for certain disastrous events in the life of the woman who serves as the real-life prototype, the "model" for the heroine of his fiction.

Both the live Suvorin and the fictitious author Chuikin are put on trial for crimes committed in their fiction. What are the implications of this charge? A close reading of these two trials, one fictitious and the other real, can tell us a great deal about the intimate and yet uneasy relationship between the writer and the law. The concepts of authorship and authority revealed by Suvorin's real-life trial and Akhsharumov's fictitious one are significant not only in literary or aesthetic terms. The last part of the chapter explores the political and social implications of the problems of authorship and authority in late-nineteenth-century Russian society as a whole.

In Akhsharumov's novella the prosecuting attorney says that "the author's power is, of course, unlimited, but only insofar as it acts within its appointed sphere, from which it may not leave if it does not wish to conflict with other powers."[2] Suvorin's trial and sentence and the banning of his book clearly represent an effort on the government's part to carry out the threat implicit in the words of Akhsharumov's fictitious prosecutor. The government used the blunt instruments of trial, banning, and imprisonment in order to limit the author's power. But as Suvorin's trial reveals, these apparently simple and straightforward techniques of regulation and punishment depend on a more subtle process, one that the government would sooner deny than admit to. In order to make its indictments and write its sentences, the law becomes enmeshed in literary interpretation, which it then transforms into literary regulation, defining and policing the boundaries of some proper "appointed sphere" for literature. Literature too participates in this process of regulation. As Akhsharumov's *The Model* shows, the writer and the police are not always on opposite sides of the law. *The Model*

---

2. N. D. Akhsharumov, "Naturshchitsa—Iuridicheskaia fiktsiia," *Otechestvennye zapiski* 164 (February 1866): 585. Henceforward, all citations parenthetical in text.

also represents an effort to control the borders of literature, by confining it to an "appointed sphere."

In this chapter and in chapter 6, on Siniavskii, we will examine how the literary trial is premised on a set of assumptions about the relation between the defendant and the narrator and or the fictitious characters in the literary work. The least sophisticated kind of prosecution simply assumes a relation of identity. The narrator and the characters are presumed to speak directly for the defendant. Here the law crosses swords with the dominant trend in literary criticism. For example, Bakhtin, as we have already seen, describes the "right" of the novelist "not to be himself." The historical person of the author and the persona of the novelist are distinct. Wayne Booth argues that each time a writer writes, he creates "an implied version of 'himself'"[3] that is not only different from the implied selves of other writers, but also different from other versions of his "second self." More radical versions of the disassociation of the historical person from the author have been argued by Derrida, Barthes, Foucault, and Siniavskii, who in various ways disrupt the concept of the single unified subject responsible for his or her writing.[4]

Several critical studies, relying on Foucault and Derrida as a point of departure, show that the literary trial raises complex questions about authorship and authority, language and meaning. Dominick LaCapra's "Madame Bovary" on Trial is an example.[5] LaCapra argues that the literary trial brings forward conventions of reading dominant in a given historical period and, moreover, provides that reading of the author's works which not only has material consequences for the author's life, but shapes his or her future literary production. Flaubert's novel radically questions legal assumptions about the individual, his her intentions, and his or her acts. It challenges legal assumptions about interpretation and evaluation. In Flaubert's trial, the law cannot admit that its grounds are challenged; otherwise, the process of judgment would have to be suspended. The framework of the trial, in LaCapra's terms, "threatens to explode." The "relation between text and context tends to

---

3. Wayne Booth, *The Rhetoric of Fiction* (Chicago: University of Chicago Press, 1961), 70–71.

4. For example, Foucault's "What Is an Author?" (1969) challenges the notion of the author, substituting in its place "a complex and variable function of discourse stripped of its creative role." See *Language, Counter-Memory, Practice,* ed. Donald Bouchard, trans. Donald Bouchard and Sherry Simon (Ithaca, N.Y.: Cornell University Press, 1977), 138. I will discuss Derrida and Barthes in greater detail in chapter 6.

5. I am grateful to Elizabeth Constable for introducing me to this work.

be reversed: it is no longer the context that provides determinate boundaries for interpreting and evaluating the text."[6] We will explore a similar problem of the text threatening the context in Akhsharumov's *The Model.*

Susan Stewart's *Crimes of Writing: Problems in the Containment of Meaning* uses a similar set of critical tools to examine the history of alternative models of authorship and authority suggested by literary crimes from the eighteenth century to the present. Stewart argues that the development of copyright law in the eighteenth century and the rise of Romanticism fix certain notions of what constitutes an author. The "particularizations of literary form, the specification of a certain kind of literary textuality, comes to acquire qualities—as practice of writing—that the law presumably will not share."[7] The law has to remain outside of what it oversees. Writing is legally defined as a "commodity" and a form of speech. Writing is linked "to the author's body." The concept of the author becomes linked to the notions of originality and authenticity. Stewart shows that what the law produces as "crimes of writing"—plagiarism, graffiti, and pornography—can also be seen as alternate forms of "authorial subjectivity." When the law punishes the author's body because of a crime committed in the author's fiction, the law presupposes that the particular historical individual, the author, is responsible for all the operations of language, all the associations and references that produce meaning. To use Stewart's language, but in a slightly different context, the law makes the author "responsible for an unbearable originality" (22).

When we insist on authenticity and originality in our model of the author, we may end up condemning the author for a heavy burden of legal responsibility. In Akhsharumov's story the judge asks the author Chuikin to state whether he was responsible for the fate of his real-life "model." The judge instructs the defendant to speak "clearly, in a literal sense without any metaphor or figurative meaning." The injunction against metaphor is significant. The second self, or the implied author,

---

6. Dominick LaCapra, *"Madame Bovary" on Trial* (Ithaca, N.Y.: Cornell University Press, 1982), 31.

7. Susan Stewart, *Crimes of Writing: Problems in the Containment of Representation,* 21. For a discussion of the intersection between legal and aesthetic developments in eighteenth century England giving rise to the concept of the author, see Mark Rose, "The Author as Proprietor: *Donaldson v. Becket* and the Geneology of Modern Authorship," in *Of Authors and Origins: Essays on Copyright Law,* Ed. Bram Sherman and Alain Strowel (Oxford: Clarendon Press, 1994), 23–55.

who is like but is not the author and is a product of an operation of language, stands in some figurative relation to the author. Putting the historical person on trial for what the narrator or one of the fictitious characters says is a fixing and a making literal of this figure. We will explore this process of literalization both in the trial of Aleksei Suvorin in 1866 and in the trial of Andrei Siniavskii in 1966.

Literature and Reality

The history of Russian literary aesthetics in the 1860s plays an important role in both of the trials discussed in this chapter. In the dominant form of mimesis in this period of Russian literature, much of the work of literalization of the author had already been accomplished by writers and readers. What I have described as a figure or trope of the author, a mere operation of language, was given a far greater significance by the reading public. Literature was understood by authors and readers, including, of course, government officials, as an attempt at making the reader do something. It was "serious" in Austin's sense of the term.[8] Characters enjoyed a life beyond the written page, and authors' second selves were invested with a larger-than-life aura.

As Irina Paperno has shown in *Chernyshevsky and the Age of Realism,* Russian readers of the 1860s understood literary fiction to have an almost unmediated relation to reality, and a crucial function in their every day lives.[9] Two principles dominated the aesthetics of Russian realism. Art was to represent life as truthfully as possible, but, furthermore, it was to affect life by offering readers models for imitation. As Paperno writes, "the literary model possesses a remarkable power to organize the actual life of a reader" (9). Realist aesthetics also attributed to literature an equally remarkable power to change society. The Russian satirist M. E. Saltykov-Shchedrin wrote that "literature predicts the laws of the future, produces the image of the man of the future."[10]

---

8. I am paraphrasing J. L. Austin, who distinguishes between serious and nonserious uses of language. Poetry and literature, according to Austin, belong to the latter category: in poetry there is "no attempt to make you do anything." See J. L. Austin, *How to Do Things with Words,* 2d ed. (Cambridge, Mass.: Harvard University Press, 1962), 104. I argue here and especially in chapters 5 and 6 that Russian literature attempts to make its readers do things.

9. See Irina Paperno, *Chernyshevsky and the Age of Realism: A Study in the Semiotics of Behavior* (Stanford, Calif.: Stanford University Press, 1988), 8–20.

10. Quoted in Paperno, *Chernyshevsky,* 10.

Paperno emphasizes that an "outgrowth of the basic principles of realism was a far-reaching confusion between the realms of literature and real life" (11). Critics discussed the heroes and heroines of fiction as if they were real people. Aksharumov's story *The Model,* as we will see, directly attacks the principles and ramifications of Russian realist aesthetics—the modeling of real-life on literature, the capacity of literature to change reality, and the confusion of the two realms.

Two works of fiction published in the early 1860s played a central role in this interaction between literature and reality: Turgenev's *Fathers and Sons* and Chernyshevsky's *What Is to Be Done.* Since Akhsharumov's *The Model* engages the realist aesthetics promulgated by Chernyshevsky and others in the late 1850s and early 1860s and also specifically responds to Chernyshevsky's novel, a brief description of its contents is called for. To paraphrase Paperno, *What Is to Be Done* is a socialist utopian love story with minute prescriptions for rearranging the daily lives of its readers. A fictitious marriage rescues the heroine, Vera Pavlovna, from her mother's attempt to force her into an unwanted marriage to a wealthy but unsavory older suitor. Lopukhov, the platonic husband, does not take advantage of his conjugal rights but instead reeducates Vera Pavlovna, who establishes a sewing cooperative. When she falls in love with another man, Lopukhov conveniently withdraws. Vera's dreams didactically emphasize the political message of the novel. The fourth and final dream contains Chernyshevsky's well-known vision of the Crystal Palace, a utopia in the utopia of the novel as a whole, in which labor, diet, recreation, education, and sex are all rationally managed.

As Paperno shows, Chernyshevsky's novel had a direct impact on the lives of its readers. Wives left their husbands if the latter were found to be ideologically deficient. Adultery became acceptable in certain circles. Chernyshevsky's novel also had a striking impact on Russian literature. Dostoevsky's *Notes from Underground,* for example, parodies the notion that human happiness can be rationally organized. As we will see, Chernyshevsky and his novel play a prominent role in the work of both Suvorin and Akhsharumov.

Literary Authority

Chernyshevskian realism of the 1860s can be distinguished from what Edward Said calls the classical realist novel of the nineteenth century. In his study *Beginnings: Intention and Method,* Said emphasizes that realist writers retained their awareness of the illusory nature of the reality their novels created. He uses two terms that have a direct bearing on the problems to be discussed in this chapter: "authority" and "molestation." *Authority* refers to the capacity to enforce obedience, but insofar as it is related to the term *author,* authority also refers to the capacity to engender or father. Later we will see that Akhsharumov explicitly takes up the problem of the realist author's paternal power to enforce obedience. For now, the crucial part of Said's definition comes under his term *molestation.* Said writes:

> that no novelist has ever been unaware that his authority, regardless of how complete, or the authority of a narrator, is a sham. Molestation, then, is a consciousness of one's duplicity, one's confinement to a fictive, scriptive realm, whether one is a character or a novelist.[11]

Neither the Chernyshevskian realist nor his distant offspring, the socialist realist of the 1930s, nor the law accepts the limitations of this definition. In Suvorin's trial, the law denies that the fictive, scriptive realm is beyond its jurisdiction. There is no distinction to be made between statements made in that realm and in other contexts. I will argue that the law takes the author seriously, attributing to him both power and authority over readers: the power to do harm, as in damaging the reputation of particular individuals, and the authority to influence readers to take up courses of action perceived as dangerous to the state.

The Author on Trial

Suvorin was a playwright, drama critic, publicist, and publisher. His career in Russian belles lettres spans the political gamut from radicalism to extreme conservatism. In his early years he published in the radical journal *Contemporary* and worked together with Chernyshevsky. Later, Suvorin became increasingly associated with right-wing and nationalist circles; his newspaper, the *New Time (Novoe vremia),* published his own and Vasilii Rozanov's notorious anti-Semitic pieces from

---

11. Edward W. Said, *Beginnings: Intention and Method* (New York: Basic Books, 1975), 84.

the 1870s through the period of the Beilis blood libel trial. Suvorin's controversial novel *It Takes All Kinds* is from the earlier period.

The novel is set in the mid-1860s, during the time that Alexander II instituted his reforms. This period was marked by student unrest, the circulation of revolutionary proclamations, arrests of prominent radical leaders, and the Polish rebellion. All of these events are reflected in the novel. One of the protagonists is a former seminary student, Il'menev. In typical fashion for a hero of the times, Il'menev, like Turgenev's Bazarov, studies the natural sciences; unlike Bazarov, he circulates revolutionary leaflets and is pursued by the police. The other male protagonist, Prince Ivan Shchebynin, also a devotee of Bazarov, used to associate with nihilist circles. Shchebynin conceals his marriage to a radical young woman from his aristocratic set. He is estranged from his wife. During the course of the novel, he pursues two women simultaneously: "Meri," an aristocrat, who falls in love with Il'menev, and Liudimila Ivanovna. The figure of Liudmila Ivanovna is a variant of Vera Pavlovna from Chernyshevsky's *What Is to Be Done.* She lives alone, supporting herself by translations and portrait painting; she organizes a fairly successful sewing enterprise for women—"not up to the measure of Vera Pavlovna's," interjects the narrator—and preaches free love. By the end of the novel, Il'menev escapes his pursuers and leaves St. Petersburg for Siberia, to free his father, imprisoned for murdering his master. His ultimate destination is America, where he plans to get rich felling timber.

Suvorin was charged with "(1) printing opinions about the decrees and instructions of governmental institutions that are offensive and aimed at undermining society's trust, (2) approving actions forbidden by law, with the purpose of provoking a lack of respect for the law, and (3) offending the highest layer of society."[12] The St. Petersburg Circuit Court found him guilty of all charges and sentenced him to two months in prison. Under the first charge, the circuit court identified several passages. The first group of these have to do with relations between the government and the press. Liudimila Ivanovna describes an editor who follows the orders of whatever government ministry pays him well enough. She suggests that censorship has been lightened, but the editors of the leading publications have taken the task of censorship upon

---

12. I take the statement of the charge from A. Liubavksii, *Novye russkie ugolovnye protsessy,* vol. 1 (St. Petersburg, 1868), 86. I rely on Liubavskii's account of the trial throughout.

themselves. The government prosecutor apparently did not note the obvious irony of arresting a book and its author on the charge of reproving the government for its repressive relations to the press. According to the court, Suvorin's novel showed that the government gave out the appearance of tolerating a free press while persisting in the constraints of the previous era. The arrest shows that these constraints had in fact not been lifted.

Under the same category of offensive opinions about government institutions, the court also looked to passages in the novel depicting the behavior and beliefs of fictitious government officials. For example, an agent of the Third Section, the secret police, commenting on the newly reformed method of investigation, says that the practice of torture, which existed "under previous tsars a long time ago . . . was a good thing."[13] To give another example, a civil servant "who possesses not a low, but a high, rank," to use the language of the novel, kisses the hand of his boss on command. According to the court, these images suggest that the government selects "base" and "untalented" people for its service.[14] In putting Suvorin on trial, the government of Alexander II sought to protect its image as a liberal-minded government of reform.

The charge that Suvorin approved illegal acts stemmed in large part from the portrait of the "nihilist" Il'menev. In one scene Il'menev recalls the recent agitation in which he had played a leading part. He remembers the crowds, the women orators, the police and asks, "was this life or the appearance of life?" (183). He remembers that when distributing proclamations, he encountered a man who pointed out their utter worthlessness, and that he, Il'menev, gave his entire allotment of proclamations to a passerby for cigarette paper.

Il'menev also recalls scenes of corporal punishment that he had witnessed: "the emaciated body" of his father being beaten with a knout (186). He remembers the public punishment of a criminal, his "bespectacled, sickly, wan face," how the executioner threw the prisoner's hat to the ground, how the criminal was fastened with iron rings to the pillory but then unaccountably freed. The crowd shouted their farewells; one young woman threw a bouquet and was immediately

---

13. A. Suvorin [A. Bobrovskii, pseud.], *Vsiakie: Ocherki sovremennoi zhizni* (St. Petersburg, 1866), 82. Henceforward all citations to be given parenthetically in the body of the text.

14. Liubavskii, *Novye russkie ugolovnye protsessy*, 98.

arrested. It is likely that Il'menev's memory refers to Chernyshevsky, who wore glasses, and who in 1864 underwent a mock execution. The details of the iron rings and the pillory are the same.[15] As these scenes pass through Il'menev's mind, he admits to himself that the "masses" have rejected him and his fellow activists; he asks himself "for whom are we destroying ourselves" and thinks of the tears shed by "our wives and mothers" (188).

Under the charge of offending the nobility, the circuit court referred to several passages in the novel. For example, a nobleman recalls a young peasant woman, whose blouse opened to reveal her breast. In another passage, the narrator provides a parodic family tree of the Pribalovs, the family to which "Meri" belongs: "During the reign of Mikhail Romanov, one of their forebears was beaten with a knout; another was beaten by Peter himself with his big stick; a third was beaten on the cheeks by Biron" (149). Biron was court favorite in the first part of the eighteenth century associated with a policy of terror.[16] As we saw in chapter 1, the Russian nobility abhorred corporal punishment, which was reserved for non-noble classes. Without giving credence to the court's charge that Suvorin was legally culpable for this passage, it is clear why his image of the "Pribalov" family pedigree struck a nerve.

Limited Authorship

Suvorin's trial and his subsequent appeal reveal several conflicting configurations of author, writing, and authority. In Suvorin's appeal, the unified production of the text, originating in the single act of a single author, breaks down. Suvorin claimed that he should not have to bear personal responsibility for the crime he was alleged to have committed. The book was "arrested" after it was printed but before it was distributed. The printing of the book should only be considered "preparation for a crime" and not its completion, according to Suvorin. The appeal challenges what we might call an idealist image of the author as the creator of meaning that is immediately and invis-

---

15. For a reproduction of an eyewitness drawing of the event, see Paperno, *Chernyshevsky*, 97, fig. 8.

16. See Nicholas V. Riasanovsky, *A History of Russia*, 2d ed. (New York: Oxford University Press, 1969), 271–72.

ibly dispersed to a disembodied community of readers.[17] The appeal emphasizes instead the material nature of the book industry. The author cannot be considered the sole source of the meaning of his work, since he depends on the printer and the distributor for the dissemination of his meaning. In another literary case of the same time period, the government did in fact prosecute the typesetter. K. K. Arsen'ev, a prominent liberal, who went on to write several treatises on the law and the press, served as Suvorin's attorney. Arsen'ev pointed out a similar flaw in the prosecution's argument. In order for someone to be offended, the offense has to be enunciated. But in the case of the printed word, publication is a necessary first step. Arsen'ev argued that since the book was never published, the law could not identify the victim suffering the offense. No one could be said to be offended, because no one received the message, we might add. In a subsequent study of the law of the press, Arsen'ev wrote: "Until a thought is put into circulation, it is not subject to culpability or prosecution of any kind, no matter in what form it was expressed— regardless of whether it was in a letter, a drawing, or a printed work."[18] Expression is incomplete without circulation. The law, we might say, imagines the author enthroned in divine isolation, creating and destroying whole worlds with a single word. Suvorin's and Arsen'ev's arguments reveal a network of relations that dethrone the author's position and throw obstacles in the path of the transmission of meaning.

In other parts of his appeal, Suvorin asked that the offending passages be stricken so that the work could be published. He also claimed to have been misunderstood. In those passages having to do with the press, he was not criticizing the government, but those editors who do not know how to use their new position.[19] Suvorin said that the passages devoted to Il'menev's reminiscences do not express the author's approval of his actions, but his condemnation, and the weeping of the mothers and sisters is not a reproach directed at the government, but at the revolutionaries.

---

17. For idealism as the "official aesthetic ideology" at Flaubert's trial, see LaCapra, *"Madame Bovary" on Trial*, 51.

18. Arsen'ev, *Zakonodatel'stvo o pechati*, 66.

19. Liubavskii, *Novye russkie ugolovnye protsessy*, 99.

Interpreting Plain Russian

The government prosecutor, N. O. Tuzingauzen, responded by pre-cluding further discussion of how to interpret the passages in question or any other passages in the novel. This part of his speech is worth quoting, because it reveals how the government reads literature:

> The court is not an arena for polemics. . . . We will say only that the circuit court and the prosecutor in citing certain passages from the work under investigation interpreted the meaning that was placed in them according to the sense that words and expressions gener-ally have in Russian. If the author, however, claims that he wanted to express something completely different from what his readers understood, this leads only to the conclusion that his work was written very ambiguously.[20]

The meaning of Suvorin's words and expressions is clear to anyone who speaks Russian, and no interpretation is necessary. The court regards the novel as it might any other document that under examina-tion, such as a contract. At the same time, however, the novel is not just another document, according to the court, because its ambiguities may conceal something more dangerous. If interpretation is called for because the author meant the opposite of what his readers understood, that too is criminal. The possibility that the court itself is engaged in a process of interpretation is one that the prosecutor will not admit to. The prosecution's reading of the novel seems to adhere to Derzhavin's prereform dictum that the court is nothing but the act of the criminal compared with the laws. The novel takes the place of the act.

If we look more closely at the statement, we see that the prosecu-tor's claim involves more than what first appears. Tuzingauzen's claim is not that the law has the same understanding of Russian as everyone else, but a special privileged access to it. The law is a kind of superdic-tionary that knows in advance what any possible combination of words and expressions means. The author charged with responsibility for how his words are interpreted is also denied that responsibility. In charging the author and not the printer, distributor, and bookseller, the law proceeds as if the book were an oral utterance. But at the trial the

---

20. Ibid., 103–4.

law privileges the printed word over the author's oral testimony. The novel, says the law, in the manner of a very strict New Critic, contains everything the author wanted to say, and no subsequent statements can modify what has already been said. The novel is made to pass sentence on itself.

The prosecutor goes on to charge Suvorin not only with ambiguity but with criminal intent. Having denied the possibility of irony except to criminalize any form of ambiguity, the prosecutor then shows that he can interpret a passage ironically. The passages in question are digressions addressed from the first-person narrator to the reader:

> Dear reader, and you, respected censor, having scanned—as you must—these pages, we are at the launching pier. In a few minutes, you can say with a clear conscience: the book is loyal. . . . You are not mistaken. The most peaceable disposition guided my pen when I hastily jotted down my remarks. I was sincere, I did not try to deceive, and I hope did not give work to your red or blue pencil, O guardian of the press, when, in accordance with your obligation, you leafed through the pages of my tale. You can say that everything turned out well and release my tale to stroll about in society or to lie under layers of dust on the shelves of the booksellers. (235–36)

The prosecutor also singled out the last pages of the novel, entitled "A Few Words to the Reader," which contain a disclaimer similar in tone to the passage just cited: "I called this trifle a tale. This is not true. It's not a tale, but simply remarks, excerpts from a diary written at various times under various impressions, connected into a living thread by a plot that is rather unskillful" (264).

Pushkin

The first-person address to the reader and the censor and the characterization of the novel as "excerpts from a diary written at various times under various impressions" have the unmistakable ring of Pushkin. The dedication that opens *Eugene Onegin* reads:

> Accept this collection of motley chapters
> Half funny, half sad

Simple-minded and ideal
The careless fruit of my amusements
Insomnia, light inspiration.

The prosecutor says that judging from Suvorin's afterword, we might suppose that *It Takes All Kinds* is "the harmless fruit of an idle imagination . . . written without any preconceived idea."[21] In this line the prosecutor picks up on the Pushkinian allusion, taking it a step further. Suvorin's "excerpts from a diary written at various times under various impressions" alludes to the first part of the dedication we quoted, "Accept this collection of motley chapters," and the prosecutor's phrase "harmless fruit" refers to the second part of the dedication, "the careless fruit of my amusements." The prosecutor's "harmless fruit" *(bezvrednyi plod)* rhymes with Pushkin's "careless fruit" *(nebrezhnyi plod)*. The prosecutor and the defendant seem to be engaged in a playful and, we might even say, Pushkinesque duet.

But the conclusion to the exchange brings the play to an abrupt end. For the prosecutor Suvorin's allusions to Pushkin constitute a form of literary imposture. Suvorin poses as a gentleman author of the previous era who creates "little trifles" out of idleness. Tuzingauzen says in effect to Suvorin, "I know my Pushkin, and you're no Pushkin." Pushkin, in the eyes of the law, was no Pushkin either. He was subject to particularly harsh surveillance and censorship under Nicholas I.[22] According to the law, Pushkin's own "light inspiration" was also a pose. The law characterizes literary play and intertextuality as an attempt to deceive. For Tuzingauzen, Suvorin's *It Takes All Kinds* is not only not Pushkinesque, it is not even art, having "no artistic value." The prosecutor suggests that Suvorin is guilty of both political crimes and literary misdemeanors, that is, the violation of aesthetic norms. The prosecutor reads Suvorin's novel as nothing other than a political pamphlet aimed at making readers sympathetic to ideas both foolish and illegal.[23]

---

21. Quoted in ibid., 102.

22. For a study of censorship under Nicholas I, see Sidney Monas, *The Third Section: Police and Society under Nicholas I* (Cambridge, Mass.: Harvard University Press, 1961), in particular 141–209.

23. Liubavskii, *Novye russkie ugolovnye protsessy*, 102.

Confession

In the afterword from which we have been quoting, we find the follow-ing passage:

> I know very well that I take a risk in publishing this work. . . . Now is the time of suspicion—suspicion about socialism, separatism, cosmopolitanism, about "a broad conspiracy entangling our fatherland in a strong net," and so forth. . . . In order to attract sus-picion, it is sufficient to have some degree of sympathy with a per-son who is called disloyal. (265)

According to the prosecutor, this passage is highly suspicious. In his appeal, Suvorin had tried to emphasize sentiments of loyalty expressed by various characters in his novel. But for the prosecutor these passages are only "a means of justification in case the book became subject to criminal prosecution."[24] The passage above, in which the narrator describes his awareness of the risk he takes, reveals to the prosecutor that Suvorin was anxious that he would be brought before the law, and rightly so. For the prosecutor, Suvorin revealed his true colors in the scene of public punishment witnessed by Il'menev. The details of the scene leave no doubt as to the identity of the criminal, says Tuzin-gauzen, without mentioning Chernyshevsky by name, as if the name itself had some sort of totemic power.

For the prosecutor the narrator's expression of anxiety—"I know I take a risk"—is tantamount to a confession. There is, however, another reading, which makes the confession far less reliable. In *Problems of Dos-toevsky's Poetics* Bakhtin describes a phenomenon peculiar to confession that he calls the "word with a loophole." In this type of speech, the speaker anticipates what the interlocutor will say in order to resist the interlocutor's negative evaluation. The speaker deliberately makes himself out to be worse than he is, sullying his image in the other's eyes, in order to forestall the interlocutor. Dostoevsky's *Notes from Underground*, in which the narrator advertises his spitefulness and unattractiveness, exemplifies the word with the loophole. In the Suvorin passage, the speaker anticipates the prosecutor's condemna-

---

24. Quoted in ibid., 105.

tion, articulating, but not admitting to, the condemnation in advance. The word with a loophole, far from an admission of guilt, "leaves open the possibility for altering the ultimate final meaning of one's own words" (233). The speaker sullies his image in order to invite the interlocutor to dispute the negative self-definition. The confessional word with a loophole produces no final, stable self-condemnation but instead sets in motion an infinite regress, in which no definition is possible. This phenomenon is an extreme example of the author's second self that we spoke of earlier. In the word with the loophole, the author's projection of himself in literary discourse fragments the unitary self. The legal culpability of the historical person based on such discourse comes under question.[25]

In his final speech to the appeals court, Suvorin said, "I, the author of the narrative, am constantly being equated with its protagonists. . . . If we assume this condition for all authors, then we would have to say that there are almost no books or authors whom we ought not to call criminals."[26] The first author on his list of criminals is Pushkin, as if to say, my allusion to Pushkin was not an effort to escape what you construct as criminality, since according to your definition of literature and crime the two are very nearly identical. The conflation of the historical person of the author with the dramatis personae of his fiction is a common feature of literary trials.[27] One hundred years after Suvorin's trial, Soviet prosecutors will show the same deliberate confusion in their case against Andrei Siniavskii.

For the prosecutor the novel is a confession of guilt. Suvorin's writing is both a crime and a metacommunication about the crime. It contains a statement of his intention to commit a crime, the crime itself, and an admission that the crime was committed. The government is not really a New Critic, as I suggested earlier, but a postmodern critic like Stanley Fish, who says that interpretation is not a matter of construing, but of constructing, meaning. The law completely rewrites Suvorin's writing. Defining the novel as a speech act, the government allows for only two addressees: the censor and the prosecutor. Didn't Suvorin sin-

---

25. For a related discussion of the problematics of confession (with reference to Bakhtin, Rousseau, de Man) in American criminal law, see Peter Brooks, "Storytelling without Fear? Confession in Law and Literature," in Brooks and Gewirtz, *Law's Stories*, 114–34.

26. Liubavskii, *Novye russkie ugolovnye protsessy*, 128.

27. For a discussion of how the prosecution conflated author, writer, and narrator in Flaubert's trial, see LaCapra, *"Madame Bovary" on Trial*, 61.

gle out the censor for special mention in the ending of his novel? According to the government, the writer writes in isolation, but not the divine isolation of Romanticism. The writer writes his novel, which is a confession of guilt, in the punitive isolation of the interrogation room. In the eyes of the law, the writer is a criminal. In Suvorin's case, the appeals court was apparently moved by some of the arguments made in his defense. His crime was not considered in a state of preparation, as he asked, but neither was it counted as having been completed, as the circuit court had found. The appeals court settled on a middle course, finding Suvorin guilty of "attempted crime." His prison sentence was accordingly lightened from two months to three weeks. His novel was ordered to be removed from circulation and destroyed.

Juridical Fiction

Although N. D. Akhsharumov (1819–93) is a minor writer in the canon of Russian literature, his fiction and criticism were well known to Russian readers of the latter part of the nineteenth century. From a military family, Akhsharumov received his education at the famous Imperial Lyceum, which many Russian writers, including Pushkin, attended. He matriculated for a time at the University of St. Petersburg, served briefly in the War Ministry, and then retired to a career in letters.[28] Like his far better known contemporaries Dostoevsky and Tolstoy, Akhsharumov published in the "thick" journals of the time, the encyclopedic literary and political periodicals, such as *Notes from the Fatherland* and the *Russian Herald.* Dostoevsky was well acquainted with Akhsharumov's work. In 1864, Dostoevsky's journal the *Epoch* featured Aksharumov's novel, *A Tricky Business*, about the travails of publishing a journal. Very few of Aksharumov's works were collected and republished, and there are no English translations.

In general terms, the conceit of *The Model* has a familiar ring to twentieth-century readers, especially fans of Philip Roth.[29] In Akhsharumov's story, the fictitious author can't make progress on his novel because the heroine rebels against him. She takes him to court to

---

28. See S. A. Vengerov, *Kritiko-biograficheskii slovar' russkikh pisatelei i uchenikh,* vol. 1 (St. Petersburg, 1889), 988–92. Dmitrii Akhsharumov, Nikolai's older brother, was a member of the Petrashevskii circle and was arrested with Dostoevsky.

29. Another variant may be seen in J. M. Coetzee's *Foe.* The heroine claims that Daniel Defoe plagiarized her letters and stole her story. I am grateful to Linda Kauffman for pointing this out to me.

compel him to change the plot that he has written for her. In Roth's novel of 1986, *The Counterlife*, various protagonists rebel against the version of the novel that the author/narrator/hero creates. "Maria" threatens to leave the hero, Nathan, and to leave the book. "She conceives of herself as my fabrication," writes Nathan.[30] In Roth, the contestation over who tells the story and the multiple selves that are thereby created for the hero are celebrated as devices that underscore the constructed nature of the novel's "reality." I will argue that in Aksharumov's work the author's trial achieves a similar effect but serves the more polemical purpose: it attempts to discipline realist authors of the Chernyshevskian school.[31] Akhsharumov suggests that such authors ought to be held responsible for the influence their fictions exert. *The Model* is an exercise in literary self-regulation. Its antirealist aesthetics directly parallels the official aesthetics evidenced by the prosecution at Suvorin's trial. At Suvorin's trial, the prosecutor attempted to create a clear distinction between his legal procedures of determining guilt and what he called literary "polemics." There is no place for literature or literariness in the law, but the law is competent to judge literature. As we saw, the effort to sustain the barrier between law and literature failed. The prosecutor called upon his own knowledge of Pushkin, for example, in order to make his charges against Suvorin stick. A similar problem unfolds in Akhsharumov's story. What belongs to literature and what to law, what is to be taken seriously in Austin's sense and what is not—become confused.

The Model opens with a brief notice that the fascinating and mysterious author Chuikin has disappeared. He had been in the middle of writing a story, which was appearing serially in one of the literary journals, but before his disappearance the story unaccountably ceased publication. An account of the events leading to the author's disappearance, most of which have to do with the troubled progress of the story he was writing, constitutes the main action of *The Model*.

In its opening paragraph the story takes aim at the "aura of sanctity," to use Paperno's language, attached to the image of the author in the 1860s. Chuikin is a gloomy, strange character, stooped and thin, his

---

30. Philip Roth, *The Counterlife* (New York: Penguin Books, 1986), 312.

31. *The Model* is not Akhsharumov's first foray into literary battle. In 1859 he published an article sharply critical of "the poisonous influence of the realist school." See V. S. Nechaeva, *Zhurnal M. M. i F. M. Dostoevskikh "Epokha" 1864–1865* (Moscow: Nauka, 1975), 137.

gaunt face framed by "masses of tousled dark hair, like an orangutan's" (549). In contrast to the author's enlightened views about women's emancipation, his physiognomy bears traces of "de-evolution," a point readily grasped by Russian readers of the time, engaged in debates about the significance of Darwin's theories of evolution. The name *Chuikin* itself suggests someone on the lower rungs of the merchantry—*chuika* refers disparagingly to this class of person.

The model to which the title refers is the model for the heroine of Chuikin's work. The "model," Alishcheva, in her thirties, with two small children, is married to a civil servant much older than herself. Chuikin persuades her into a program of personal emancipation prescribed by Chernyshevsky in *What Is to Be Done*. She changes her circle of friends to include a woman who has a child out of wedlock, and she begins to attend lectures on physiology and political economy. Upon her husband's death, Alishcheva moves in with her lover, Bragin, who attempts to convince her to hand her children over to the care of a public institution. The raising of children, he claims, is the obligation of society, "in which they will live and which they will serve" (575). When she balks, her children die. This is a hyperexaggerated example of the realist author's authority to enforce obedience. It is a commonplace to speak of an author punishing a character for her sins. Anna Karenina's suicide is an example. Aksharumov realizes the commonplace explicitly. After she loses her children, Alishcheva takes Chuikin to court in order to force him to return her children to her. The story culminates in Chuikin's trial.

As we have seen, realist literature was to take models from real life, transform them into "new people," and return them to life as models for readerly imitation. In *The Model*, Akhsharumov blurs the boundary between the real person, Alishcheva, whom Chuikin calls his model, and the fictitious heroine of his (Chuikin's) story. The narrator suggests that Alishcheva is nothing more than a shadow of the heroine of Chuikin's unfinished work, who has somehow escaped the confines of the printed page. The narrator remarks that there was nothing remarkable in Alishcheva's appearance, nothing that "attracts or repels; she was simply the typical strong thoroughbred woman" (551). Her facial features resemble a mark of punctuation. Her "eyebrows met, forming something similar to a question mark" (551). Her face bears traces of the printed page.

Who is Alishcheva? What is Chuikin's relation to her—advisor and

friend, or creator? Alishcheva writes in her diary, addressing Chuikin:
"You control me like no sultan ever controlled his slave! I and my children and everything that surrounds me belong to you from head to toe!
. . . With one stroke of your pen you can expunge me from the ranks of
the living" (561–62). Alishcheva comes to be persuaded that she is
entirely the product of Chuikin's authorial invention. But perhaps
Chuikin's power over Alishcheva is nothing more than her fantasy? Or
is Alishcheva's "reality" nothing more than Chuikin's fantasy?

Given the immediate context of Chernyshevskian realism, it seems
fairly obvious that Akhsharumov uses the puzzle about Alishcheva's
relation to Chuikin in order to challenge the notion that realist literature
takes models from real life, enhances them, and then "returns" them to
readers as models for imitation. Chuikin does not offer alternatives but
imposes them tyrannically on his model/heroine, overstepping her
wishes in the name of historical progress. According to the omniscient
narrator, Chuikin wanted to portray a woman who "enters the new
path" not by accident, and "not under the alien influence of inculcated
ideas, but freely" (546). But to claim that his story is based on real life,
Chuikin takes measures to persuade his model to act according to the
dictates of his authorial vision. In one scene, Chuikin complains to
Alishcheva that her "conservatism" impedes the progress of his story.
She fears that change will ruin her children: "I'm not going to make
myself and the children unhappy so that your story will come out more
interesting" (552). Chuikin responds that it is not for the sake of art, but
"in the interest of the great historical movement" (552). Chuikin threatens Alishcheva. If she does not act as he wishes, he will redo her character, substituting another woman in her place, who will assume all her
"rights," including her rights over her children—which Alishcheva
calls "force" and "extortion" (553).

When Alishcheva responds by threatening to expose him and have
him judged in a court of law, Chuikin switches registers, now addressing her not as his creature, but as a "real" person—who has gone mad.
He tells her: "A shaved head and a straitjacket threaten you" (570). The
"author" forces a change in the heroine by threats, intimidation, and
finally, seduction. Chuikin, thwarted in his attempt to force Alishcheva
along to the next step of emancipation, introduces the mysterious figure of Bragin to induce her to do so. The omniscient narrator describes
Bragin as a "lever without which there was hardly any possibility of
moving his heroine in a logical fashion along her new path" (565). The

narrator goes on to remark that Bragin is quite similar to Chuikin, only "enhanced and idealized" by Chuikin's own "creative inventiveness" and Alishcheva's love (565). Bragin is nothing more than a "figurehead, behind which two things were concealed: in the first place, the author himself, and in the second, the spring of the action" of the story (566). At one point in the story, Chuikin and Bragin merge into one another. Bragin looks into the mirror and sees Chuikin.

Once Alishcheva "crosses her Rubicon," as the narrator puts it, and has sex with Bragin, things take a turn for the worse. Bragin, like Chuikin, insists that Alishcheva give up her children to public care. When Alishcheva refuses, the children die one by one. Alishcheva suspects Chuikin's authorial interference and turns to a lawyer for help. The implicit but nonetheless central question as to how we ought to interpret the story—whether Alishcheva is "real" or not—becomes explicit in its ending, a trial scene. The trial takes place in a fantastical "court of conscience," complete with judge, jury, defense, and prosecution.

Literature on Trial

In recapitulating the events of the story, the trial scene rehearses several competing versions of the story's meaning. In this imaginary trial of literature, legal and literary interpretation are inextricably linked. Any decision about the heroine's suit against her author is a decision about the meaning of the story. Her attorney opens with a statement about the "human rights" of fictitious characters. Until this time, no fictitious character has reached her awareness of her human rights and decided to "protest against their infringement" (590). Zenkovich tries to blur the boundary between the fictitious and the real person. His approach relies on the basic tenets of the realist aesthetics of the time. First, no poet creates a fictitious character ex nihilo. Aesthetics does not tolerate a character who is completely new and unlike anything that has ever existed before; such a character would be a "monster." Characters are "taken entirely from life," and the poet merely creates the circumstances in which the character is to act. Society is very involved in the fates of these characters and does not doubt their "real existence." The reading audience of a Chernyshevskian-type novel does not acknowledge a separate "fictive" realm created by the work, as we have seen.

Zenkovich, suggesting a note of Sade in Chuikin's relation to

Alishcheva, tells the jury that as soon as she confronted Chuikin, she fell completely under his power: "he led me around by a leash" and awakened passions in her that she never before had experienced. He argues that the delays in the publication of the story correspond to the struggles of "the victim against her tormentor," struggles that the published version conceals. Zenkovich concludes by demanding that the court free Alishcheva from Chuikin's hold over her, that she be materially compensated for her sufferings, that her children be returned to her, and that the court take measures to safeguard "private persons" *(chastnye litsa)* from "seizure and oppression from belletrists" (601).

Chuikin's lawyer refutes the complaint against his client in its entirety, pointing out the absurdity of the charge. How could a character from a novel take an author to court? "If Alishcheva were not before you and therefore outside the novel, if she did not exist independently of the author's fantasy . . . there could be no case, because a fictitious character cannot act other than within the boundaries of the author's intention." Since such a claim is patently absurd, the defense lawyer argues, then the only complaint that the plaintiff can have is that Chuikin exerted an influence over her. But influence over another and responsibility for that person's actions are not the same. Chuikin's novel may have foretold events that did actually occur in Alishcheva's life, but neither Chuikin nor his novel can be said to have caused these events.

The defense changes his tactics. Zenkovich argues that he never meant to suggest that Alishcheva is bound by some mysterious power to Chuikin, or that she is the heroine of an unfinished novel. The power by which Chuikin directed her actions is none other than the power of literature itself, which "is capable of changing the point of view of masses of people and submitting society to itself" (622). There can be no distinction between Chuikin's role as author, the creator of a fictitious character similar to Alishcheva, and his role as Alishcheva's friend and confidant.

The judge instructs the jury to consider whether Chuikin can be held responsible for the harm ultimately caused to Alishcheva by the fiction he wrote and the advice he gave her. The judge suggests that Chuikin exploited Alishcheva's belief that he controlled her actions. After she noticed the great similarity between his novel and her life, she fell under his influence, acting as he directed so that he could then describe those acts in his novel. Alishcheva came to believe that she could not contravene Chuikin's instructions. Is it possible that Chuikin failed to take note of her belief? The judge states that Chuikin could have intervened at the very beginning to dissuade Alishcheva of her "illusion," but failed to do so. Alishcheva's illusion was necessary to Chuikin as an "instrument with which he could control Alishcheva's will" (631). Whether Alishcheva is the "heroine of an unfinished novel" or merely resembles one is irrelevant. What matters is Chuikin's failure to respond to her mistaken belief about her status.

The judge continues his examination of Chuikin, emphasizing not Alishcheva, but Chuikin's relation to her. Did Chuikin need a "citizen under his command, selflessly fighting for the civic cause, or only a model for the heroine of his story, or both together?" (631). The judge reminds the jury that Chuikin's novel followed the course of events in the plaintiff's life step by step. The jury must decide whether it is possible that "the course of events that he [the author] foresaw to a certain degree, in the life of the plaintiff, was not in general predicted by the novel, and that Chuikin, as the author of the novel and as an artist, did not try to bring the two sides together into an artistic unity, having, as we already know, a dramatic role in both" (632). Chuikin took upon himself the godlike role of authoring a life in an immediate sense. Why be satisfied with the literary imagination of a new woman when he could create the new woman in the flesh? The judge asks whether it is possible that Chuikin "did not use the living exemplar constantly turning before his eyes?" What is on trial is not the fate of "the heroine of an unfinished novel," but an author fascinated with his power to realize his metaphors in the flesh of another living person.

Law and the Author

The judge's characterization of Chuikin paints a disturbing picture of the author as a Pygmalion in love, not with his creation, but with his power.[32] Zenkovich, the heroine's lawyer, also makes a statement about power, which we have already quoted: "the author's power is, of course, unlimited, but only insofar as it acts within its appointed

---

32. For a discussion of the Pygmalion theme in nineteenth-century Russian literature, see Irene Masing-Delic, "Creating the Living Work of Art: The Symbolist Pygmalion and His Antecedents," in *Creating Life: The Aesthetic Utopia of Russian Modernism*, ed. Irina Paperno and Joan Delaney Grossman (Stanford, Calif.: Stanford University Press, 1994), 51–82.

sphere, from which it may not leave if it does not wish to conflict with other powers" (585). Implicit in Zenkovich's statement is a Romantic aesthetics that in one of its modes sharply separates literature from daily life and politics. The "appointed sphere" within which the author is free to act is the realm of the imagination. Romantic literature and philosophy of the late eighteenth and early nineteenth century envisioned a godlike creative power for the artist's imagination, which brings into being an endless proliferation of new artistic forms.[33]

Akhsharumov came to maturity in the height of Russian idealism and Romanticism in the late 1830s and 1840s, and the influence of these movements can clearly be seen in his work. The scene of Chuikin writing captures a Romantic sense of the mysterious process of artistic creation—with a demonic twist. Out of a fog there appear figures who move, walk, and speak. Chuikin looks on approvingly, but sometimes "in a rage, with a sweep of his hand, he drove all this rubbish from the scene, and then in one instant, everything disappeared back into the fog, the fog itself disappeared, and in its place pages covered with lines of writing, along which a hand, wildly waving a pen, drew a gigantic X" (572). Chuikin, we might say, has overstepped not legal but aesthetic bounds by attempting to unite the creative power of Romantic artist with the political and social program of the realist writer.

In *The Model* Chuikin's trial is a hyperextension of the notion of the author's responsibility for meaning. But the trial's ending unravels the closure that the law seeks to provide. The jury, addressing Chuikin, finds him guilty on four counts:

1. Of the abuse of your authorial rights, which you tried to extend farther than their natural boundaries;
2. Of the abuse of your influence, which you gained by means of deceit, over a woman who served you as the model or the heroine of your novel;
3. Of the seduction and ruin of this same woman;
4. Of the death of her children. (633)

The court sentences Chuikin to "exile from the world of real life" and consigns him to live "forever in the world of abstract thought." We

---

33. See M. H. Abrams, *Natural Supernaturalism: Tradition and Revolution in Romantic Literature* (New York: Norton, 1971), 169–95 and 431–37.

leave the scene of the courtroom not knowing how to interpret what transpired there. Chuikin protests that the only "court of conscience" society has known up to this point has been literature itself.

There is a strong hint that the whole scene is a product of Chuikin's authorial invention. We have just discussed the mysterious scene of Chuikin writing. When he writes, Chuikin stares off at some "transparent fog" in which glimmer a multitude of figures. Chuikin has only to fix his gaze at any one figure in order for it to emerge from the fog into "the sharp feature and finished form of live reality" (527). With one wave of his hand the figures disperse back into the fog. At the trial's conclusion, all the members of the court rise from their seats "horror struck" and "crowd together in a pile" (633). Chuikin leaves the court, and the story ends.

During the trial, the judge confronts Alishcheva with documentary evidence in the form of death certificates, which prove the real, irrevocable deaths of her children. Alishcheva suggests that the death certificates may also be fictitious—not forgeries, but products of the same authorial invention that made her children ill in the first place. The judge replies that "there is nothing left but to assume that I and everything that is taking place at this moment, all of this is the novel" (616). As Alishcheva says, "the novel can swallow everything." We may take Alishcheva's reading of the death certificates either as a symptom of her delusion—or of her profound grasp of the truth. Her fears interrupt the flow of the narrative, and we are reminded that we are reading a work of fiction. Alishcheva experiences Said's "molestation," that is, "consciousness of one's confinement to a fictive . . . realm." As we have seen, she is *molested* in the full sense of the word, both physically and psychologically. In this work, even the most abstract precondition of literary fiction, the consciousness of the fiction, is realized in a literal way and is experienced as a form of brutalization by the heroine. We will return shortly to the significance of gender in this relation.

The Model is a story about a writer writing a story whose heroine takes him to court in order to compel the writer to change the plot. During the trial the question of the writer's culpability for the events in the heroine's life depends on which of two competing interpretations of the story the judge accepts. *The Model* is a story about the impossibility of its own interpretation. We never know how to resolve the questions it raises. The distinction between its "literal truth," that is, the story of a heroine who escapes the pages of her novel, and its figurative truth—

the story of a heroine who wishes to escape the influence of Russian realist literature of the 1860s—ultimately loses its meaning. Literal and figurative meaning are blurred, just as legal and literary interpretation are blurred in its trial scene. The boundaries between the two processes of interpretation, one seeking finality and closure, the other open-ended and unfinalizable, cannot be maintained.

Authorship and Self-Authoring

Even as Akhsharumov's story puts the fictitious author on trial for overstepping the boundaries of literature's "appointed sphere," it threatens the basis upon which such a trial could be conducted. While they share a Romantic and idealist image of the author, Tuzingauzen would not want Akhsharumov on his side. In *The Model* distinctions between author and character, original and copy, break down. Bragin is a stand-in for Chuikin, a device that conceals the "spring of the action." Akhsharumov's fascination with the theme of the double, and his own doubling relationship with Dostoevsky, can be seen in a curious literary fact. In 1850 Akhsharumov published "The Double" in *Notes from the Fatherland* four years after Dostoevsky had published his own "Double" in the same journal. In 1858 Akhsharumov published a tale called *The Gambler;* eight years later, Dostoevsky published a novella under the same title.

The Model turns the notion of authorial responsibility on its head, since the author is revealed as an effect of writing, and not a being with a unified identity. The story self-reflexively exposes the mechanisms whereby the illusion of reality is created, revealing the behind-the-scenes struggles concealed by the published version of Chuikin's novel. The scene of the writer creating and destroying worlds at a word—the image of the author shared by the prosecution at Suvorin's trial—is revealed as an illusion. In *The Model* the heroine rebels at her author's attempts to refashion her identity, to force her out of her role of wife and mother into the role of emancipated woman. Ironically, she comes to fulfill the author's program but turns it against him, seeking emancipation from his authorial rule. The heroine rebels against the author, and the author is put on trial. To use Said's Nietzschean language, the text is a site upon which a struggle of the wills is inscribed, and not a repository of an author's intention. Legal culpability for crimes of fiction depend on clear-cut and stable definitions of authorship, intentionality, and originality. In *The Model* the contest over the plot radically undermines these concepts. The author as a being whose intentions are enacted in a text cannot be recovered. We are left with a far more elusive image of the author, whose identity is fragmented and multiple.

The problem of identity receives particular attention one of Aksharumov's earlier works, his novel of 1861, *Another's Name*. The hero, an illegitimate son defrauded of his inheritance, settles on the expedient of taking on "another's name" in order to keep his illegitimacy a secret. Grigorii Alekseevich Lukin becomes Grigorii Alekseev by switching passports with Alekseev when the latter dies. The passport, the official document guaranteeing identity, becomes the means of subverting the law. We should note that using a stolen passport was such a common crime that it comes under special discussion in the statutes of 1864. The story repeatedly uses the metaphor of writing as a signal of the empty conventionality of behavior and indeed the conventionality of identity itself—created not by integral selves in interaction with each other, but by the manipulation of signs. At one point early in the story, Lukin's fate hangs on whether a doctor examining Alekseev will report that the initials on the dead man's cigarette case do not correspond to the passport Lukin has placed on his body. A few letters make all the difference. During a conversation in the salon of one of St. Petersburg's most fashionable hostesses, Lukin comments that it is not difficult to read people's faces

> when there is really something written on the face, and especially when the truth is written there, but what if it is silent like a blank sheet or, still worse, lies?[34]

Whoever can manipulate these special forms of writing can elude both the pitfalls of the law and society's unwritten codes. Imposture is another "crime of writing."

In the course of the story the imposter hero Lukin/Alekseev becomes as indispensable to the hostess as he does to her husband, a highly placed government official. Lukin quickly learns "the complicated machine of the higher administration with all its curlicues, fantastic formalities, and punctilious details."[35] Law is reduced to a

---

34. N. D. Aksharumov, *Chuzhoe imia: Roman v trekh chastiakh*, pt. 2, *Russkii vestnik* 31 (February 1861): 709.

35. *Russkii vestnik* 32 (March 1861): 667.

curlicue, a playful and decorative stroke of the pen. The exercise of crime and the conduct of official duty are joined together into one vast game of writing.[36] Ultimately, however, Lukin loses the game. His new persona consumes him, and he becomes the criminal the law says he is.

Authority Figures

The problems of authority, authorship, and identity encapsulated by Suvorin's trial and Akhsharumov's work are not limited to the sphere of literary aesthetics. The problem has broad implications for Russian society in the 1860s, a decade of upheaval, marked by political terror. In April 1866, just two months after *The Model* was published, Dmitrii Karakozov, a member of a radical political organization, attempted to assassinate the tsar.[37] But even leaving aside political terror, the emancipation of the serfs and the legal reform initiated by the government of Alexander II contributed to the overall sense of the dismantling of traditional forms of authority. New procedures, for example, held that "no one can be arrested other than in cases defined by law," and, similarly, that no one was to be subject to punishment except by means of sentence from the appropriate court. In criminal cases, "each one bears responsibility only for himself" (*PSZ* 41476:276). Akhsharumov's story and Suvorin's trial reveal the difficulties involved in establishing who this "self" is in the case of an author charged with a crime of fiction. Full equality before the law was not granted by the reform of 1864 inasmuch as different classes of persons were subject to different regulations. Neither was full protection from the law guaranteed, since governmental interference in the judiciary, particularly criminal cases, continued. But to some extent, the provisions contained in the reform safeguarding the rights of persons subject to legal investigation and prosecution alter the way individuals interact with figures in authority.

The legal protections alter what Lotman and Uspenskii define as

36. One of the installments of *Another's Name* appeared in the same issue as an article on the need for reform in criminal investigation. Both the article and the novel show how skilled criminals could manipulate the formal categories and procedures of the law to their own advantage. See N. Polozov, "Neskol'ko slov ob ugolovnykh sledstviiakh," *Russkii vestnik* 31 (February 1861): 715–77.

37. For more on Karakozov and organized terror, see Franco Venturi, *Roots of Revolution: A History of the Populist and Socialist Movements in Nineteenth-Century Russia,* trans. Francis Haskell (Chicago: University of Chicago Press, 1960), 331–53.

the traditional Russian concept of self-giving. The individual gives of himself or herself to the ruler without stipulating conditions and receives the ruler's beneficence. The person is defined not so much by limits, but by proximity to the sacred figure of the tsar. The legal protections against unlawful search, seizure, arrest, and imprisonment set limits on the tsar's power. Some minimal legal concept of the person as a being with rights emerges from these new provisions. Akhsharumov's *Model* reflects some of these issues. The fictitious author Chuikin, reflecting on Alishcheva's challenge to his authority, attributes her rebellion to the rebelliousness of the age: "That's the nineteenth century! Everywhere there is freedom! Everywhere there is emancipation! It's gone beyond the boundary of every decency! The clearest and most unquestionable right of one person over another—and they don't want to leave that in peace!" (571). For Chuikin, intoxicated with his own sense of power over Alishcheva, "rights" are tantamount to rights over another.

The question of "authorial rights" for Chuikin boils down to absolute power. Alishcheva's husband dies after he realizes that his life, even in its most intimate scenes, is displayed on the pages of a journal for all to read. Alishcheva, in love with Bragin, hesitates about sexual relations with him. In order to force this next stage of her emancipation, Chuikin threatens to take full advantage of his "authorial rights" over Alishcheva: "You know that you are in my power and that this power is limitless; that I can destroy you with a word, I can force you to suffer as you have never suffered before. . . . I can put you before me like a statue, without clothes, and feast my eyes on you" (569–70). The author's creative word devolves into an invasive, degrading, masculine gaze. Authorial omniscience is grotesquely transformed into malevolent omnipotence. As we recall, Chuikin also threatens to incarcerate Alishcheva in an insane asylum—suggesting a relation between omniscient narrative authority and regimes of punitive discipline.

In the trial scene, Akhsharumov plays with the notion of the paternal authority of the realist author, making explicit the failure in the normal mechanism of the author's filial relation to his characters. The defense states:

> the prosecution looks at the author as a father of all the people that he introduces on the scene, and this means that Mr. Chuikin did nothing less than seduce his own spiritual daughter. (620)

The family romance of the author and his characters is perverted.[38] The author/father commits the crime of incest with his "daughter." Aksharumov playfully intertwines the image of the abusive father into his fantastical narrative about an author overstepping the boundaries of his authority. The relative states of sickness and health, of narrative order and authorial filiation, and of social order and parental filiation thus reflect each other. Violence and excess on both planes—the narrative and the social order—spread from the top down. The image of the author as a source of a stable world of verisimilitude comes undone, just as the image of the ruler and the father as the source of a stable world of relations begins to erode.[39] In *The Model* the author loses his stable identity. Chuikin disappears into Bragin, who is a figurehead, a stand-in for Chuikin himself. The doubling of the author's image stages the absent father. Multiple copies replace an absent original.

Gender and Authority

In *The Model* Akhsharumov imagines the breakdown of normal authorial filiation in terms of sexual abuse. The image of authorial incest raises a question about authority, narrative, and gender, which, while not the main theme of this study, deserves at least a brief discussion.[40] As Irene Masing-Delic points out, "radical realists" such as Chernyshevsky "usually took women as the objects of their human-transformation projects."[41] The Pygmalion story depends on an opposition between a virile and masculine authority, which creates form and meaning, and a passive, feminized materiality. In Akhsharumov's parody, the female rebels, but not without having to subject herself to the same kind of authority from which she seeks protection. In order for Alishcheva to

---

38. For the significance of the "family romance" in politics, see Lynn Hunt, *The Family Romance of the French Revolution* (Berkeley and Los Angeles: University of California Press, 1992).

39. The elaborate scenarios of domestic bliss and fatherly love initiated by Tsar Nicholas I, which continued throughout the nineteenth century, underscore the significance of the family romance in Russian political life. The staged scenes of family happiness may be seen as masking the reality. See Richard Wortman, *Scenarios of Power: Myth and Ceremony in Russian Monarchy* (Princeton, N.J.: Princeton University Press, 1995), 333–78, especially 335.

40. A good starting point for a theoretical discussion of this question is found in Teresa de Lauretis, *Alice Doesn't: Feminism, Semiotics, Cinema* (Bloomington: Indiana University Press, 1984), 103–57.

41. Masing-Delic, "Creating the Living Work," 59.

escape Chuikin's power, Zenkovich, her lawyer, instructs her to hand herself over to the authority of the law, embodied in none other than the lawyer himself. Zenkovich says:

> give your signature that from this day forward until the end of the case, you acknowledge yourself under its [the law's] control and obliged to it in everything, not doing anything without its knowledge and agreement. If you only give this signature . . . then all his power will disappear and he will stand on the same level as you, as a defendant. (586)

Alishcheva, designating herself "the heroine of an unfinished novel," signs a document promising to obey Zenkovich in everything. The remedy proposed by the lawyer mimics the offense committed by the author. Zenkovich appears in some sense as yet another mask for the all-powerful Chuikin. The heroine moves from the jurisdiction of one to another, without ever being able to author her own story. "He was my author and the author of everything that happened to me," says Alishcheva, in reference to Chuikin. The law, no less than the writer Chuikin, authors and authorizes the heroine's behavior. Equality before the law, in the startling ending of the passage, means being equally under suspicion as one who is accused of a crime. The status of legal subject to which Alishcheva aspires offers no relief from her condition as "the heroine of an unfinished novel."

The image of the abusive father, which appears as a trope for the abusive author in Akhsharumov resurfaces in Dostoevsky's journalism as a symptom of the collapse of the Russian social order. Dostoevsky takes up this question of the crimes of parents against their children, particularly fathers against daughters, in his *Diary of a Writer*. The image of the female abused and beaten and subject to insanities brought about, according to the norms of the time, by her very condition as female—pregnancy and passion—this is the scenario in which Dostoevsky inscribes himself as the Diarist. Competing with the law's interpretations of female criminality, Dostoevsky gives the apparently inchoate actions of his real-life heroines form and meaning and, in so doing, fashions himself as an authoritative and powerful figure.

Chapter 4

Dostoevsky's *Diary*:
A Child Is Being Beaten

For you a character is created, like a novelist, like a storyteller, and
you go and believe my novel. It's a game of artistry, psychology, eloquence. But because of this toy, the fate of a man can perish! Have
we gathered to listen to the novel of a fashionable writer or to the
fate of a man?

A character is created, his thoughts and feelings are connected—
all very well constructed. But what if it's something completely different?

—Fetiukovich, in the notebooks for *The Brothers Karamazov*[1]

In *The Diary of a Writer*, his unique one-man monthly journal, Dostoevsky is fascinated by the new jury trials and the new institution of the
bar.[2] He had already written about the law in his journalistic work of
the early 1860s and in his fiction up to 1876, the year he began publish-

---

This chapter, along with chapter 5, is a greatly revised and expanded version of my article, "Russian Law and Literature: A Study in Cultural Thematics," *Studies in Law, Politics,
and Society* 15 (1996): 315–34.

1. F. M. Dostoevskii, *Polnoe sobranie sochinenii v tridtsati tomakh* (Leningrad: Nauka,
1972–90), 15:365. Henceforward all citations to be given parenthetically in the body of the
text by volume and page number.

2. Dostoevsky's announcement for the *Diary* in 1875 indicated that its format would
be that of "our weekly newspapers." The announcement continues: "But this will not be
a newspaper; out of its twelve issues (for January, February, March, and so on) there will
be formed something whole, a book, written by one pen" (22:136). The *Diary* came out
every month in 1876, the first year of its publication. In 1877, May–June and July–August
were combined issues. In April 1877, Dostoevsky announced the cessation of the *Diary* for
reasons of health, but the main reason was to work on *The Brothers Karamazov*. In 1880 the
sole issue appeared in August, containing Dostoevsky's famous Pushkin speech. For a
general discussion of the *Diary*, see Joseph Frank, introduction to *The Diary of a Writer*,
trans. Boris Brasol (Santa Barbara, Calif.: Peregrine Smith, 1979); and Gary Saul Morson,
introduction to *A Writer's Diary*, trans. and annotated by Kenneth Lantz (Evanston, Ill.:
Northwestern University Press, 1993).

ing the *Diary*, and would write about it in *The Brothers Karamazov*, for the sake of which he temporarily suspended publication of the *Diary*. In the *Diary*, Dostoevsky, like other observers, is dismayed by what he sees as a high number of acquittals, and by the use of what were then fashionable new defense strategies, such as temporary insanity, and the argument that a hostile social and economic environment was responsible for individual crimes. Dostoevsky discusses four different legal cases of his time.[3] The Kronenberg case (which Dostoevsky mistakenly spells "Kroneberg," *Diary*, February 1876) and the Dzhunkovskii case (*Diary*, July–August 1877) both involved what we now call child abuse. In both, the parents were acquitted. The Kairova case (*Diary*, May 1876) also produced an acquittal. Kairova attacked her lover's wife with a razor. In the Kornilova case, which Dostoevsky first discusses in May 1876, a pregnant woman assaulted her stepdaughter by throwing her out of a window. Dostoevsky returns to the case on four subsequent occasions: in October and December 1876 and in April and December 1877.

Dostoevsky's response to these cases and, more generally, to the new legal institutions brought about by the reform of 1864 is marked by inconsistency and even outright contradiction.[4] On some occasions, he seems to abhor lawyers and the institution of the courts as an evil, but elsewhere he speaks of the results brought by the reforms in more favorable terms, describing the new jury system as an edifying force, as "a moral school for our society and people" (23:19). The extreme negative reaction can be found, for example, in Dostoevsky's discussion of the Kronenberg case. But in several of his discussions of the Kornilova case, Dostoevsky embraces the legal process wholeheartedly. He actively intervened in the case and, largely through his discussion in *The Diary of a Writer*, helped to secure Kornilova's ultimate acquittal. As we will see, his arguments on Kornilova's behalf are based on the plea

---

3. V. A. Tunimanov suggests that these legal entries form one of the *Diary's* main constitutive layers; the other two are politics and literature. Tunimanov also points out that the legal pieces of the *Diary* "are one of the most important stages of the 'creative history' of *The Brothers Karamazov*." See V. A. Tunimanov, "Publitsistika Dostoevskogo *Dnevnika pisatelia*," in *Dostoevskii khudozhnik i myslitel': Sbornik statei* (Moscow: Khudozh. lit., 1972), 167.

4. Most scholars see only hostility on Dostoevsky's part. Walicki finds that Dostoevsky was "deeply suspicious of barristers" and believed, like Count V. L. Panin under Nicholas I, that lawyers "try to bias the court, not by law, but by eloquence." See Walicki, *Legal Philosophies*, 15. For more on Russian writers and the reform, see also Wortman, *Russian Legal Consciousness*, 288.

of temporary insanity, a defense strategy that he otherwise will hold suspect—in the *Diary,* in *Crime and Punishment,* and in *The Brothers Karamazov.* In the latter work, one of the characters offers a lengthy tirade about temporary insanity *(affekt)* as "that for which everything is forgiven" (15:17).[5]

I will suggest in this chapter that underneath the contradictions in Dostoevsky's responses to the court cases he discusses there is a fundamental continuity, which has to do with Dostoevsky's personality, not his actual or historical personality, but the public persona that he constructs with the writing of the *Diary.* According to Igor Volgin, the *Diary* is personal not just in that it contains autobiographical entries, but insofar as it always and everywhere is about Dostoevsky himself. Volgin writes that the *Diary* is personal from beginning to end, and that its hero is Dostoevsky. It is Dostoevsky's personality that "fills in the lacunae" between Dostoevsky's conflicting ideological positions.[6] Volgin emphasizes the importance of reading the *Diary* in its historical context, and of understanding the interactions between Dostoevsky and his reading audience. The persona that Dostoevsky constructs must be understood in terms of its capacity to persuade an audience, that is, its rhetorical force. Dostoevsky fashions an authoritative role for himself in the *Diary* by constructing a narrative about himself. This underlying autobiographical narrative unfolds in Dostoevsky's discussion of the Kronenberg, Kornilova, Kairova, and Dzhunkovskii cases. I will show that the main contours of this narrative mirror the themes of the cases, namely, childhood and parenthood. Dostoevsky the author of *The Diary of a Writer* authors himself as a child of, and as a father to, a new Russia. These two stages are not always chronologically distinct from one another.

The passage that serves as the epigraph to this chapter suggests the outlines of Dostoevsky's strategy in the *Diary.* In the passage, Dmitrii's

---

5. Gary Saul Morson argues that the *Diary* is self-conscious about its own gaps: as "threshold art" poised between the genres of utopia and antiutopia, it is destined to be inconclusive, offering only "an intensified dialectic of utopian 'pro' and anti-utopian 'contra.'" See Morson, *The Boundaries of Genre: Dostoevsky's Diary of a Writer and the Traditions of Literary Utopia* (Austin: University of Texas Press, 1981), 26–31, 56–68.

6. See I. L. Volgin, *Dostoevskii—Zhurnalist (Dnevnik Pisatelia i Russkaia obshchestvennost')* (Moscow: Izdatel'stvo Moskovskogo universiteta, 1981), 67. See also Tunimanov, who writes that in the *Diary,* "Dostoevsky's I is vividly . . . emphasized: the I of a polemicist, a teacher, a prophet, of a person with an interesting and complex biography." "Publitsistika Dostoevskogo *Dnevnika pisatelia,*" 205.

defense attorney argues that the prosecution's artistry creates an obstacle to the apprehension and representation of the truth. As we saw earlier, Richard Weisberg argues that for Dostoevsky "verbose legal eloquence" undermines values and morality. But it is precisely as a
"novelist" that Dostoevsky will read and rewrite the characters of the
real-life protagonists in the court cases he discusses, using his own narrative fiction as sources for his new creations. Although Dostoevsky
takes great pains to distance himself from the political program of
Chernyshevskian realism, he no less than Chernyshevsky subscribes to
its fundamental artistic tenet. Notwithstanding his great artistic exper-
imentation in polyphony and dialogism, for Dostoevsky, as for Chernyshevsky and other writers of his time, the purpose of the artistic work
is to mold reality, to shape and "organize" the lives of its readers. The
boundary between the art work and "real life" is blurred. This extraliterary program is especially apparent in the *Diary*.

In his reading of the Kronenberg case, and in *Diary* entries that
immediately surround his discussion of this case, Dostoevsky positions
himself as one with the suffering child in this case, and by extension, as
one with the suffering child as a figure for Russia. In taking this position, Dostoevsky retroactively creates a new class identity for himself;
that is, he overcomes the gap that separates him as a member of the
educated upper classes from the peasantry. At the same time, he reinvents for himself and his reading audience what it is to be Russian. A
second reading of these sections of the *Diary* reveals another side to
Dostoevsky's creative reimagination of himself and of Russia: the role
of pain and violence in this process.

The Cases

The *Petersburg Gazette* for January 19, 1876, called the Kronenberg case
"the most outstanding fact of our social life in recent times." Stanislav
Kronenberg, a nobleman, was accused of "torturing" his seven-year-
old daughter. Kronenberg had an affair with a woman who, unknown
to him, became pregnant. She went to Geneva, where she left her
daughter with some peasants. Kronenberg, who discovered the child's
existence some time later, had her placed in the custody of the local pas-
tor. Three years later he went to Geneva to take the girl home to Russia
with him, at the urging of his new mistress. It was after this "accidental
family" was settled in a Petersburg suburb that the trouble began. The

yard keeper made out a complaint at the local police station that the father "frequently and cruelly beat his young daughter" (*Petersburg Gazette,* Jan. 14, 1876). The case came to trial.

The defense lawyer was the renowned Vladimir Spasovich, whose cautionary thoughts about his profession we have discussed in chapter 2. Spasovich discredited the complaint brought by the servant woman by suggesting that the little girl and the servant were in some kind of collusion. He used medical experts who testified that the marks left on the girl's body provided no evidence of a threat to her life. The statutory definition of torture in Russia in 1876 required that the physical attack represent such a danger. Beyond this criterion, the Russian law, unlike the Polish law, as Spasovich argued, was imprecise about what constitutes torture. This point about the superiority of Polish over Russian law could hardly have struck a responsive chord in Spasovich's broader public audience beyond the courtroom, given the animosity that prevailed between Russia and Poland for much of the nineteenth century; as recently as 1863, there had been a rebellion in Poland against Russian rule. Spasovich concluded that the blows inflicted by the father did not fit the legal definition. In response to the question—"Was the nobleman Stanislav Kronenberg guilty of the following, that during the summer of 1875, he consciously and intentionally subjected his minor daughter to torture, consisting in the repeated infliction of blows that left bruises, and consisting in the cruel, tormenting and prolonged punishment with rods?"[7]—the jury returned a verdict of not guilty.

Dostoevsky and many others were outraged. Dostoevsky attacked Spasovich's "talent" and rhetoric, which, in his view, transformed the victim into a laughing, red-cheeked thief with "secret vices" (22:57). The *Week (Nedelia)* makes explicit what Dostoevsky only suggests: the alleged "secret vices" for which the father disciplined the child were bedwetting and masturbation, the latter being the a typical vice of the nineteenth-century child.[8] Two contrasting images of the child emerge: the suffering victim, the "little one," "the creature with the face of an

---

7. *Peterburgskaia gazeta,* no. 17, January 25, 1876.

8. *Nedelia,* April 15, 1876, no. 3, 145. For references to the history of masturbation as a disease in the nineteenth century, see Eve Kosofsky Sedgwick, "Jane Austen and the Masturbating Girl," in *Questions of Evidence: Proof, Practice, and Persuasion across the Disciplines,* ed. James Chandler, Arnold Davidson, and Harry Harootunian (Chicago: University of Chicago Press, 1994), 112 n. 13.

angel," as Dostoevsky puts it (22:67), and the oversexualized liar and thief, the budding delinquent, as Spasovich apparently was able to convince the jury.

The St. Petersburg newspapers, in responding to Spasovich's defense, attempt to tar him with the same brush that he had used against the little girl, as if to suggest that the reason he could persuade a jury that the victim was a wanton criminal was that he himself belonged to a moral universe, in virtue of his profession and his nationality, in which a seven-year-old could indeed very well be a criminal. The *St. Petersburg Times (Sanktpeterburgskie vedomosti)* describes Spasovich's arguments as overly refined, imbued with the supersophistication of "ancient Roman morality." At a more visceral level, the newspaper objects to Spasovich himself, to his client, Kronenberg, and the entire court proceeding, all of which it characterized as alien, not Russian. "Kronenberg does not really belong to Russian society. . . . in him we can see the image of a purely Western, half-French nervousness." To paraphrase the newspaper, a man has beaten his daughter, and the whole apparatus of the courts quite inexplicably comes into play: witnesses, expertise, the prosecution, the defense, and "a solemn verdict," which permitted the little girl's tormentor to go unpunished. "And in sharp contrast to all these foreign morals, habits, witnesses, there enters upon the scene the local element of the simple people in the person of the cook and the yard keeper and other simple women." In these ordinary Russian women, the "feeling of pity boiled over." Dostoevsky too finds the cook and the yard keeper to be the "most attractive people in the whole case" (22:62). The *St. Petersburg Times* emphasizes the contrast between the Russian feeling of pity and the foreign expertise of the officials of the court and of the defense lawyer. "Why all these references to the nuances of the opinions of the experts?" "Why all this philosophizing about what constitutes torture?" "The jury must judge according to human feeling and not by examples from judicial practice."[9] Dostoevsky says something very similar: "But tell me, why should we be concerned that the sufferings and torment of this little girl do not fit the legal definition of torture letter for letter" (22:65).

The press, for the most part, finds that in the Kronenberg case, legality was served, but not justice. The *Judicial Herald (Sudebnyi vestnik)* pointed out that the prosecution was more to blame than the defense

9. P. Boborykin, "Voskresnyi fel'eton," *Sanktpeterburgskie vedomosti*, February 1, 1876, no. 32.

lawyer, since it admitted that the father only sought to discipline his child. Legally, it could not be shown that the child's "physical inviolability" had been impinged upon, since the prosecution made no attempt to prove that Kronenberg intended to humiliate her. The law required that such an intent be proved in order to establish torture, since the state gave broad leeway to parental power.

Just beneath the surface of the case lies an anxiety about sexuality. The sexuality of the female child must be erased; the girl is a sinless angel, an innocent. Public feeling about the child's innocence or vice is tied to issues of Russian identity, innocence being Russian, and vice being Western. The youth and innocence of the girl is tied to a self-definition of Russia as a youthful and innocent nation, in contrast to an older, depraved Europe. Kronenberg, more European than Russian, suffered from "nervousness" and beat his daughter for fifteen minutes, "unconsciously and beside himself," in a transport of rage, as Dostoevsky reports (22:67). The most important figure on the map of national identity is that of the compassionate Russian servant woman, in whom Dostoevsky found the "keen gaze of an observer, a gaze full of inner torment at the suffering of an offended creature of God" (22:62). But during the trial the mythologized Russian people, seduced by the brilliance of the defense lawyer, betrayed themselves. The jury acquitted Kronenberg. As far as Dostoevsky is concerned, Kronenberg is a false father and Spasovich is a false authority, a pretender. In whom or what true parental and legal authority are constituted remains an open question.

In Dostoevsky's view the Kronenberg case shows how a lawyer's talent leads him to stray from the simple facts, that is, that a child had been cruelly beaten by her father. In Dostoevsky's discussion of the Kornilova case the opposite is true. Dostoevsky shows that we cannot get to the truth without straying from the simple facts. Kornilova reported to the police that she threw her daughter from a window in order to take revenge on her husband. For Dostoevsky in October 1876 these facts require a more profound understanding, which only he, with his special novelistic vision, can provide. Dostoevsky writes that "it's not in the subject, but in the vision" (23:141). For now we may note a surprising privileging of the eye over the ear in this line. What has become of Dostoevsky the inventor of polyphony? We will return to this point later.

Dostoevsky's sympathetic attentiveness to the facts of the

Kornilova case in October marks a significant change from attitudes he had previously held. In May 1876 Dostoevsky responds to the Kornilova case with horror and dismay. He writes a self-styled parody *(karikatura)* of what a clever lawyer could do for Kornilova in the way of a defense. The lawyer would describe

> the hopelessness of the situation . . . a young wife married to a wid-
> ower, either forcibly or by mistake. Here would come pictures of
> the impoverished daily life of poor people, eternal work. She, a
> simple, innocent, an inexperienced girl, . . . thought she was mar-
> rying for joy, but instead of joy—she got laundry, cooking, bathing
> the child—"gentleman of the jury, she naturally had to hate this
> child. . . . in a desperate moment, in an attack of insanity, beside
> herself, she grabbed the girl. . . . Gentlemen of the jury, who of you
> would not have done the same thing? Who of you would not have
> thrown [*ne vyshvyrnul*] the child out of the window?" (23:19)

Dostoevsky quickly adds, however, that here is something "too strange" about what Kornilova did, and that a "subtle and profound analysis" of the case would be required, which might even lead to a softening of Kornilova's fate. In the next chapter of the May issue, in which Dostoevsky describes his visit to a foundling home, the Kornilova case becomes emblematic of the neglect and abuse of chil-dren. Dostoevsky invents a noun, *vyshvyrki*, loosely, "outcasts" from the verb *throw off (vyshvyrnut')*, using it to describe all the children in the home.[10] He uses the occasion of his visit to comment more generally on crimes committed by women against children, commenting ironi-cally on an acquittal that a Russian jury had recently made in a case of infanticide. Dostoevsky suggests that the jurors may have been influ-enced by the literary figure of Goethe's Margaret, who also commits infanticide.

But in October 1876 the Kornilova case means something else to Dostoevsky. He rehearses the details of the case and then poses a ques-tion. "Here are the facts, what could be simpler, but nonetheless, there is much that is fantastic here, isn't that true?" (22:263). The "fantastic" element is supplied, according to Dostoevsky, by the psychological

---

10. I am grateful to Charles Isenburg for pointing this passage out to me.

effect of Kornilova's pregnancy. Dostoevsky defends Kornilova on the grounds of temporary insanity due to pregnancy. In a sense, Dostoevsky turns outs to be the object of his own previous "caricature" of Kornilova's imaginary defense lawyer. This process is repeated again in December 1877. In that issue, as we will see, Dostoevsky assumes the role of his old adversary Spasovich and tries to establish what does and what does not constitute the "systematic" abuse of a child—all of this in defense of Kornilova. The Kronenberg and Kornilova cases curiously mirror each other.

In order to trace this mirroring, we will begin with the October 1876 Kornilova entry and Dostoevsky's psychological defense. Dostoevsky argues that Kornilova, who was pregnant at the time she committed the crime, might have been suffering from a special form of temporary insanity *(vremennyi affekt)* due to her pregnancy. Dostoevsky reports that the examining physician determined that Kornilova acted "consciously," and that therefore legal incompetence could not be shown (23:138). Dostoevsky argues that even "lunatics" rarely perform actions "unconsciously." He asks his readers to consider the kinds of actions that might be performed consciously, but without legal culpability. He recalls a story he heard in childhood about a lady in Moscow who developed a "passion for stealing" every time she became pregnant. Dostoevsky tells us, "It is well known that a woman at the time of pregnancy is very often subject to certain strange influences and impressions" that sometimes take on "extraordinary, abnormal, almost absurd forms" (23:138). Had Kornilova not been pregnant, Dostoevsky writes, she would perhaps have contemplated, but not committed, the crime. The very possibility that the pregnancy was the determining factor should have been enough to convince the jury to act mercifully, Dostoevsky concludes.

The new pathological entity that Dostoevsky creates has much in common with views prevailing in Russia and Europe about a woman's mental state during pregnancy, childbirth, and the postpartum period. For example, Nikolai Tagantsev's course on Russian criminal law notes that psychiatrists had observed cases in which "under the influence of pregnancy psychiatric changes occur that have the character of psychiatric illnesses." He cautions that the so-called cravings associated with pregnancy should not lead to a determination of reduced legal competency. Furthermore, pregnancy is often used as a way of concealing the

execution of premeditated crimes, which are the result of "bad inclina-
tions, egotistical calculations, and the imitation of fashions."[11] However, childbirth may cause a temporary suspension of the mother's
psychic and physical strength, which can result in her failure to take
adequate measures to protect the life of the newborn. In her study of
sexuality in fin-de-siècle Russia, Laura Engelstein finds that "Russian
juries in the last quarter of the nineteenth century were almost twice as
likely to dismiss charges of infanticide as of other forms of murder."[12]
The reasons had to do with the perception of childbirth as a time of particular distress for the mother, and if the child were illegitimate, one of
social stigma as well.

A. Liubavskii's three-volume compendium of Russian criminal
cases published in St. Petersburg in 1867 describes three cases of infanticide in which the female defendants were found to be suffering from
some form of "temporary insanity" (prekhodiashchee pomeshatel'stvo)
related to pregnancy. For example, the peasant woman Varvara Erkhova was tried for burning her infant son to death in the stove. The
medical authority in the case observed signs of "severe hypochondria"
in Erkhova after the crime, including long periods of weeping, speaking to herself, and withdrawal from others. On the basis of this evidence, and on the medical "fact" that "temporary insanity is often
encountered during pregnancy and in the period immediately following birth," the medical authority concluded that Erkhova "committed
the crime in an attack of acute and temporary insanity."[13] In light of her
predisposition toward this illness, however, they recommended that
Erkhova be closely watched when pregnant. Exempt from the law's
harshest penalty, the woman is nonetheless subject to a quasi-legal
supervision. Engelstein argues that infanticide is the quintessential
female crime in Dostoevsky's era because it reveals the duality with
which the woman's legal status was then regarded. To paraphrase her
argument, according to the medical and legal experts of late-nineteenth-century Russia, the sexual impulse that guided women's lives
left them especially vulnerable to criminal impulses, yet incapable of
true criminal intentionality.[14]

---

11. Tagantsev, Russkoe ugolovnoe pravo, 458.
12. Engelstein, The Keys to Happiness, 107 n. 37.
13. A. Liubavskii, "O krest'ianke Varvare Erkhove, suzhdennoi za sozhzhenie v
pechke svoego rebenka," in Liubavskii, Russkie ugolovnye protsessy (St. Petersburg, 1867),
3:349.
14. See Engelstein, The Keys to Happiness, 106.

In part through Dostoevsky's intervention, Kornilova's conviction is overturned. As Igor Volgin's research has shown, Dostoevsky's plea for mercy on Kornilova's behalf led to an appeal procedure. The grounds for the appeal were based on a legal formality: the same individual had testified both in the capacity of witness and expert. At the subsequent retrial, a jury trial, which Dostoevsky himself attended, Kornilova was acquitted, notwithstanding the prosecutor's instruction to the jury "not to yield to the influence of 'certain talented writers.'"[15] The prosecutor uses "talent" here as a term of opprobrium with regard to Dostoevsky in the same way Dostoevsky had used it with regard to Spasovich.

Dostoevsky returns to the Kornilova case in the December 1877 issue of *The Diary of a Writer*. Stung by an attack of his defense of Kornilova published in the *Northern Messenger*, he is forced to defend himself. In so doing, he ends up repeating some of the strategies that Spasovich had used in his defense of Kronenberg—strategies that previously had outraged Dostoevsky. As Dostoevsky reports it, the *Northern Messenger* argued that Kornilova "systematically beat" the child for a year. Dostoevsky replies that the child was indeed beaten, by both parents, not out of "cruelty," but out of "ignorance" (26:97). Kornilova had beaten her stepdaughter so hard on one occasion that welts were raised, but this was out of ignorance about how to train her not to wet her bed at night. "Systematic" and "cruel" beating, therefore, could not be established. Spasovich had used similar reasoning in his defense of Kronenberg: the father beat his daughter only to rid her of "secret vices"; the expert testimony of the doctors, the precise description of the welts and bruises on the child's body, and the vagueness of the law itself, all taken together, showed that "torture" could not be proved. In the Kornilova case, Dostoevsky plays the role of doctor and lawyer and more all at once. He positions himself as an authority on corporal punishment, its motivation, and its severity.

Dostoevsky had, in May 1876, created a parody of a defense plan, emphasizing Kornilova's "eternal work"—and now in December 1877, Dostoevsky unwittingly quotes himself, citing Kornilova's "eternal work" (26:100). What are we to make of this apparent volte-face? Why has Dostoevsky permitted himself to become one with his own caricature of a clever, talented defense lawyer? I suggested at the beginning

---

15. Quoted in Igor Volgin, "Pis'ma chitatelei k F. M. Dostoevskom," *Voprosy literatury* 9 (1971): 196.

of this chapter that the contradiction between his earlier and later views might be seen as part of an autobiographical narrative that relates Dostoevsky's development into author of, and authoritative figure behind, *The Diary of a Writer*. Dostoevsky constructs himself first as a child in the *Diary* of 1876 and then as a father in the *Diary* of 1877. Where he speaks from the position of the child, he resists the authority of the lawyer and of the father, and then when he becomes a symbolic father, he embraces, in a different form, the authority that he had previously resisted. The second stage, being a "father," depends on the first even though the representation of the two stages overlaps in *The Diary of a Writer*; as we will see, Dostoevsky must first be a "child" in order to become a father.[16]

Childhood: Dostoevsky Is Being Beaten

We will begin with "Dostoevsky the child." In his discussion of the Kronenberg case itself and in the other essays that frame this discussion, most notably, "The Peasant Marei," which immediately precedes Kronenberg, the theme of childhood, which figures prominently in the 1876 *Diary*, is especially important.[17] In the piece, Dostoevsky "remembers" how the drunken carousing of his fellow convicts sickened him at first; he ran out of the barracks, where he met the Polish political prisoner, Mirecki, who said "Je hais ces brigands." But a memory from childhood saves him. When he was a child playing alone in the woods in his father's estate, he had become frightened by the cry "A wolf is coming!"—which he may have only imagined—and had run, "beside himself" with fear, to the peasant Marei, who was plowing a field. Marei made the sign of the cross over him and touched him with his earth-stained finger.

It is in the memory of Marei that Dostoevsky the convict can overcome his feelings of repulsion for his fellow prisoners, each one of whose "scarred and branded" faces could conceal another "Marei." In recounting the childhood episode, Dostoevsky emphasizes Marei's

---

16. For a discussion of how sons become fathers in Dostoevsky's fiction, see Michael Holquist, "How Sons Become Fathers: *The Brothers Karamazov*," in *Dostoevsky and the Novel* (Evanston, Ill.: Northwestern University Press, 1977), 165–93. His argument relies on Freud's *Totem and Taboo*.

17. William Rowe notes that 32 percent of the 1876 *Diary* "deals primarily if not exclusively with children and childhood." See his *Dostoevsky: Child and Man in His Works* (New York: New York University Press, 1968), xi and 3–40.

"tender, maternal smile" and "delicate, almost feminine tenderness" (22:49).[18] Dostoevsky retroactively constructs his time in Siberia as a moment of rebirth. He authors himself not as the son of his biological father, but of Marei, and of all others who might be a "Marei." In the concluding lines of "The Peasant Marei," Dostoevsky contrasts himself with Mirecki, who "could not have reminiscences about any Marei's and could not have any other view of these people [the convicts] other than 'Je hais ces brigands'" (22:50). On the basis of his Russian childhood, Dostoevsky is able to construct a filiation with his fellow convicts, and by extension, with the Russian people, something that is not available to a foreigner such as Mirecki.[19] Dostoevsky re-Russifies himself as a figurative child of Russia, creating himself anew as a child of "Marei." Dostoevsky overcomes the class boundary that had previously separated him from ordinary Russians, as a member of the educated upper class.[20]

In the Kronenberg piece Dostoevsky constructs a similar filiation between the little girl and the servant Ul'iana Bibina, who felt compassion for her, and notwithstanding the common people's typical terror of the courts, made out a complaint against the father, out of pity for someone else's child (22:62). The yard keeper stated that after the beating of July 25, the girl sat alone and wouldn't talk to anyone. In this statement, Dostoevsky finds the "keen gaze of an observer, a gaze with inner torment at the suffering of an offended creature of God" (22:62). Dostoevsky suggests that he too shares this gaze. Spasovich had hinted that the little girl and the servant were in some kind of conspiracy, but Dostoevsky points out that the two could not speak with one another, since the child spoke only French. The lawyer's skill is all "sparkle and effect," all external, but the servant woman's pity is prior to speech and the distortions produced by rhetoric.

Dostoevsky suggest a parallel between his childhood encounter

---

18. For a discussion of Marei as a mother figure, see James L. Rice, "Psychoanalysis of 'Peasant Marei,'" in *Russian Literature and Psychoanalysis,* ed. Daniel Rancour-Laferriere (Philadelphia: John Benjamins, 1989), 252–54.

19. Rice reveals that Mirecki's mother managed to obtain a release for her son. He aptly comments that "it would seem that in 'Marei' Dostoevsky appropriated the Pole's maternal salvation, transposing it into the vision of a "motherly peasant protector for himself" (ibid., 254).

20. For a discussion of "Marei" and the problem of conversion see Frank, *Dostoevsky,* 116–27. For more on "Marei," see Robert Louis Jackson, "The Triple Vision: 'Peasant Marei,'" *Yale Review* 67 (winter 1978): 225–35; and my "Dostoevsky in Siberia: Remembering the Past," *Slavic Review* 50 (1991): 858–66.

with Marei and the Kronenberg girl's relation with the servant. Each unfolds in a primitive, presocial, prelinguistic state, in which the father, the law, and authority in general are conspicuously absent, and feminine compassion predominates. Dostoevsky's love/hate affair with Rousseau has already been established, and some of it clearly emerges here.[21] Pity is the presocial virtue envisioned by Rousseau in his *Discourse on the Origin of Inequality*. Dostoevsky's valorization of the presocial is accompanied by an attack on social institutions. The family is *"made,* and not given . . and no rights or obligations are given" (22:70).

Dostoevsky's attack on authority reaches a climax in the conclusion of his discussion of the Kronenberg case. One of Spasovich's arguments was that if the jury were to convict Kronenberg, they would call into question their own authority as jurors and would ill serve the state. The state is only as strong as the families that sustain it. The family, Spasovich said, can ultimately be reduced to a principle of paternal power.[22] Dostoevsky rejects this line of reasoning, and especially the link between the power of the state and that of the family: "We love the family as a sacred object when it is indeed sacred, and not only because the government stands firmly upon it" (22:72).

By the end of the Kronenberg piece, we have returned to a point of origin, a beginning. Everything that is new and innocent is valorized, not by the child, but Russia itself, and Dostoevsky himself, whose innocence is won by suffering, and whose identification with the child and with the simple Russian people is reconstructed from his past. Dostoevsky creates an opposition between an old world and a new and proclaims Russia to be a "young" and "fresh" nation. The theme of Russia's youthfulness runs throughout the February issue. Dostoevsky finds childlike qualities not only in the *narod,* the people, but in society *(obshchestvo),* whose ideological quarrels he likens to childish bickering (22:41). In foregrounding the new, Dostoevsky dismantles everything that belongs to the old. The authority of the father, upon which, according to Spasovich, the state rests, is suggestively likened by Dostoevsky to an old idol, for which the new Russia no longer has any need. Even though jury trials and professional attorneys like Spasovich are very new in Russia in 1876, Dostoevsky associates the law with what is old

---

21. See Iurii Lotman, "Russo i russkaia kul'tura XVIII-načala XIX veka," in Jean-Jacques Rousseau, *Traktaty* (Moscow: Nauka, 1969), 603.

22. The newspaper *Nedelia* observed that with this concept of the family, "we have not gone very far from the ideals of the *Domostroi*" (*Nedelia,* April 15, 1876).

and worn out. The law is "a young school of the withering of the heart" (22:73).

Spasovich's argumentation, in its literalness and in the blame that it places on the little girl, is associated by Dostoevsky with ancient Jewish law as it is portrayed in the New Testament. Dostoevsky asks, addressing Spasovich: "How can you impose such a burden of responsibility on such a little one, which perhaps you yourself do not have the strength to bear?" (22:68). He continues, "'They impose heavy, unbearable burdens,' remember these words." The reference is to Matthew 23:4: "they bind heavy burdens, hard to bear, and lay them on men's shoulders, but they themselves will not move them with their finger." "They" are the Pharisees, who elsewhere in the New Testament are referred to as "lawyers" (Luke 11:46).

We can summarize Dostoevsky's reworking of the Kronenberg case. Kronenberg is a false father, and Spasovich is a false authority who generates a false narrative, one that comes from the letter, and not the spirit.[23] But the idealized scenes that Dostoevsky creates—of himself alone with Marei, of the Kronenberg child alone with the yard keeper with her gaze full of inner torment—are also incomplete. The notebooks for the *Diary* for 1876 contain the words "Children in general. Children with father and without fathers in particular" (22:140). Children cannot remain without fathers.

How will Dostoevsky transform himself from child to father? In the Kronenberg piece, Dostoevsky directly refers to his Siberian experience to question the medical testimony as to the severity and painfulness of the little girl's beating. As Dostoevsky recounts it, the absence of significant scarring five days after the beating, according to the medical experts, showed that there was no danger to the child's life. But in Siberia, Dostoevsky tells us, he saw men who had undergone one or two thousand strokes of the rods whose backs were almost completely healed after six days. Therefore the lack of physical evidence on the Kronenberg girl's body does not mean, as Spasovich tried to show, that she did not suffer.

The reference to the beatings that Dostoevsky witnessed conceals more than it reveals. The reference suggests an image of Dostoevsky as victim, or at the least, a potential victim of corporal punishment. In the

---

23. For another discussion of the Kronenberg case that focuses on Dostoevsky's critique of Spasovich and the professionalization of justice, see Gary Rosenshield, "Dostoevskij and the Kroneberg Case," *Slavic and East European Journal* 36 (1992): 415–34.

second volume of his biography of Dostoevsky, Joseph Frank points out that during Dostoevsky's lifetime, it was widely rumored that the author himself had been beaten as a prisoner in Siberia, and that as a consequence, he began to suffer epileptic attacks.[24] In *Notes from the House of the Dead*, Dostoevsky's quasi-fictitious memoir of his time in Siberia (the first-person narrator is imprisoned for the murder of his wife), we find a prolonged treatise on punishments. The narrator becomes ill and endures a lengthy stay in the prison hospital, where he encounters prisoners who have run the gauntlet and received the number of strokes they were sentenced to, or some portion deemed safe by the prison doctor. The narrator describes his "greedy" curiosity:

> I was agitated, confused, and frightened. . . . I wanted to know . . . immediately all the degrees of the sentences and of their execution, all the gradations of their execution. . . . I asked a lot about the pain. I wanted to find out definitively how great the pain was and with what it could be compared. It's true, I don't know why I sought this out. . . . But no matter whom I asked I could never get an answer that satisfied me. It burns, like fire burns—that's all I could find out, and that was only answer that everyone gave. (4:152–54)

These excerpts show a desire for knowledge that borders on a desire for the experience itself. What drives this desire? As a nobleman, Dostoevsky was technically exempt from corporal punishment.[25] To be beaten would be shameful, painful, and possibly, lethal. Bogoliubov, the political prisoner on whose behalf Vera Zasulich fired her shots, died from his beating.[26] For Sukhovo-Kobylin, as we have seen, the horrifying symbolic "branding of his name" represents the absolute limit of his free self-fashioning. In contrast, beating represents a critical stage in Dostoevsky's reinvention of himself. To be beaten would effect the transformation in his rhetorical position from one of distance from the Russian people to one of union with them—in one stroke. This transformation is crucial to Dostoevsky's self-fashioning in *The Diary of a Writer*. In *Notes from the House of the Dead*, the narrator's need to know

---

24. Frank, *Dostoevsky*, 78–79.

25. Laws of 1863 and 1871 softened the severity of beatings administered to convicts in Siberia. See Taganstev, *Russkoe ugolovnoe pravo*, 977.

26. See Engelstein, "Revolution," 39.

is insatiable, but never satisfied, and the work ends without the closure even of a figurative brotherhood between the narrator and the ordinary prisoners. In contrast, in "The Peasant Marei" we have a happy ending, and in *The Diary of a Writer*'s legal cases Dostoevsky knows more than the medical experts. The uncertainty, fear, and even longing are spent. Dostoevsky recoups from this powerful mixture the certainty to say that Kronenberg's daughter suffered from her father's beating and that Kornilova's stepdaughter did not. He takes the side of the victim and of the executioner simultaneously, ultimately speaking from the position of the executioner.[27] As victim of the mock execution imposed by Nicholas I for his participation in the Petrashevskii circle, and as the would-be victim of corporal punishment, Dostoevsky entitles himself to pronounce the executioner's sentence—here and elsewhere in the *Diary*, and especially, in the Kairova case, as we will see.[28]

In the July–August issue of the *Diary* for 1877 Dostoevsky suggests that Russia itself is without a father, without law, without a charismatic center. He speaks of the "loss, on the part of Russian fathers, of any general idea in relation to the families, general for all fathers, that would bind them together" (25:178). He goes on to say that "the very presence of this general . . . idea . . . is the beginning of order, that is, of moral order" (15:178). Russia cannot remain in its feminized, presocial state, gazing with "inner torment" at her children, but unable to help them. Russia cannot remain without whole, integrated families, without social organization, and without language. It must ultimately utter its "new word," as Dostoevsky likes to say (as, for example, in the July–August 1877 issue). A new father is needed, a new voice of male authority, and Dostoevsky, having legitimized himself as one with the suffering child in the Kronenberg case, and in other *Diary* entries as one

---

27. I am grateful to Barbara Heldt for discussing this point with me.

28. Mikhail Yampolsky makes a related point. "In a paradoxical fashion . . . the ethos of Russian humanistic literature approaches the ethos of the overseer, the doctor, the investigator, the pedagogue and in the final account the informer—with the ethos of that abstract Other, who is located at the heart of the structures of power and each time takes on a new concrete embodiment. The gigantic humanistic pathos of Russian literature in such a case can be understood as the ideology of its unconscious concealment of this its identification with the point of view of the Other-Father-God-Ruler." "Vina-Pokaianie-Donos," *Russian Culture in Transition: Selected Papers of the Working Group for the Study of Contemporary Russian Culture, 1990–1991*, ed. Gregory Freidin, Stanford Slavic Studies, vol. 7 (Stanford, Calif.: Stanford University Press, 1993), 222–23.

with the suffering Russian people, will be able to offer himself for that role.[29]

Fatherhood

The final stage of development in the self-fashioning of Dostoevsky's authority is represented in the July–August 1877 discussion of the Dzhunkovskii case. The parents were charged with having singled out three of their children for special ill-treatment. The children were not provided with adequate food (they ate from the servants' table); they were kept in unheated rooms; they were beaten (Dostoevsky writes "with such cruelty that it was terrible to look at"); one of them was beaten especially severely by his mother because he brought his hungry sister a potato from the kitchen for her breakfast (25:183). As in the Kronenberg case, the parents were acquitted. In this case, Dostoevsky's strategy is to speak from the position of the father and of the state. He remarks that when people are acquitted, sometimes the chairman of the court takes the opportunity to make some comments of an edifying nature, in order that the accused may avoid trouble in the future (25:188). Dostoevsky says that he will play the role of the chairman, who, he adds, speaks "on behalf of all of society and on behalf of the government." At the end of his remarks, he repeats that in making the speech from the position of the chairman of the court, as it were, he is fulfilling his "obligation," and speaking on behalf of society, the government, and the "fatherland" (25:192). In the Kronenberg piece, the child was valorized; it is children who "humanize" adults by their mere presence among them. But here in the Dzhunkovskii case, Dostoevsky makes gods out of fathers, who must, he says, "always be spiritually on a mountain" for their children "as an object of love . . . respect . . . and imitation" (25:190). In the Kronenberg case, Dostoevsky rejects the reasoning that the state depends on strong families. But in this case, the child is subsumed to the state; children are the "future Russia" (25:192).

Dostoevsky, having uttered his paternal and authoritative word in the Dzhunkovskii case in July–August 1877, will continue in the same vein in his final discussion of the Kornilova case in December 1877. Significantly, he characterizes his intervention in the Kornilova case as

---

29. Morson, in contrast, emphasizes the apt fit between Dostoevsky's perception of the fragmentation of the Russian family and what he takes to be Dostoevsky's deliberately fragmented writing in *The Diary of a Writer*. Morson, *The Boundaries of Genre*, 9.

"fatherly": "chopping off heads is easy according to the letter of the law, but understanding truthfully, humanely, and in a fatherly way is always harder" (26:106). The "fatherly" understanding that Dostoevsky showed toward Kornilova led to her retrial.

Dostoevsky's self-proclaimed "fatherliness" toward Kornilova is really more than that. He plays judge, teacher, and husband as well. The Kornilovs came to visit Dostoevsky after her release from prison. Mr. Kornilov told Dostoevsky that the first thing he did when his wife arrived home was to read to her from the Gospels. Mr. Kornilov is a predictable type, Dostoevsky tells his readers in the December 1877 *Diary.* He could not have done otherwise. Dostoevsky imagines Kornilova's reaction to the moral lesson. "Here is the person upon whom she depends, raising himself over her in the highest halo of a judge; he is merciless in her eyes because of the way that he too autocratically invaded her soul" (26:104). Note the political language, the parallel drawn between the unlimited, invasive power of the autocrat and the husband. But there is an important sense in which Dostoevsky himself claims a similar power over Kornilova. Dostoevsky claims to be quoting Kornilova's response to her husband. But it is more likely that he is quoting himself. The words that Dostoevsky puts into Kornilova's mouth resemble those he had invented for the hero of *The Devils,* Stavrogin, who says: "I hate spies and psychologists, at least those who climb into my soul (11:11).[30] To be known by another is invasive and threatening; to have this knowledge is to have a certain power. Recall the narrator in *Notes from the House of the Dead,* whom no one will open up to about the pain of corporal punishment.

But Dostoevsky himself is guilty of this sort of invasiveness. He has already given Kornilova her moral lesson. Her husband's version is an inept repetition of what Dostoevsky thinks he has already accomplished. He has gone to teach her how to live in Siberia, should that be her fate, on the evening of her retrial. During that visit, he warns her against the temptation of prostitution. He describes the visit in the same December 1877 *Diary.* His Siberian experience provides him with a certain expertise. "Her marriage destroyed, in a foreign place, alone, defenseless, still attractive, and so young—how could she resist the temptation?" (26:105). Kornilova's child will follow her mother's foot-

---

30. See Bakhtin's discussion of this and other similar passages in Dostoevsky in *Problems of Dostoevsky's Poetics,* ed. and trans. Caryl Emerson (Minneapolis: University of Minnesota Press, 1984), 59–61.

steps, according to Dostoevsky, "she will be *compelled* to inherit her mother's career" (26:105). By using the word "inherit" *(nasledovat')* Dostoevsky hints at theories of criminal degeneracy popular in his time; his reading of Kornilova and her daughter reveals a Lamarckian twist. One generation inherits the traits acquired by the previous one. The same experience of incarceration in Siberia has very different consequences for the male and the female. What positions the male protagonist, Dostoevsky, squarely within the symbolic center of the liberal Russian culture—oneness with the suffering Russian people—places the female on the periphery, within a marginal realm of deviant sexuality.[31] In *The Diary of a Writer* Kornilova's suffering is purely natural and has no transformative effect, unlike Dostoevsky's, which enables him to acquire a different and superior relationship to the center of symbolic power. Becoming a father to Russia requires that Dostoevsky discipline unruly female sexuality—I use Foucault's term loosely.[32] As we have already seen, Dostoevsky argues that Kornilova's crime may be the result of her pregnancy. By placing her actions in a medical context, and calling them the result of "temporary insanity due to pregnancy," Dostoevsky tames an otherwise unpredictable and volatile female condition.

The Rights of Authorship

Dostoevsky begins his *Writer's Diary* for May 1876 by telling his readers that he is being asked to write about the Kairova case. Anastasia Kairova, an actress from a theater in Orenburg, confessed to having attacked her lover's wife with a razor. The victim, Velikanova, survived. At the trial, the defense argued for temporary insanity. Kairova was acquitted, an outcome that, according to Dostoevsky, displeased

---

31. For another discussion of Dostoevsky's response to the Kornilova case see Eric Naiman, "Of Crime, Utopia, and Repressive Complements: The Further Adventures of the Ridiculous Man," *Slavic Review* 50 (1991): 513–20.

32. Foucault's discipline cannot be the result of the actions of a single individual. Foucault speaks of power as "a moving substrate of force relations," which does not result from the choice of an individual subject (*The History of Sexuality*, 93). Foucault reiterates that power is not to be found in the single sovereign or even in the law, but in a "multiple and mobile field of force relations, wherein far-reaching, but never completely stable effects of domination are produced" (102). Dostoevsky cannot by definition constitute such a field. Whatever institutional base he was seeking to create in the *Diary* was at least in part a kingdom not of this world. For another view, see Irina Paperno et al., "Symposium," *Slavic Review* 53 (1994): 209.

many of his readers. He goes on to quote one particularly irate letter, which I shall return to later. Dostoevsky got his information about Kairova and her trial from the newspapers, for example, the *Voice (Golos)* and the *New Time (Novoe vremia)*.

In *Golos* Dostoevsky could have read the following about the Kairova case. In 1874, retired naval lieutenant Vasilii Aleksandrovich Velikanov managed a theatrical troupe in Orenburg, near Kazan. The actors that his agent had engaged had never acted before. Among them was Anastasia Kairova, a young woman without previous theatrical experience, who had come all the way from Petersburg. By the spring of 1875, he was bankrupt—a typical fate for theatrical entrepreneurs in the provinces. Velikanov left Orenburg for Petersburg, accompanied by Kairova, with whom he had formed an intimate relationship. His wife, Aleksandra, an actress, stayed behind in Orenburg. Velikanov and Kairova lived together, first in Petersburg, and then in Oranienbaum, a Petersburg suburb, where a dacha was rented under his name, but with Kairova's money. At the end of June 1876, Aleksandra Velikanova arrived in Petersburg and made it known to her husband that she wished to live with him. Velikanov told Kairova that his wife was going to go abroad for several years. On July 2, Kairova went to Petersburg, taking some of her things out of Velikanov's apartment, but returned on the fifth and spent the weekend with him. On July 7, a Monday, Kairova and Velikanov left together for Petersburg, but on the same day, Velikanov returned alone and proposed to his wife that she spend the night in his apartment in Oranienbaum, which she agreed to do. After supper, Velikanova went to sleep in her husband's bedroom, a room that Kairova thought of as hers; he took the adjoining room. That same night Kairova appeared at Velikanov's apartment. Upon learning from the cook that Velikanov's wife was spending the night, Kairova went upstairs, where Velikanov's sister had a room, undressed, and then entered the bedroom where Velikanova was sleeping. Kairova struck Velikanova several times on the head, throat, and chest with a razor but was stopped by Velikanov and his sister. A medical examination of Velikanova determined that her wounds were serious, but not necessarily lethal, and a subsequent examination, made one week after the attack, concluded that Velikanova's physical condition was "satisfactory." During the ten-month interval between the crime and the trial Velikanova returned to the stage.

In the preliminary investigation, Kairova made a full confession.

She admitted that she had carried out the attack, with the premeditated intention of killing Velikanova. She told the court investigator that she planned either to cut Velikanova's carotid artery, or to drive a nail through her ear to her brain. Kairova said that she bought the razor on July 7, in Petersburg, on Nevskii Prospect, and sharpened it four hours before she appeared at Velikanova's bedside. Kairova said that she committed the crime out of love for Velikanov, and out of the desire to save him from what she considered the extremely bad influence of his wife. During the trial, Kairova denied that she acted with premeditation. She said, "The razor was bought just in case—for me, for her, for whomever" (*Voice*, May 11, 1876, no. 188).

The case was heard on April 28, 1876, in the Petersburg Circuit Court. Four questions were put to the jury: (1) Did Kairova inflict wounds with a razor on Velikanova with the premeditated intention of killing her, but was stopped by Velikanova and her husband? (2) Did she inflict these wounds, for the same purpose, in a fit of anger *(v zapal'chivosti i razdrazhenii)*? (3) Did Kairova act in a fit of madness *(umoizstuplenie)* that was precisely established? (4) If she acted not under the influence of madness, then is she guilty of the crime in the first or second question? To both the first and the second questions, the jury answered "no, she did not inflict the wounds," and left the remaining questions unanswered. Kairova was acquitted. It is of crucial importance to note that the jury was not asked whether Kairova carried out the attack without the intent to murder Velikanova. Dostoevsky and others point out that the jury had no choice but to acquit if they did not want to convict Kairova of attempted murder with premeditation, a crime with a more serious penalty than attempted murder without premeditation.

What dominant themes emerge from the trial? Testimony about Kairova's mental state before and after the crime, including her family history, plays a central role. This testimony comes not only from medical experts, but from those who observed Kairova during her imprisonment, from her mother, and from other witnesses. An acquaintance of Kairova's, a certain Gladkov, who knew Kairova for twelve years, testified that she "sometimes was like a madwoman [*sumasshedshaia*]. . . . once she threw herself on him and tore out a clump of his shirt with her teeth" (*Voice*, April 30, 1876, no. 119). Kairova's mother, according to the paraphrase given in *Voice*, said that her daughter had an "excitable and irritable character from earliest childhood on, that from the age of five she had 'fits' [*pripadki*] and was constantly sick." Her character was "despotic." The mother goes on to say that Kairova's father drank heavily; her maternal uncle did the same, "lost his reason and shot himself"; her mother's cousin killed his wife; and Kairova's paternal grandmother was a "madwoman." Kairova's mother said that Kairova worked for the editorial board of a newspaper in Petersburg but had to give up her job because of illness; she joined the Orenburg troupe because she and her mother had nothing to live on.

This testimony goes to show that Kairova might have been acting in a state of *affekt*, temporary insanity, when she attacked Velikanova, which would limit the degree of her criminal responsibility. From the perspective of the defense, the mother's testimony shows that Kairova inherited a predisposition to abnormal behavior. The medical experts at the trial questioned Kairova's mother to establish that up to a year and a half before Kairova's birth, her father drank heavily, that he suffered fits during this time, in which he would lose consciousness, and his arms and legs would jerk. Kairova's mother says that during her pregnancy with Kairova she didn't feel as she usually did in her other pregnancies, that she had "fits and felt a strong need to drink wine."

The mother's testimony requires further comment. It seems unlikely that she had read Dr. Henry Maudsley's theory about the relation between alcoholism and insanity in the parent and the resulting "pathological degeneration of the mind" found in the immediate offspring and in subsequent generations. Maudsley's *Responsibility in Mental Disease* was published in English in 1876. However, the questions asked by the medical experts and the defense strategy in general show the influence of Maudsley, whom defense attorney Utin explicitly discusses, along with Kraft-Ebbing and others. We can assume that Kairova's mother received some sort of coaching from Utin, whose purpose was to provide Kairova with a temporary-insanity defense. However, the mother's testimony shifts the responsibility for her actions during her pregnancy away from her will and conscious actions. Something about this particular pregnancy causes the urge to drink. The mother says that during her pregnancy with Kairova she didn't feel as she usually did in her other pregnancies, that she had "fits and felt a strong need to drink wine." Can it be that even as an unborn child, Kairova exerts her "despotic personality," compelling her mother to drink? This prenatal display of deviant behavior turns the tables on Maudsley's notion of "pathological degeneration" from parent to child.

At the very least, the overall impression left by the mother's testimony is a peculiar one. The defense strategy here and elsewhere backfires.

Another witness, Voskresenskii, a prison official, testified under questioning from the defense that Kairova suffered "hysterical attacks" during her periods. She would lie on her bed, "roll about and howl." Furthermore, Voskresenskii says, she had false ideas about the circumstances leading to her imprisonment.

The defense attorney Utin, while admitting that the medical experts didn't agree as to Kairova's mental state, draws together the testimony of the laymen to leave one impression in the mind of the jury: that up to and including the time Kairova committed the attack, she had no control of her actions. His argument is, at one level, a version of "she had to be crazy to love this man." For example, Utin says: "If this woman were completely healthy, normal, she would have understood, in her right mind, that it is impossible to love such a man as Velikanov, impossible to sacrifice your life for him" (*Voice,* May 3, 1876, no. 122). Velikanov drank; he said at the trial that he loved Kairova only as a woman, but loved his wife for her spiritual qualities. It also emerged at the trial that Kairova saved him from debtor's prison. Utin goes on to say: "But passion took possession of her, destroyed, swallowed her mind and forced her to play out this terrible game. Utin describes the moment when Kairova discovered Velikanova in the dacha:

> If she had been told that Velikanov was not home, then she perhaps would have killed herself at that moment. But she encountered that scene so eloquently described by the prosecutor: she arrives at their dacha, she is told that Velikanov's wife is there; she goes to the bedroom and sees what's going on there [reporter's paraphrase]. "Really, gentlemen of the jury, is it possible for a woman to remain calm? She would have to be a stone . . . The man she passionately loves is in her bedroom, in her bed, with another woman! Her feelings were a stormy torrent which destroy everything which falls in its path; she rages and could destroy everything around her. If we ask this torrent what it is doing, why it does evil, could it answer us? No, it is silent" [reporter quoting Utin].

There are several layers to this portion of Utin's speech. At one level, Kairova is the embodiment of new scientific theories about the psychology and physiology of female criminality in late nineteenth century Russia. For example, I. Foinitskii, a law professor, argued that women are inherently incapable of premeditated crimes because they cannot carry out the planning and deliberation that goes into such crimes.[33] Women commit crimes out of sudden outbursts of strong emotions.

But at another level, Utin borrows a literary image for his client's defense. Kairova appears as the typical hero—not heroine—of literary Romanticism. Heroines are the objects of contestation, not the contenders. At one point, Utin remarks that had Kairova and Velikanova been men, their rivalry would have ended in a duel. In other words, there is a socially acceptable, albeit violent mechanism, for men to resolve their conflicts over women. The *Voice* reporter paraphrases: "But inasmuch as women do not fight duels [*mezhdu damami dueli ne polagaetsia*], in order to extricate herself from her situation Kairova was led fatally to crime." Noblemen still fought duels at the time of the Kairova trial.

Utin makes a hero out of Kairova. She achieves, in this moment of passion, a complete transfiguration. She is wholly merged with nature; not a trace of self-consciousness—the bane of the Romantic hero— remains. Utin's image of the jealous Kairova as a raging torrent *(potok)* recalls Lermontov's image of the jealous Arbenin, who warns his wife:

> I was born
> with a soul that seethes, like lava
> Until it melts, it's firm
> like a stone. . . .
> but it's no fun to meet its stream [*potok*]! Then,
> don't expect forgiveness.

(106)

Utin's choice of literary models, whether his source is Lermontov or some other author, is outdated. By 1876, the Russian reading public had already encountered a new type of rational hero in Chernyshevsky's *What Is to Be Done.* The Romantic hero, with his outwardly calm mask, ready to explode for the thrill of it, was a thing of the past.

But Utin may very well have relied on the outdated taste of his audience to win his case. In using the image of the raging torrent and other, similar images—at one point, he refers to Kairova as a lioness defending her young, that is, Velikanov—he depends on the low level of his audience's literary expectations. For Dostoevsky, Utin is simply

---

33. I. Ia. Foinitskii, "Zhenshchina-prestupnitsa," pt. 1, *Severnyi vestnik*, no. 2 (1893), 135.

"careless." He is busy with many cases and has little time to worry about his diction. Dostoevsky imagines Utin and other busy attorneys rationalizing their overblown style as follows: "I'll get rid of it when the time comes; the grand style is good enough for this . . . 'gallery'" (23:13). The "gallery" refers to the cheapest seating area in a theater, the one furthest from the stage. According to Dostoevsky, lawyers think that spectators at the jury have the same bad taste as those who sit in the gallery. Dostoevsky writes: "Mr. Defense, of course, courted the bad taste of the jury" (23:13).

Utin's image of Kairova is ultimately reductive. The Kairova who worked for a St. Petersburg newspaper, who signed a contract to act in Velikanov's theater, who saved Velikanov from debt and worked to arrange an imperial subsidy for his theater—this Kairova, apparently skillful at negotiation, planning, and strategy, is reduced to a raging "torrent" of sexual passion and jealousy, utterly without consciousness of her actions, and without the capacity for speech: the "torrent" could not say why it does evil. When Kairova makes a brief statement at her trial, she is preeminently rational. She explains why the details of her family history as given in her mother's testimony were not presented before the court in a formal document. While she was in the hospital for pretrial psychiatric evaluation, her mother prepared a document and proposed to the doctor in charge that the information be corroborated. But the doctor refused, saying that "it would be useless." At the close of her trial, Kairova says: "I only wish to remove the stain of mistrust from my mother's testimony" (*Voice*, May 3, 1876).

Utin's defense strategy, which doubtless helps to secure his client's acquittal, is ultimately equivocal. He convinces his audience that Kairova should not be held accountable for her actions; yet, if we take him seriously, Kairova should not be left without supervision, either. Utin depicts Kairova as a sexual criminal, both helpless and dangerous. Kairova is acquitted, but she remains guilty in the eyes of Dostoevsky's reading public and others as well.

Dostoevsky's anonymous correspondent describes the "profound disgust" he felt when he read about the Kairova case:

> This case, like a camera lens, brings into focus a picture of the uter-
> ine instincts, the path to which had been formed for the main char-
> acter (Kairova) by cultural preparation: her mother gave herself
> over to drunkenness during the pregnancy, her father was a drunk-

ard, her brother lost his mind from drink and shot himself, her cousin killed his wife, her father's mother was insane—and out of this culture arose a personality despotic and unbridled in her uterine desires. Even the prosecution . . . asked itself: is she not insane? The experts in part reject this and in part allowed the possibility of insanity not in her personally, but in her actions. But what shows through this entire trial is not a madwoman, but a woman who has reached the ultimate limits of the rejection of all that is sacred: for her the family does not exist, nor the rights of another woman— not only to her husband, but to life itself—everything is for her alone and her uterine lust.

She was acquitted, perhaps, as a madwoman. . . . At least her moral depravity was attributed not to progress of thought, but to psychiatric illness.

But in the "lower part of the public seating area, occupied *exclusively by women,* applause was heard" [*Birzhevye vedomosti*].

What was the applause for? The acquittal of a madwoman, or for the triumph of an explosively passionate nature, for cynicism, appearing in a woman?

Ladies applaud! Wives, mothers! They ought not to applaud, but to weep at such a desecration of the ideal of a woman!

(N.B. Here are omitted several lines that are too harsh [Dostoevsky's note].)

Are you really going to pass over this in silence? (23:5)

The letter from Dostoevsky's correspondent reads like a parody of the defense speech, and of what Dostoevsky calls "liberal humanism." He or she uses the word "culture" where we might expect "nature": the "path of cultural preparation," that is, Kairova's family history, led her to her crime against Velikanova. Kairova, the letter writer suggests, is a textbook case of the inherited predisposition to crime, which in her manifests itself as unbridled sexual impulses. Kairova must bear the blame for the legacy she was born with, and for the sexual instincts that all women suffer from to a greater or lesser degree.

Again, to quote Dostoevsky's correspondent, "this case, like a camera lens, brings into focus a picture of the uterine instincts." The choice of metaphor is highly suggestive. The phenomenon of women's hypersexuality needs only the right technology to bring it into focus, the technology of the camera, or, the technology of the new courts. Surely

Kairova herself never imagined that her best acting role would not be in the theater at all, but as a photographer's model. She is a walking still of criminal Woman.

The *Voice* reporter's description of Kairova fits the bill: Kairova is "dark, with strong, even coarse features, no longer young, her face is long and pale, with broad cheekbones; her breast is almost sunken" (May 11, 1876). When she speaks, she is practically inaudible. The hedging qualifiers "even," "almost" suggest that the author of this description acknowledges the possibility of another take on Kairova. Her features need not be termed coarse; her bosom is not necessarily sunken. Some other adjectives may be appropriate. But nuances do not interest the reporter. His Kairova is the living image of a passion that is spent, but still dangerous. The reporter informs his readers that Velikanova, the victim, is under doctor's orders to stay away from the trial. One look at her attacker could lead to hysterical episodes.

Dostoevsky responds directly to his anonymous correspondent:

> You say that Kairova's crime was not thought out, did not come from the head, was not bookish, but that here there was simply "woman's business" [*bab'e delo*], very straightforward, very simple, and that on her bed in addition lay her rival. (23:9–10)

For Dostoevsky things are not so simple. In order to understand what happened, Dostoevsky goes back to the scene of the crime and imagines what didn't happen. He transforms the still into a moving picture. According to Dostoevsky, Kairova could have become frightened at what she had done and turned the razor on herself. Or, Dostoevsky writes:

> What if, finally, she not only did not get frightened but, on the contrary, feeling the first drops of hot blood, leaped up in a rage and not only finished killing Velikanova, but began cursing the corpse, cut off the head, the nose, the lips, and only then, suddenly, when the head was already taken from her, guessed: what had she done? (23:10)

There are several literary representations that could have prompted Dostoevsky's image of Kairova decapitating the corpse of Velikanova. Euripides' *The Bacchae* is one possibility. Kairova takes the role of

Agave, who decapitates her own son, and only after she holds his head in her arms does she finally realize what she has done. Dostoevsky transforms the "uterine lust" described by his correspondent into one of the most grotesquely violent images in his entire corpus. In suggesting this possible outcome of Kairova's crime, Dostoevsky resorts to the same sort of tactics that he finds so reprehensible in the defense lawyer, namely, courting the bad taste of his reading audience. The exaggerated monstrosity of the image he creates indicates the degree of anxiety provoked by the Kairova case. Dostoevsky's reading of the case, no less than that of his correspondent, offers a moral lesson on the disastrous consequences of women's sexuality outside the discipline of marriage and family.[34]

Conclusion

Women—real, historical women—play roles in the *Diary* that Dostoevsky did not imagine in his fiction.[35] Who can best read and interpret their behavior, if not Russia's most compassionate spectator? In both the Kairova and Kornilova cases Dostoevsky enters into a competition of sorts with the prosecution, defense lawyer, and the medical experts. This competition centers around who is most qualified to understand the behavior of the female defendant. But to understand and to interpret another's behavior, as Dostoevsky very well knows, and as we

---

34. For another discussion of this passage and Dostoevsky's approach to Kairova as a whole, see Gary Saul Morson, *Narrative and Freedom: The Shadows of Time* (New Haven: Yale University Press, 1994), 142–45. Morson argues that Dostoevsky's point is to disrupt what everyone else had taken for granted: the necessary link between Kairova's intention and the final form her action took. Morson emphasizes that Dostoevsky wants to show that in taking the weapon and attacking Velikanova Kairova did not know what she was going to do next. Morson names Dostoevsky's technique in this passage and elsewhere "sideshadowing." Sideshadowing reveals "multiple potentials changing from moment to moment" (145). In contrast, I am arguing that Dostoevsky's interpretation of Kairova and Kornilova does not emphasize the multiple potentials of a given moment but a single potential, women's capacity for crime and violence. If Dostoevsky were primarily interested in "sideshadowing" Kairova's attack against Velikanova, he might have chosen a scenario without the Bacchic violence of corpse mutilation and decapitation. Dostoevsky's projection of Kornilova's infant daughter inheriting her mother's career as a prostitute clearly does not conform to Morson's model of sideshadowing.

35. For a discussion of women in the *Diary* and in Dostoevsky more generally, see Nina Pelikan Straus, *Dostoevsky and the Woman Question: Rereadings at the End of the Century* (New York: St. Martin's Press, 1994).

have seen in *The Devils*, is to have power over the other. To have knowledge of another is to risk having power over another, interpreting, as
Dostoevsky does, according to his own models of female sexuality, easily flows into controlling, disciplining, and finally, authoring—as we
have seen from Dostoevsky's transformation of Kornilova into a prostitute and Kairova into Agave.

In the same December 1877 issue that concludes the Kornilova
case, Dostoevsky points with pride to the correspondents he has
acquired over the course of the publication of the *Diary*. He says that he
considers his correspondents as "collaborators" (26:126). He has begun
to dispense advice to many of them. Dostoevsky has authored his own
authoritative role as the Diarist and claims to have authored his own
reading audience, to have fathered a community of like-minded readers who will become the new Russia.

As we have seen in chapter 3, according to Edward Said, the realist novelist is guided by a double sense of inventiveness and
"restraint." Said uses the terms "authority" and "molestation" for these
two factors. For Said, *authority* suggests the power to institute and to
"enforce obedience." Its relation to the word *author* suggests the series
of meanings: to father, engender, and beget. The realist novelist does all
of these things in his or her work, but always with the awareness that
in comparison to reality, the work produced is an "illusion," and that
the authority that goes into its making "is a sham" (Said, *Beginnings*,
5–6). Dostoevsky's *Diary* suspends the boundary between realist fiction
and journalism, and in so doing suspends the boundary between the
author's "fictive, scripted realm" and reality. Dostoevsky, explicitly
calling on his skills as a novelist, creates a fiction about Kornilova and
her infant daughter becoming prostitutes in Siberia and Kairova muti-
lating the corpse of her rival. It is in these fictions that the violence of
"fathering" and authoring come to the fore: a symbolic violence, to be
sure, but one that has the capacity to compel his reading audience to
conform to his vision of the dangers of unruly female sexuality. The
emergence of a new authoritative voice, "the beginning of order" that
Dostoevsky writes about elsewhere in his *Diary*, turns out to be Dostoevsky's own self-engendering as a symbolic father to Russia. As his
essays on Kornilova and Kairova reveal, that process very much
depends on a specific type of symbolic and gendered violence.

As we have seen, Dostoevsky, the witness to corporal punishment
in Siberia, and vicarious witness to the beating of the little girls in the

Kronenberg and Kornilova cases, pronounces himself more knowl-
edgeable about torture than the lawyers and the medical experts and
declares that in the first case, the little girl suffered too much, and in the
second case, hardly at all, even though her stepmother threw her out of
a window. Dostoevsky moves from identification with the victim in the
first case to identification with the executioner in the second, speaking
almost as a doctor in the service of the state, who presides over the
administration of corporal punishment or torture. Juxtaposed to one
another, Dostoevsky's responses to the two stories are irreconcilably
contradictory. Freud tells us that in the fantasy "a child is being
beaten," the beating is for the fantasizer a substitute and a punishment
for the illicit love felt for the father.[36] The fantasizer gets what he wants
and gets punished for it, but the punishment is what he wants—this is
a circular story that goes nowhere. Dostoevsky, however, untangles the
knot. Out of the contradictions of wanting to be the child and the father
simultaneously (and the child and the father to Russia simultaneously)
comes a coherent linear narrative about Dostoevsky, first a child and
then a father to a new Russia.

What is fictitious or, better, illusory is the linear progression from
child to father, from chaos to order. The capacity of the literary author
to fashion himself or herself as an authority may have to do with the
capacity to tell stories of a particular kind, stories with a coherent linear
pattern, in which order and meaningfulness, having been threatened,
are restored, and violence masked. We have considered what contribu-
tion to the practice of law literature's multivoicedness and multivalence may make. We have considered how law itself, particularly, as it
is embodied in jury trials, is an arena of change, contestation, and discontinuity. Law makes society's conflicts and fissures visible, reveals
irreconcilably competing claims. Dostoevsky is a master storyteller in
The Diary of a Writer not because he gives voice to law's polyphony. On
the contrary. Dostoevsky succeeds because he provides homogeneity
and closure to a fragmented public space. He reenchants public life by
telling the kind of story we want to hear, a story of progress, with a
clear beginning, middle, and, above all, happy ending.

---

36. See Sigmund Freud, "A Child Is Being Beaten," in *Collected Papers*, trans. Joan
Riviere, vol. 2 (New York: Basic Books, 1959), 171–201.

Chapter 5

Testimony and Testament: Solzhenitsyn and the Scar of the Gulag

Solzhenitsyn was an inmate of the Gulag from 1945 to 1953. His crime was having written a few negative remarks about Stalin in a letter to a friend. He was indicted under article 58, point 11 of the Soviet criminal code, participation in an organization for the purpose of propaganda, agitation, or the dissemination of literature leading to the weakening of Soviet power. As Solzhenitsyn explains in *The Gulag Archipelago,* the fact that "there were two of us" left him vulnerable to the charge of participation in an "organization." Although the book contains some elements of personal narrative, which are important to its overall structure, the scale and scope of the work far exceeds that of a single life. Solzhenitsyn's *Gulag Archipelago,* a massive work of three volumes, chronicles the rise and operation of the Soviet labor camp system, tracing its internal laws and language, mechanisms, institutions, procedures, and regimes—all of which serve to transform the prisoner into "excrement and dust," as the author says.

Solzhenitsyn at one point uses the old-fashioned word "archivist" *(letopisets)* to describe his role. But this term does not adequately convey the range of his project. Solzhenitsyn describes the Gulag as a vast but invisible and silent world just beyond the familiar landscape of so-called normal Soviet life. He seeks to make this world visible and material for his readers. He also shows that normal life depends on the Gulag and is fully implicated in it. The rise of the Soviet state, Solzhenitsyn claims, is the rise of the Gulag; the history of the Soviet Union is, to use his metaphor, "the history of our sewage system." The produc-

---

This chapter, along with chapter 4, is a greatly revised and expanded version of my article, "Russian Law and Literature: A Study in Cultural Thematics," *Studies in Law, Politics, and Society* 15 (1996): 315–34.

tion of the Soviet body politic is the production of the individual body as waste product.

The Gulag Archipelago brings into stark and dramatic focus several crucial issues about law, writing, and violence. The operations of literary narrative, the operations of the law, and the operation of violence intersect. The writing of the work is itself a crime, as Solzhenitsyn tells us. In September 1965, he was threatened with the "arrest" of his work and the destruction of his archive.[1] *The Gulag Archipelago* is a form of legal testimony in that it seeks to establish the crimes committed by the Soviet state. It purports to contain "no fictitious persons or events" (1:9). Solzhenitsyn is a survivor of the Gulag, a witness to its abuses, and a witness to the testimony of others. In addition to what he "took out of the Archipelago on my skin, in my memory, in my ears and eyes," the author credits the "stories, reminiscences, and letters" of 227 others whose names he cannot mention (1:10). It is significant that the body and its pain are a source of testimony.

Here we must pause to consider one of the central problems posed by Solzhenitsyn's text. It denies that it contains any fiction whatsoever, yet the work bears the subtitle "an experiment in artistic investigation." When Solzhenitsyn speaks of the "arrest" of his work, he uses the Russian word for "novel" *(roman)*. What is the relation between art, fiction, and the fact? On another plane altogether is a question about the accuracy of Solzhenitsyn's facts. I am not interested in evaluating them; others, such as Roy Medvedev, have done so and found them wanting.[2] What I wish to explore instead is the rhetorical problem of how Solzhenitsyn establishes his facts, what role his art and his aesthetics play in this process.

In order to establish his facts and the facts of other witnesses, Solzhenitsyn must disestablish other facts. He challenges the facts provided by Soviet science, Soviet law, and official Soviet history. In order to make his statements, Solzhenitsyn must define the conditions under which the statements can be made. Solzhenitsyn creates his own epistemology—knowledge comes from pain. He creates his own parodical

---

1. Aleksandr Solzhenitsyn, *Arkhipelag GULag, 1918–1956: Opyt khudozhestvennogo issledovaniia,* 3 vols. (Paris: YMCA Press, 1973–75), 579. Henceforward, all citations will be given parenthetically in the text by part and page number.

2. For example, Medvedev alleges that Solzhenitsyn "distorted many details of Yakubovich's testimony." Yakubovich was one of the defendants at the Union Bureau trial. See Roy Medvedev, *Let History Judge: The Origins and Consequences of Stalinism,* rev. ed., trans. George Shriver (New York: Columbia University Press, 1989), 272–77.

ethnography in the chapter "The Zeks as a Nation" (pt. 3, chap. 19). He reinvents the technology of writing. *The Gulag Archipelago,* like the Gulag that it describes, constitutes its own self-made world. The *Gulag* is unlike the conventional form of testimony heard before a court of law because it itself must constitute its own court. Solzhenitsyn is witness and lawyer and judge.

In revealing how the Soviet state uses the Gulag to construct its power and authority, *The Gulag Archipelago* constructs its own power and authority, upon which it relies in order to establish the veracity of its statements—but not only that. Like Russian realist authors of the 1860s and the socialist realist authors of the 1930s and 40s, Solzhenitsyn wants not only to tell us something, but to make us do something. Near the end of the *Gulag* Solzhenitsyn tells us that words ought to be connected to acts: "If the word isn't about anything and doesn't lead to action, then what is it? A dog's barking at night in the village" (7:513).[3] In previous chapters, we have seen the degree to which Russian literature takes itself "seriously," in Austin's sense. Readers are familiar with the concept of the performative speech act, as in the example of the minister who in saying that a couple is married, makes them so. I will argue that *The Gulag Archipelago* moves from the denotative to the performative. Solzhenitsyn's work is ultraserious. His "experiment in literary investigation" seeks to impose itself on the reader with the binding force of law.

The Gulag Archipelago is a narrative that generates its own nomos. Robert Cover argues that laws and legal institutions are grounded in narratives that give them meaning. By means of narrative, laws resonate—or fail to resonate—with the values of the groups that are under their purview. Law creates patterns of meaningful action beyond mere obedience. In a country such as the United States, Robert Cover writes, "the precepts we call law" are nested in a hierarchy and hedged round with social control, "but the narratives that create and reveal the patterns of commitment, resistance, and understanding . . . are subject to no formal, hierarchical ordering, no centralized, authoritative provenance."[4] In the totalitarian society of the Soviet Union, these master narratives are controlled by the government and are made to exert a force of control not only over the individual's relation to the law but

---

3. For another discussion of this line in particular and the third volume of the *Gulag* as a whole, see Sidney Monas, "GULag and Points West," *Slavic Review* 40 (1981): 444–56.
4. Cover, "Supreme Court 1982 Term," 17.

over the production of literary narrative. To put it simply, there is only
one master narrative. As the work of Katerina Clark has shown, the
officially sponsored doctrine of socialist realism not only dictated the
form and content of literature and the arts, but created a larger mythological pattern, by means of which behavior was to be ordered and
understood. Socialist realist literature, according to Clark, generates the
myths that sustain the political order. The party replaces the family, and
ordinary historical time takes on a sacral character.[5]

The link to politics is important. Socialist realism is more than a set
of officially sanctioned stories and artistic techniques. It not only offers a
way of understanding the individual and the world, but seeks to
"reforge" the individual and change the world and defines the writer as
an "engineer of the human soul." In setting these extraliterary goals, the
socialist realist aesthetic of the 1930s has much in common with its fore-
bear, the Chernyshevskian realism of the 1860s, which we discussed in
chapter 3. Evgenii Dobrenko rightly calls socialist realism a "discourse
of power."[6] Solzhenitsyn's work resists the master narrative of Stalinist
culture and the heroic cast of its plots. But his purpose is not only to
destabilize and disestablish. The text re-creates its own "patterns of
commitment and understanding," its own moral precepts and meaning.
The Gulag Archipelago, as I will show, seeks to establish its own mono-
lithic nomos out of its narrative. I will trace in particular how it depends
on and departs from socialist realist aesthetics in this process.

My argument in this chapter has a simple structure. I am going to
describe the main features of Solzhenitsyn's testimony, what he says
about the Gulag. To use an old-fashioned set of terms, I begin with the
content of the work, and then I will turn to its form, its distinctive features as an artwork, in order to see how the *Gulag* tries to re-create its
readers and bind them into a new set of commitments.

An Impossible Knowledge

The Gulag Archipelago seeks to produce knowledge in its readers of the
Gulag—knowledge that had been, by and large, secret. The central

---

5. See Katerina Clark, *The Soviet Novel: History as Ritual* (Chicago: University of
Chicago Press, 1985), especially 39–41.
6. Evgenii Dobrenko, *Metafora vlasti: Literatura stalinskoi epokhi v istoricheskom
osveshchenii* (Munich: Verlag Otto Sagner, 1993). 33. For an English translation of another
work by the same author that pursues similar themes, see "The Literature of the Zhdanov
Era," in *Late Soviet Culture: From Perestroika to Novostroika,* ed. Thomas Lahusen with Gene
Kuperman (Durham, N.C.: Duke University Press, 1993), 109–37.

episode of the frame introducing parts 1 and 2 relies on an article in the journal *Nature,* published by the Academy of Sciences. The remains of a prehistoric salamander were discovered frozen in the ice of the Kolyma River. The remains were so fresh that the workers at the site "consumed them with relish"—Solzhenitsyn tells us that this is what the "learned correspondent reported" (1:6). The real meaning of the correspondent's remark could hardly be known to readers of the journal, or even to the correspondent himself, even though he was an eyewitness to the event. Even though the Gulag archipelago transverses the country that contains it, most inhabitants of the larger country have only a vague knowledge of the archipelago. Solzhenitsyn writes: "Only those who have been there know everything" (1:7). But they do not speak. The meaning of the prehistoric frozen meal can be grasped only by those who had themselves suffered the experience of the workers at Kolyma, that is, the members of the numerous tribe of zeks, labor camp inmates. All of the massive knowledge of the Gulag that Solzhenitsyn's eighteen hundred pages seek to provide can be compressed to this one instant of ravenous hunger. The truth of the Gulag is the fact of this hunger. But witnessing it provides no guarantee of understanding, and hence, giving adequate testimony about it. This episode brings into focus one of the fundamental strands of Solzhenitsyn's testimony: the suffering of the body.

The second major strand of Solzhenitsyn's testimony is the realm of the imaginary: that which is fantastical or fictive, but in the strange world of the Gulag is not unreal. Solzhenitsyn's factual testimony about the Gulag shows how fiction is a fundamental part of Gulag discipline and power. Several examples will help illustrate how the two themes of suffering and fiction work together. The first comes from the history of the concentration camp on the White Sea island of Solovki, established in 1921. According to Solzhenitsyn, the camp at Solovki contained the embryonic form of the Gulag as a whole. The testimony of the atrocities committed at Solovki is overwhelming. Prisoners were forced to sleep standing up; they were issued sacks instead of clothes; they, instead of horses, were used to drag boats, carts, and sleighs; they were tied to horses and dragged through the forest; they were left naked outdoors in the summer to be consumed by mosquitoes; they were thrown down 365 steep stairs. Shootings were carried out in broad daylight; when infectious diseases broke out, whole barracks were locked in until everyone died (3:51).

Solzhenitsyn juxtaposes this testimony of atrocity with descrip-

tions of what he calls "the fantastic world" of Solovki. The acronym for
the administrative unit responsible for Solovki and other camps is
SLON, the Russian word for "elephant." An elephant was depicted on
the flower bed outside the building housing the Solovki camp administration. The same "rebus" was used on the camp scrip. Solzhenitsyn
comments: "What a pleasant home-grown masquerade!" (3:37). For
one year the camp journal was published under the title *Slon*. Solzhenitsyn notes that the leader of the camp artistic troupe was named Kunst.
This coincidence is for him part of the "fantastic world."

In the Gulag world as a whole the real and the unreal change
places. In part 1, chapter 2, Solzhenitsyn describes arrest as "a blind-
ing flash and shock from which the real instantaneously retreats to the
past, and the impossible attains all the rights of the real" (1:18). Arrest
is the painful eruption of the unreal world of the law into the life of
the individual. Solzhenitsyn suggests what can be called an aesthetics
of arrest: "when the speeches of orators, theatrical works, and
women's fashions seem to have come right off the conveyor belt,
arrests take on variety" (1:23). He gives as examples the arrests of
patients in the hospital, arrests carried out by railroad conductors,
taxi drivers, and seeming religious pilgrims. Solzhenitsyn hints at a
deliberate artistry, what he calls an "excessive inventiveness" behind
the proliferation of the forms of arrest. Art as a special realm of
human endeavor no longer exists as such: political oratory, fashion,
and the theater come off the conveyor belt. Art is now only to be
found in the operations of the police.

Letters without Spirit: The Language of Punishment

The two sides of the Gulag—the fictitious and the corporeal—produce
and maintain each other. The prisoner's suffering, caused by the fictions the law creates, generates yet more material for the law to work
on. From the perspective of the law, the suffering of the individual is of
no account, since the individual is only an instrument of or an "obstacle" to its world-creating purposes.[7] The law names and gives meaning
to the behavior of individuals only in terms of its language of crime and

---

7. See Renata Galtseva and Irina Rodnyanskaya, "The Obstacle: The Human Being,
or the Twentieth Century in the Mirror of Dystopia," in Lahusen and Kuperman, *Late
Soviet Culture*, 69–94.

punishment. Hence, the variety of crimes and the laws needed to punish them is as infinite and variable as human behavior—as Solzhenitsyn suggests in his antipsalm to article 58 of the 1926 criminal code:

> it is great, mighty, abundant, branching, multiform. . . . In truth, there is no deed, design, action, or inaction, that could not be punished by the hand of article 58. (1:71)

The law produces crime—or, as Solzhenitsyn puts, it "where there is law—there is crime" (1:79). In chapter 1 we considered a strikingly similar line from Sukhovo-Kobylin's *The Case:* "a case can be made out of anything." The nineteenth-century fiction anticipates the twentieth-century reality. The law and its agents may be compared to artists, authors, and playwrights, who create roles and scripts and then embody them by charging and convicting particular individuals.

Solzhenitsyn draws attention to the way that article 58 proliferates, feeding on its own material in order to produce endless new mutations—new categories of guilt that are slight modifications of what has come before. The new life forms, so to speak, are to be found in a new language, consisting entirely of acronyms, what Solzhenitsyn calls "frightening combinations of capital letters." For example, the sixth point of article 58, *shpionazh* (espionage), becomes *podozrenie v shpionazhe* (suspected espionage), or *PSh*, which mutates into *sviazi, vedushchie k podozreniu v shpionazhe* (contacts leading to suspicion of espionage), or *SvPSh* (1:74–75). In the late 1940s new letters were invented, to use Solzhenitsyn's idiom: *PZ*, for "Kowtowing to the West" *(preklonenie pered Zapadom)* (1:100). The code itself is not the only means for the production of crime. Solzhenitsyn reports that according to Soviet legal hermeneutics, guilt could be determined by analogy, by descent, and by contact with "dangerous elements." New categories of crime were generated out of hints from Stalin's language. In 1950 the death penalty was restored. It could be applied to "demolitionists and saboteurs." The concept of demolition was not confined to bombing railroad lines, for example. Conversations on the tram could be seen as "demolishing the authority of the government" (1:296).

The history of the Gulag, in all of its instantiations, its laws, crimes, arrests, imprisonments, transports, and camps, is a history of the unreal and the fantastical made terrifyingly real. The law itself produces an imaginary universe of crimes that were never committed: espionage, betrayal, sabotage, and "wrecking." This universe has its own unique history and identifiable trends. Solzhenitsyn observes that in the 1930s the secret police liked to invent shameful sexual crimes, such as sodomy, for the intelligentsia. A certain Professor Pletnev was charged with vampirism. Left alone with a patient, he allegedly bit her on the chest. The author emphasizes the sexual double entendre of the term *organ*, used to refer to governmental and party agencies, including the security apparatus. The "Organs" are true to their name. Istvan Rev, writing about show trials in Hungary, comments that "pornography is a 'realistic' representation of the world of phantasmagoria, a world of appearances that is created from lies and modeled after certain low-quality fiction."[8]

Solzhenitsyn argues that the imaginary universe created by the Organs and fueled by article 58 invades the "real" world of everyday life, undermining it from within. He writes that "only the Organs know people's true position and ranks" (1:158). In the eyes of the police, people's everyday, real lives are nothing more than a charade, which can be interrupted at any time. Again, Sukhovo-Kobylin's trilogy offers striking material for comparison. In *The Death of Tarelkin*, a policeman says: " I am now of the opinion that our whole fatherland is a pack of wolves, snakes, and rabbits, who have suddenly turned into people, and I suspect everyone." Sukhovo-Kobylin's phantasmagoric fiction becomes Solzhenitsyn's phantasmagoric fact.

In describing his own sentencing, which took place without a trial, Solzhenitsyn discusses the shadowy qualities of the Organ that replaced the court. This was the OSO (*Osoboe SOveshchanie*, Special Commission). In the 1920s, sentences were handed down by troikas, the names of whose members were broadly advertised. Later, the troikas were transformed into the OSO, the true nature of which very little is known. The OSO worked out its own "code of letters" (*liternye stat'i*; emphasis added) (1:289), including *ASA*, Anti-Soviet Agitation, *SOE*, Socially Dangerous Element, *SVE*, Socially Harmful Element, and the broad *ChS*, Member of the Family. Solzhenitsyn writes that "it wouldn't be miracle if we find out that there was no OSO, no hearings, just a staff of experienced typists making extracts from nonexistent

---

8. Istvan Rev, "*In Medacio Veritas* (In Lies There Lies the Truth)" *Representations* 35 (summer 1991): 17.

minutes" (1:288). The very apparatus even of this secret, purely administrative court, may have no real existence. The free play of the signifier—of the law made of letters—produces its own unreal origin, the OSO.

In Solzhenitsyn's revelations about the workings of the Gulag we find a profound statement about the nature of power, and the nature of absolute power. We have touched on this question in the introduction to this study. Power works in part by draping itself in ritual borrowed from the realm of the sacred. Solzhenitsyn contributes to this discussion by showing how Bolshevik leaders use elements from religious tradition. The group-authored paean to the White Sea canal, built with zek labor, is an example. Solzhenitsyn remarks that this work "was published for ages to come, so that future generations would read it and feel awe" (3:79). In its very format, *Belomor: An Account of the Construction of the New Canal between the White Sea and the Baltic Sea* (1934), with its bas-relief of "the pantheon of demigods" on the front, resembles an edition of the Gospels (3:78).

Solzhenitsyn's testimony about the definition of political crimes under Stalin emphasizes the religious semiotics of his rule. A half-literate stovemaker liked to practice signing his name. He used newspapers for this purpose, and inadvertently signed his name over an image of Stalin. The neighbors reported him, and the man received ten years for "Anti-Soviet Agitation" (3:86). A tailor who stuck a needle in the newspaper hanging on the wall in front of him received ten years for "terror," because the needle landed in Kaganovich's eye (3:287). In the Soviet state, the signs by which power displayed itself became hyper-invested with value.[9] The signs and symbols of power, in these examples, images in the print media, become tantamount to the person in whom power resides. The scenario of power extends from the Kremlin into the print media, in which images and the words of the ruler are imbued with his aura. Any indication of lack of respect for the signs is equivalent to an attack on the person of Stalin or his delegates. The sign and the referent change places.

---

9. In a somewhat different sense, Krystyna Pomorska speaks of the narrowness of the code according to which the fictitious characters of Solzhenitsyn's novels must live, and hence "its strong palpability; in other words, the more attention paid to the system of communication, the stronger its semiotic character." See Pomorska, "The Overcoded World of Solzhenicyn," *Poetics Today* 1, no. 3 (1980): 65.

The Theater of the Law

Even before the show trials of the 1930s, Soviet authorities used various popular theatrical forms to communicate specific political messages to a mass audience. They reinvented traditional Russian street theater during the trial of the Socialist Revolutionaries in 1922. Troupes of clowns traveling throughout Moscow in decorated automobiles described the betrayals committed by the SRs in rhymed couplets. Petrushka, the traditional clown-puppet of Russian street theater, beat with a club other puppets made up to look like the most prominent defendants.[10] Petrushka, whose theatrical role previously had been to disrupt public order and decorum, now served the state.[11]

Solzhenitsyn and other observers consider the 1930 trial of the so-called Industrial Party to be a dress rehearsal for the "Great Terror" that followed. Solzhenitsyn remarks that with this trial, the "standard" performance was reached, and it could then be repeated "every season according to how the chief artistic director dictated" (1:401). Siniavskii too, we should note, will speak of Stalin as a theatrical director, but in a different context. There were eight defendants, mostly from the State Planning Commission. Prominent among them was the well-known scientist Leonid Ramzin, who was later discovered to have authored many of the accusations against his fellow defendants. The defendants were accused of "wrecking" Soviet industry on the planning and operational level, which would have led to an economic crisis. But far more grandiose was their alleged conspiracy to overthrow the Soviet government. Plans to drain swamps, for example, were part of a more sinister program to pave the way for invasion from abroad. The prosecution alleged a center of operations consisting of the eight defendants, contacts with two thousand engineers, workers, and peasants throughout the country, and agreements made with the president of France. Solzhenitsyn, like other observers, notes the complete lack of documentary evidence in the prosecution's case. The fabricated story, according to Solzhenitsyn, is somehow familiar. He compares it to Verdi's *Aida*. In act 1, Radames, the general of the Egyptian army,

---

10. See V. Voitinskii, *Dvenatsat' smertnikov: Sud nad sotsialistami-revoliutsionerami v Moskve* (Berlin: Izdanie zagranichnoi delegatsii P. S. R., 1922), 42.

11. For this characterization of Petrushka's traditional role, see E. Kuznetsov, ed., *Russkie narodnye gulian'ia po rasskazam A. Ia. Alekseev-Iakovleva* (Leningrad: Iskusstvo, 1948), 59–62.

together with his officers and captains, is positioned on stage. Two thousand soldiers are painted on the backdrop.

Solzhenitsyn emphasizes the literariness of the plot and compares the defendants to performing artists, who are forced to enact roles. He notes the suspiciously smooth, seamless, and seemingly endless flow of their testimony: "repentance pours out of one's breast in whole monologues, and one wants to talk, talk, expose, flagellate. . . . the defendants talk, talk, explain, and then still later ask to talk, in order to fill in what was left out" (1:380). Earlier, in his chapter on investigation, Solzhenitsyn remarks that intellectuals gave themselves away during interrogation by telling stories that were too coherent (1:130). The interrogator's criterion for verisimilitude and Solzhenitsyn's coincide. In Solzhenitsyn's words, Krylenko, the main prosecutor, decided at one point to change from Stanislavsky's system to the theater of "improvisation" (1:390). The defendants were asked to describe their lives up to their crimes. This move nearly "spoiled all five acts," because it turned out that "hirelings of bourgeois intelligence" all came from poor families and thus did not have the bourgeois motivation that the prosecution imputed to them.

The show trials represent one form of the unity of the aesthetic, the political, and the judicial characteristic of Soviet culture. Solzhenitsyn emphasizes that the trials consolidated politics and law, the functions of the defense and prosecution, judge and jury into one totalized process. They can be considered one vast socialist realist performance, a version of the mass spectacles and celebrations that were a crucial part of revolutionary and Stalinist culture.[12] Leopol'd Averbakh, one of the most important theorists of the proletarian-art movement of the twenties, wrote in 1928 that the theater, especially the mass-theater movement, which reached a vast audience, could exert a far greater influence over the public than literature. The artistic works of the proletarian playwright, aimed at the mass spectator, were to act upon his "thoughts, psyche, and feelings, directing them towards communism."[13]

The mythological scale of the conspiracy in the trial of the Indus-

12. For a discussion, see Alexander Zakharov, "Mass Celebrations in a Totalitarian System," in *Textura*, ed. Alla Efimova and Lev Manovich (Chicago: University of Chicago Press, 1995), 201–18.

13. Leopol'd Averbakh, *Kul'turnaia revoliutsia i voprosy sovremennoi literatury* (Leningrad: Gosudarstvennoe izdatel'stvo, 1928), 39.

trial Party, the harnessing of nature for the demonic purpose of the overthrow of the Soviet government, is the other side of the coin of the heroic mythologies of socialist realism. The titanic power of the Soviet hero to create a new world out of nothing meets its match in the titanic power of the enemy to destroy.[14] The show trials communicated to the public the power of the Soviet state by dramatizing its larger than life triumphs over its enemies.

The Gulag as Mass Art

A politicized theater and a theatricalized politics characterize Stalinist culture. Solzhenitsyn reports that the world of the Gulag had its own forms of theater and agitprop performances. For example, simulated preparations for the execution of the death penalty were used as a means of extracting information from prisoners. Solzhenitsyn also describes the plays performed by camp inmates. He terms these a "double performance." First, the prisoner must imagine herself or himself as a free artist and then must enact the particular role demanded by the script to be performed. Solzhenitsyn speaks of his own participation in a camp ensemble as "humiliating" (3:486). A certain parallel to the serf theater of imperial Russia may be drawn.

His example of theatrical performances at Solovki reveals an important connection between the operation of punishment and the aesthetics of the 1920s. An exhausted couple dancing the fox-trot represented the dying West, and a smithy painted on the backdrop represented the new workers' nation. The piece is titled *The Rails Hum* (3:38). Without imputing blame to the avant-garde movements of the 1920s, and without suggesting that Solzhenitsyn does so, it is nonetheless striking that in this image a certain grim coincidence unfolds. The constructivists and futurists had sought too construct reality, to reach beyond the aesthetic to the real and shape the real aesthetically. An example can be found in Vsevolod Meyerhold's "biomechanics," a set of techniques by means of which the actor was to improve the functioning of his own body, thus bringing about the new man under communism.[15] The metaphor of the "new man" is realized in the biome-

---

14. For a discussion of titanism in socialist realism, see Dobrenko, *Metafora vlasti*, 39–41.

15. See Irina Gutkin, "The Legacy of the Symbolist Aesthetic Utopia: From Futurism to Socialist Realism," in Paperno and Grossman, *Creating Life*, 184.

chanically improved actor. In a similar fashion, in the Gulag performance, the metaphor of the dying west is fulfilled in the body of the prisoner. The prisoner representing the dying West is dying in reality. Punishment realizes the metaphor of artistic representation.

According to Solzhenitsyn, the practices of at Solovki were not organized into a deliberate system. It was not clear where everything was leading. The camp administration was subsequently purged and shot. Solzhenitsyn argues that the definitive systematic form of the Gulag was given it by Naftalii Aronovich Frenkel', "a Turkish Jew" (3:74). Roy Medvedev disagrees with this version of events, as well as what is in his view Solzhenitsyn's undue emphasis on Frenkel's Jewishness and that of other key figures of the camp system.[16] According to Solzhenitsyn, it was Frenkel' who suggested to Stalin that socialism be built by means of the forced labor of prisoners, and that the system of camp rations be tied to work quotas (2:84). Solzhenitsyn takes pains to elaborate the ideological component of the forced labor projects, such as the Baltic–White Sea and the Moscow-Volga canals. He relies heavily on I. L. Averbakh's *From Crime to Labor,* published in 1936.[17] Solzhenitsyn quotes Averbakh's definition of Soviet corrective labor: "the transformation of the most foul human material into fully valued active builders of socialism."[18] The transformation was to take place by means of "concentrated labor on gigantic objects, which shock the imagination by their grandeur" (2:104).

The grotesque coincidence of life and art at Solovki becomes the deliberate policy of so-called rehabilitation through labor, adapted for the Gulag as a whole. The zek whose labor produces these "gigantic objects" is imagined as a spectator, a spectacle, and the raw material out of which the spectacle is constructed. As spectator, the laborer beholds the gigantic objects in their finished state. As raw material, the laborer's forced work on the object is work on himself. The prisoner's agency in building the object is really a form of passivity, since the purpose of building the object is only the prisoner's enforced transformation. In the passage from Averbakh we see a version of the concept of human

---

16. Medvedev, *Let History Judge,* 507. For a discussion of Solzhenitsyn's attitudes toward Jews, see Daniel Rancour-Laferriere, "Solzhenitsyn and the Jews: A Psychoanalytic View," *Russian Literature and Psychoanalysis,* Ed., Daniel Rancour-Laferriere (Amsterdam) Philadelphia: John Benjamins, 1989), 143–70.

17. I am unable to provide information as to the possible relation between I. L. Averbakh and the more famous Leopol'd Averbakh.

18. I. L. Averbakh, *Ot prestupleniia k trudu,* quoted in Solzhenitsyn, 2:103.

society as a totalized artwork. The completed project is not primarily the "gigantic object," but the newly transformed "active builder of socialism." The state is both artist and spectator of its own creation. In *The Total Art of Stalinism,* Boris Groys writes that "the Communist party leadership was transformed into a kind of artist whose material was the entire world."[19]

We can make a connection between this concept of the person as material to be reworked and our earlier discussion of the special status of the sign in Soviet totalitarian culture. As we saw earlier, the person of the ruler is projected forward by means of totemic signs. The consequences for the individual are lethal: the ordinary person becomes a surface upon which the signs are inscribed. The horrifying law made of letters is written in the flesh of the prisoner. Kafka's "In the Penal Colony" comes to mind. Solzhenitsyn, while not referring to Kafka, describes how in eighteenth-century Russia, the empress Elizabeth replaced capital punishment, with, among other punishments, the branding of the word *thief (vor)* on the convict's face (1:433). As we saw in chapter 1, the prospect of branding is horrifying, painful, and degrading to Sukhovo-Kobylin. To be forever marked is to lose the possibility of self-fashioning. The so-called rehabilitation that Solzhenitsyn describes has the added horror of totalization, the complete transformation of the individual into an element of the collective. For Solzhenitsyn the transformation is not from "human material" to "active builder of socialism," but the other way around, from human personality to sheer material, to waste product. Solzhenitsyn stresses that the end result of the process is the remains of the prisoner.

Since the passage from Averbakh is key to the operation of the Gulag, to the content of Solzhenitsyn's work, it bears a fuller explication. The transformation of the prisoner into an active builder of socialism takes place by means of an operation that is at one level aesthetic. The laborer feels "the striking visual qualities [*nagliadnost*], the effectiveness, and the pathos of the object under construction" (3:104).[20] Solzhenitsyn continues the quotation from Averbakh, interpolating his

19. Boris Groys, *The Total Art of Stalinism: Avant-Garde, Aesthetic Dictatorship, and Beyond,* trans. Charles Rougle (Princeton, N.J.: Princeton University Press, 1992), 3.

20. The experimental filmmaker Sergei Eisenstein had used the term "pathos" to refer to the transformation of the spectator from one psychological condition into its opposite. Eisenstein emphasized that the spectator is taken out of himself or herself—that is, out of individuality and into an identification with the collective. Averbakh may have something similar in mind.

own commentary: "every camp inmate (who isn't dead yet) feels the political resonance of his personal work, the interest of the entire country in his labor." The individual comes to feel part of the collective. Language from *Belomor* (in which Leopol'd Averbakh played a significant role) emphasizes this moment of transformation in the prisoner.[21] We hear about the "reforging of the individual, " the entrance of the criminals into the "family of workers," their restoration to "equal members of our family of workers."[22] Gorky's speech to the canal workers at the completion of the project emphasizes the homogenizing effect of the canal construction on its workers: "The victory over nature accomplished by thousands of heterogeneous individuals of almost a hundred different races is amazing" (337). Class and occupational difference have been erased. The authors of *The White Sea Canal* observe that previously one could see in the prisoners various social types: "a criminal type, an intellectual, a typical kulak" (325). Their experience at the canal has changed them. "But we look attentively for the impress of their biographies, which has eaten into their skin and muscles; we can distinguish something new and different—something characteristic of the Belomorstroy people" (the people who built "Belomor," the White Sea Canal). As we will see, Solzhenitsyn, while not referring to this phrase, has a great deal to say about biographies that have eaten into people's skin and muscles. The photographs in the club room at the canal site show "huge, heroic, sharply lighted faces, in proud foreshortening" (325). The construction of the canal has very nearly created a new race, in which everyone looks the same.

The merging of the individual into the collective is a dominant theme in socialist realist art and literature. Evgenii Dobrenko remarks on "the desire to disperse individual configurations of bodies in the total equality of elements in one superbody" (38). He quotes a line from V. Lugovskii's "The Morning of the Republic": "I want to forget my name and calling and exchange them for a number, for a nickname, for a letter" (38). The exchange of name for number is the experience of the camp inmate. The merging of the individual with the mass is not deferred to the infinite future but happens within historical time.

---

21. For a discussion of *Belomor: An Account* as part of a modern Russian salvation tradition, see Irene Masing-Delic, *Abolishing Death: A Salvation Myth of Russian Twentieth-Century Literature* (Stanford, Calif.: Stanford University Press, 1992), 126–27.

22. *Belomor: An Account of the Construction of the New Canal between the White Sea and the Baltic Sea* (Westport, Conn.: Hyperion Press, 1977), 329.

The Testimony of the Body

It is Solzhenitsyn's point to show that the destruction of the individual and the creation of the collective takes place in real individual bodies. The destruction of the individual is not a figurative, but a literal, process. It begins in the torture chamber; sometimes it ends there or sometimes continues in the camps. Relying on statements made by victims, Solzhenitsyn contends that torture was practiced before 1938. He is very careful about establishing the most likely version of events on this point. Before 1938, interrogators needed some sort of permission, but after 1938, they could use torture at their own discretion. Robert Conquest put the date earlier, finding evidence for secret permission in 1936.[23] Both Solzhenitsyn and Conquest agree that Stalin supported the use of torture. In part 1, Solzhenitsyn describes over thirty types of torture. Unlike his description of Solovki, here the author names names, gives dates and places. The physical torture includes forcing the prisoner to speak loudly for six to eight hours, tickling, extinguishing a cigarette on the prisoner's skin, forcing the prisoner to stand or kneel, depriving the prisoner of fluids, food, and sleep, beating, and a device known as the "bridle" or "swallow," by means of which the prisoner was suspended in the air.

In *The Body in Pain*, Elaine Scarry argues that torture is not a means of gaining information. It is rather the means by which the state transforms the prisoner's body into an instrument of its own power: "having as its purpose the production of fantastic illusion of power, torture is a grotesque piece of compensatory drama."[24] The state shows its omnipotent agency by destroying the prisoner's self, world, and voice. Scarry writes that for the prisoner, the body and its pain are overwhelmingly present and voice, world, and self are absent" (46). The power of pain to dissolve the prisoner's world and self is transferred to the regime imposing the pain. The regime has the power to destroy lives and worlds. The "scenario of power" is repeated over and over in the interrogation rooms of numerous prisons.

Solzhenitsyn's writing is an effort at reclaiming the self and voice that the State seeks to eliminate. Solzhenitsyn writes "for Russia that

23. See Robert Conquest, *The Great Terror: A Reassessment* (New York: Oxford University Press, 1990), 121–22.
24. Scarry, *The Body in Pain*, 28.

has no tongue" (3:311).[25] In the context it is clear that he is referring to those Russians who did not and could not write their own memoirs and testimonies. However, from other passages, it is equally clear that the author is very concerned with the issue of the restoration of self. For example, he describes the deprivation of sleep and the deprivation of "a few minutes of private life" *(chastnaia zhizn')* at the prison in Sukhanovka. The prisoner is always being looked at and always "in the power" of the authorities (1:190). In another passage, he relates his own text to the issue of the restoration of the past, not for the nation as a whole, but for discrete individuals. The protocols signed in the interrogation cells distort this past, creating, as we have seen, a counterreality of espionage and betrayal. Prisoners were required to sign statements that they would not reveal the methods used during interrogation. The prisoner's pain is to find no voice, not even in the future. The prisoner internalizes this censorship. Solzhenitsyn writes in the conclusion to his chapter on torture that as a whole, "we are not yet certain: do we have the right to recount the events of our own personal lives?" (1:152). His writing is an affirmation of that right. The testimony of the body's pain is part of the reclamation of the self. It restores the reality of suffering to the victim, whose suffering the regime appropriates for its own purposes, that is, to affirm its power. Testimony of suffering recontextualizes the suffering as suffering for the individual.

Solzhenitsyn stresses the near impossibility of his task. Numerous problems arise. Sometimes there are no witnesses to the events. Solzhenitsyn describes illegal shootings carried out by the Soviet government in the late 1930s: "The door of the prison cell opens, you are shot at, you cry out before death—and no one besides the prison stones hears you, and no one will tell" (1:89). Because no Soviet historian will provide reliable statistics of these shootings, Solzhenitsyn relies on the "rumors" circulating in the prisons during 1939–40 to the effect that half a million so-called political prisoners and another 480,000 "criminals" *(blatarei)* were shot (1:438). The most recent version of Robert Conquest's *The Great Terror* gives the figure of one million killed in prison in late 1938, including deaths caused by prison conditions (486). Solzhenitsyn emphasizes that it is impossible to know what the death

---

25. For another discussion of the significance of this line, see Natalia Pervukhin, "The 'Experiment in Literary Investigation' (Čexov's *Saxalin* and Solženicyn's *Gulag*," *Slavic and East European Journal* 35 (1991): 495.

penalty is, that not even the executioner knows "up to the end": "Up to end only the murdered know, and that means no one" (1:446). Only the dead know, and therefore no one knows. The solution is provided—not fully—by art. The artist manages to gain some of the knowledge denied the historian and the statistician. From artists and from those who were pardoned Solzhenitsyn composes "an approximate picture of death row" (1:446).

Earlier we saw that Solzhenitsyn's use of the ordinary apparatus of historical evidence is uneven. In his descriptions of Solovki he gives few details, but in his descriptions of torture, many. In a footnote to the Solovki section, Solzhenitsyn points out that there are no memorials at the site. Tourists play volleyball where bodies where thrown after torture. History fails to provide testimony. The question then arises as to what special space Solzhenitsyn reserves for the testimony provided by art, a question that applies not only to those sections where there are no footnotes, but to the work as a whole, which, as we recall, is subtitled *An Experiment in Artistic Investigation.* Shoshana Felman addresses this issue in the context of the Holocaust. In her discussion of Camus's *The Plague* as a form of literary testimony, she writes:

> The specific task of the literary testimony is . . . to open up in that belated witness, which the reader now historically becomes, the imaginative capability of perceiving history—what is happening to others—in one's own body, with the power of sight (insight) usually afforded only by one's own immediate physical involvement.[26]

Felman refutes the historian's claim that distance is necessary to historical narration. The eyewitness who gives testimony must be implicated and involved in the events being described. The testimony of the body provides insight into material that official history and bureaucratic institutions have made unreal, abstract, and unbelievable. Felman quotes Camus's statement that the artist "testifies not to the Law, but to the body."[27]

The Gulag Archipelago is an example of the literary testimony of the

---

26. Shoshana Felman and Dori Laub, M.D., *Testimony: Crises of Witnessing in Literature, Psychoanalysis, and History* (New York: Routledge, 1992), 108.

27. Albert Camus, "Le Temoin de la liberté," in *Oeuvres complètes d'Albert Camus,* 5:188, 191, quoted in Felman and Laub, *Testimony,* 108 n. 8.

body. Solzhenitsyn explicitly and repeatedly contrasts theory, that which, as he says, is written on paper, and what is written on the camp inmate's body. Marx, Solzhenitsyn reminds his readers, wrote that the only way to correct the criminal is by forced labor. Solzhenitsyn notes that "Marx wrote this on paper, and it didn't object" (3:142). Solzhenitsyn's history of the Gulag is, in contrast, what "we felt on our skin" (3:144). The use of the first person here and elsewhere (for example, "Here is the daily life of my Archipelago" [3:204]) brings forward the immediate involvement of the author not only as eyewitness but as victim. Later, we will discuss the author's self-declared implication as perpetrator.

The individual inmate of the Gulag suffers above all from starvation. Responding to critics of *A Day in the Life of Ivan Denisovich* who charged that Solzhenitsyn exaggerated the significance of food rations, here the author devotes several pages to the theme of hunger. Hunger "darkens the brain" and forces its victim to think of nothing but "food, food, food." The zek's hunger can never be satisfied: "the person is transformed into a one-way pipe, and everything comes out of him in the same form in which it was swallowed" (3:205).

Solzhenitsyn reflects on which artistic medium more appropriately depicts the effects of hunger. Film can best capture how those on their last legs fight each other for the kitchen garbage, how they "search for fish heads, bones, and vegetable peelings" (3:205–6). Film "will show how still-joined bones lie under the orderly's blankets and die practically without moving—and are carried out" (3:205). But "slow, attentive prose will describe the gradations of the paths to death known as . . . pellagra and alimentary dysentery" (3:206). Here Solzhenitsyn describes how the teeth fall out, the gums bleed, ulcers appear on the legs, the skin peels off, diarrhea sets in that makes its victim forget everything, even his own name, pus-filled lesions appear on the face, arms, legs, trunk, "even the scrotum" (3:206–7). Solzhenitsyn remarks that the perpetrators and self-proclaimed innocent bystanders of suffering do not wish to see its history in print. As we have already seen, even some of the victims of this history wish to deny it. He himself does not expect to see his own work published. The history of disease and unimaginably unbeautiful death is written against a desired and threatened invisibility. The State's abstractions, all those whom it sentenced under its "code of letters," all those deemed "insects," enemies of the people, and betrayers of the motherland, become embodied before the reader in the countless descriptions of physical suffering. The recovery of the self, of the individual human personality, if such a thing is possible, is not to be found, however, in the testimony of the body, but in another form of testimony, to which we will return later.

The Carnival Body

A distinction has to be made between Felman's analysis of Camus's strategy in *The Plague* and what I am suggesting about Solzhenitsyn. The problem is one of scale. Felman emphasized that the reader gains insight into the experience of the other, the subject of an inaccessible history, by the vicarious experience of her or his own body. A one-to-one relationship emerges, presumably between the reader of the work of art and the other. In contrast, the reader of Solzhenitsyn is engulfed. Solzhenitsyn overwhelms the reader with images that suggest the weight, the scale, and the endless multiplication of the suffering he describes. The grotesquely distorted bodies of the Gulag are the photographic negative of the aesthetically enhanced superbodies of Soviet visual culture, as in for example, Vera Mukhina's statue from 1937, *Worker and Woman Farmer.*[28] This is not to say that the fates of individual Russians are neglected. For example, part 5 contains the lengthy first-person narration of Georgii Tenno, who escaped from a camp. Solzhenitsyn's own inner, spiritual autobiography can be traced throughout the work, as we will shortly see. But the dominant metaphors of cancer and of the body's waste products pertain to the suffering body of Russia as a whole. Solzhenitsyn writes that during the war, "the entire cancerous swelling of the archipelago turned out to be an important necessary organ of the Russian body" (3:132). The history of the Soviet Union is the history of "our canalization"; the history of arrests is the history of the production of "streams" of sewage. In Solzhenitsyn's image, human individuals were pressed or squeezed into streams of "blood and urine" that unceasingly poured through the vast sewage tunnels that fed the Gulag archipelago (1:38). The project of debunking the hyperoptimistic official history of the Soviet state, a project carried out in part by means of carnivalization—takes over the work as a whole, overshadowing the suffering of individuals.

---

28. For a photo, see Igor Golomstock, *Totalitarian Art in the Soviet Union, the Third Reich, Fascist Italy, and the People's Republic of China,* trans. Robert Chandler (New York: HarperCollins, 1990), 362.

The image of the supraindividual body and its waste products suggests a parallel with Bakhtin's collective carnival body and its hyperbolically exaggerated lower stratum. In Bakhtin, the grotesque body is never finished; it "transgresses its own limits. . . . the stress is laid on those parts of the body through which the world enters the body or emerges from it."[29] Solzhenitsyn's picture of the zek as a one-way tube through which everything exits in the same form as it enters is a horrific realization of the grotesque body. In Bakhtin, the lower stratum is also a source of rebirth: "in the images of urine and excrement is preserved the essential link with birth, fertility, renewal, welfare" (148). But for Solzhenitsyn, the sublimation of the self in the collective grotesque body is not a joyous process. The zeks on their last legs, who have no choice but to rethink everything through the lower bodily stratum, who forget their families and even their own names, feel no joy at the passing of their individuality. Compare Bakhtin:

> The individual feels that he is an indissoluble part of the collectivity, a member of the people's mass body. In this whole the individual body ceases to a certain extent to be itself; it is possible, so to say, to exchange bodies, to be renewed. (255)

Mikhail Ryklin argues that Bakhtin's book on Rabelais, which was written, as he points out, during 1935–36, "reflects the trauma of a member of the Russian intelligentsia caught in the unthinkable situation of terror and the spread of . . . collective corporeality."[30] Solzhenitsyn's massive study charts the history of this enforced collective corporeality. Ryklin suggests that Bakhtin's book provides a theoretical framework not of popular festivity, but of terror. Reading Bakhtin against Solzhenitsyn gives ample support to his claim.

The Testimony of the Soul

The Gulag Archipelago testifies not only to the facts, the sheer physicality of the Gulag, but also to the rebirth of the author's religious convictions. It is a witnessing also in the religious sense of the term. Solzhen-

---

29. M. M. Bakhtin, *Rabelais and His World*, trans. Helene Iswolsky (Cambridge: MIT Press, 1968), 26.

30. Mikhail Ryklin, "Tela Terrora (tezisy k logike nasiliia)," *Bakhtinskii sbornik* 1 (1990): 60.

itsyn, unlike Bakhtin, does not locate the possibility of rebirth in the body. However, his experience in the Gulag turns out to be a necessary stage in the process of renewal.

Solzhenitsyn's personal narrative begins early in the work, in part 1. The first part recounts his spiritual fall and his dawning realization of his past sins. Solzhenitsyn writes, "Why must one fall to the bottom of the camp in order to understand his insignificance?" (2:191). He describes how the day after his arrest he and other prisoners had to march a considerable distance. He demanded that a German civilian prisoner carry his suitcase. Solzhenitsyn writes that "this was the time to think over my past life . . . but I could not" (1:173). He thought of himself at the time as one capable of "self-renunciation" but was in fact a "fully prepared executioner" (1:175). On his arrival at his first camp, he managed to receive a reprieve from the general work assignment. He and another former officer were appointed to be leaders of a work group at a clay quarry, and he witnesses his fellow officer nearly be killed by the ordinary criminals in his charge. Solzhenitsyn comments on his desire to "get ahead," as he puts it: "at one point other ideals had been instilled in me," but from they were submerged by the conditions and general tenor of the times (3:172). His inability to control his group leads to his "fall"; that is, he must fulfill ordinary work assignments, but the fall is a blessing in disguise. He experiences moments when the work itself distracts him.

The heart of the conversion narrative unfolds as he lies recovering from a cancer operation, in a chapter titled "Ascent" ("Voskhozhde-nie"). He agrees with the observation of his companion in the ward, V. N. Kornfel'd, a converted Jew, that no punishment comes undeserved. Solzhenitsyn is now able to evaluate his former life—again in a manner quite similar to Tolstoy's depiction in *The Death of Ivan Ilich*. He sees that he was cruel to others in his youth, and that in the exercise of power as a grown man he was "a murderer." His new understanding of his life is given him not by the power of his own reason, but by "the steady radiance" of divine meaning, which illuminates every "fissure" of his previous existence. Solzhenitsyn puts his miniature religious autobiography in verse. A prose translation of the central two stanzas reads:

> Passing between life and death
> I fell and holding onto the edge,

I look in trembling gratitude
At the life I lived.

Not with my reason, not by my desire
Was its every crack illumined—
But by the steady radiance of the Almighty's plan
Which was explained to me only later.

(4:602)

The poem concludes with a triumphant "I believe again." From his new vantage point, the events of world history and the meaning of all religions become clear to him. Solzhenitsyn writes: "From that time I understood the truth of all the religions of the world and the falsehood of all revolutionary history." His final gratitude is not to God, but to the Gulag. The chapter "Ascent" ends with a twice repeated uppercase: "BLESSED BE YOU, PRISON" (IV: 604). Prison has made the events of his life legible as a narrative of religious conversion. However, as we will see later, the ring of certainty in this, the personal part of Solzhenitsyn's testimony, is belied by a lack of certainty in other aspects of his testimony.

The triptych of photographs that the author provides of himself in the very opening of *The Gulag Archipelago* emphasize the centrality of the Gulag in the formation of the author's persona. The first, taken in 1944, before his arrest, shows a youthful Solzhenitsyn in uniform, writing, with open notebook, inkwell, and pens placed in front of him. The second is captioned 1946, "there," and shows Solzhenitsyn with a shaved head and furrowed brow, staring directly at the viewer. The third, taken in 1953, with the caption "just having been freed," is quite similar to the second, but Solzhenitsyn is older, his features etched more prominently on his face, and his expression more concentrated and piercing. There is no photograph of the author at the time of the book's publication in 1973, that is, what would have been a picture of the author as the author his reading audience would know and recognize. Such a photograph would provide an undesirable symmetry. He wrote; he was "there," and now he writes again. That homogeneity would blunt Solzhenitsyn's point that the was forever irrevocably made "there" in the camps. He writes that his experience "there" was the "most important rupture in my life" (1:195).

The rupture does not close with Solzhenitsyn's departure from the

prison camp. He reinflicts it on himself regularly. The regimes and
order of the Gulag mold Solzhenitsyn.[31] Even after his release, he
observes its law, which he invests with a sacred value. Once a year, on
the anniversary of his arrest, he observes a ceremonial "Day of the
Zek," during which he eats an approximation of his prison rations.
Solzhenitsyn observes "how quickly I enter the old form" (6:483). The
old prison sensations reappear. The law of the Gulag is enacted by
means of the regulation of the body. He and others carefully preserve
the tattered remains of their prison numbers, showing them to selected
guests as if they were "sacred objects."

Solzhenitsyn's personal story bears a number of features associated with other narratives of religious conversion. These features,
which can be found in, for example, Augustine's Confessions, include a
break with a false past and the return to an originary core of goodness,
and the retrospective sense that the farther away the sinner strays from
God, the more closely he is pulled back to the divine. The setting of
Solzhenitsyn's conversion narrative is by no means unique in Russian
literature. Dostoevsky too reports the rebirth of his religious convictions while in Siberia. What distinguishes Solzhenitsyn's confession is
its grotesque echoing of the forced confessions of the show trials. In his
own account of the trial of the Industrial Party, Solzhenitsyn recalls that
the foreign pressed charged that the defendants confessed under torture. Solzhenitsyn quotes what was apparently the forced response of
one of the defendants: "I even feel better in prison than in freedom"
(1:390).

Another veteran of the camps, Varlam Shalamov, writes in his
Kolyma Tales that "truth and falsehood are sisters."[32] Solzhenitsyn takes
issue with this statement, but in the story of his spiritual rehabilitation,
and in his construction of divine justice, which so perfectly matches
earthly law, the "truth" of Solzhenitsyn's rebirth and the "falsehood" of
the state's policy of torture and forced labor come perilously close.
Solzhenitsyn quotes one official of the NKVD who said that in the

---

31. Sidney Monas, writing about Solzhenitsyn in the eyes of the West, observes that
his moral and political "stance is . . . a response to Gulag and therefore in some sense still
a part of Gulag." See "Fourteen Years of Aleksandr Isaevich," *Slavic Review* 35 (1976): 521.

32. For an introduction to Shalamov that also includes a comparison to Solzhenitsyn, see John Glad's foreword to Varlam Shalamov, *Kolyma Tales*, trans. John Glad (Middlesex, England: Penguin, 1994). For a study of Shalamov's "poetics," see Lev Timofeev,
"Poetikia lagernoi prozy: Pervoe chtenie *Kolymskikh rasskazov* V. Shalamova," *Oktiabr'* 3
(March 1991): 182–95.

remote undeveloped regions of the Soviet Union, the Gulag was often the only sign of civilization. The Gulag disciplines men, women, children and nature, leaving its stamp on an otherwise untamed landscape. It also makes possible the inner spiritual autobiography of its inmate, Solzhenitsyn.

Testimony and torture are inseparable. In the seventh and final part of *The Gulag Archipelago* Solzhenitsyn chronicles his appearance before the Supreme Soviet's special commission devoted to the corrective labor code. Solzhenitsyn will give testimony in the most direct sense of the word. Here is how the author describes his qualms:

> Everything that I truly think, as it is set forth in this book—is both dangerous to say, and completely useless. It means only losing your head in the secret silence of their offices . . . not having moved the matter forward by a millimeter. Crossing their marbled mirrored thresholds, ascending their soft carpets, I must bear upon myself paths of departure, silken threads, running through me across my tongue, ears, eyelids, and then sewn to my shoulders, to the skin of my back, and to the skin of my stomach. (6:544)

Solzhenitsyn enters the halls of the Supreme Soviet like Theseus in the labyrinth of the Minotaur. But Theseus carries the ball of string given to him by Ariadne; Solzhenitsyn's is a self-imposed torture machine, not carried, but sewn to the body, a gift not from a goddess, but an image taken from the state's interrogation chambers. Solzhenitsyn's silken threads are similar, metaphorically, in their effects to the "bridle" or the "swallow" that he describes in his chapter on interrogation, except that that device prompts speech and his preempts it. In both, pain regulates the production of speech. The silken strand is connected to his face, stomach, and back in such a way that with every movement "I feel it" (7:546). What do the threads regulate? Solzhenitsyn sets himself rules of testimony that he must not violate. First, he must praise the Party and not doubt the necessity of the archipelago. Second, he must assume that the members of the commission before whom he is to speak are devoted to the matter at hand. When he is told that prisoners are well fed, that there is in fact an excess of bread that is taken away in trucks, he wants to protest. But he cannot: "how painfully my tongue jerked, tied across my shoulders to my rear" (7:548). When he is told that increasing the size of parcels to prisoners would put working families at a disadvantage: "How the threads cut and tear me!" (7:548). Solzhenitsyn as a modern Soviet Theseus, with Ariadne's threads hideously sewn to his body, a devastating image of the incursion of the state's power into the inner recesses of the individual subject.

To save himself from perishing, Solzhenitsyn restrains himself from speaking fully. The visualization of the torture device is a method of self-protection. But the image of Solzhenitsyn sewing himself to the bridle may also serve as an emblem of *The Gulag Archipelago* as a whole. The image forces us to rethink the question of how the author who stands in opposition to a legal order nonetheless depends on that order for the construction of his authority. Solzhenitsyn's indictment of Soviet law, the suffering he endured as an inmate of the camps, and the risk he took in producing his work make him a towering figure of great moral authority. He is an insider only to the extent that he was a victim and an eyewitness to the suffering of other victims. He admits his own guilt as a perpetrator, as we have seen. He can speak because he was "there," and while he was there, far from being corrupted, he was reborn. In exposing the crimes committed in the name of law, and in revealing the infiltration of the Gulag into every aspect of Soviet life, Solzhenitsyn becomes "the writer as second government," to quote his own character Sologdin in *The First Circle.*

The image of Solzhenitsyn's sewing himself to the bridle in order to testify reveals another side of the story. The author appropriates in his imagination an atrocity carried out by the Soviet interrogator in order to fashion his own authority. The discipline imposed from without becomes necessary from within. The torture device of the interrogator is deployed on the self. The production of the text depends on a punitive self-wounding that repeats and imitates an initial wound—which in this case is imaginary. Solzhenitsyn was never the victim of the particular torture device known as the bridle. Like Dostoevsky before him, Solzhenitsyn's suffering, both vicarious and personal, gives a legitmizing frame to his text, authorizing him to speak for those who cannot. On every level of the text's operation, the production of the author's authority depends on the enormous wound inflicted by the Gulag.

The Gulag Archipelago *as Testament*

The reader too is drawn into the process of wounding and knowing. The Gulag inflicts a wound on the author, who reinflicts it on himself and then on his readers. In his discussion of the death penalty, Solzhenitsyn describes the desirability of a book "practically without letters" (1:442). Letters, as we recall, form themselves into horrifying combinations that signal the suffering and death of ordinary Russians. Solzhenitsyn's ideal book would have no letters; it would consist instead of photographs of those were shot. The reading of such a book "would lie as an eternal deposit on our heart" (1:442). Solzhenitsyn goes on to describe how a group of former zeks organized a viewing of such photographs in an apartment. He adds that these viewings should take place everywhere, so that "from all these deaths we would carry away at least a scar on our hearts" *(rubchik na serdtse)* (1:443). The scar or deposit on the heart would be an external sign that we would carry hidden in the interiority of our body, an invisible, but nonetheless material, inscription. Unlike the statistics that we forget, we would have no choice but to remember the photographs of those who were murdered. We would be permanently marked after having seen their faces. The "book without letters" would fulfill Solzhenitsyn's dream of a language that could transmit meaning without slippage or loss.

This image reveals another facet of Solzhenitsyn's project as a whole. Testimony, the act of bearing witness, becomes testament, in the biblical sense of covenant or binding agreement. The scar on the heart contains an allusion to the biblical covenant between God and humankind. In Genesis, circumcision is the sign of the everlasting covenant between God and the generations to follow Abraham: "You shall be circumcised in the flesh of your foreskins and it shall be a sign of the covenant between me and you" (Gen. 17:11). In Deuteronomy, we find a figurative reworking of the Genesis commandment. After receiving the Ten Commandments for the second time, Moses tells the recalcitrant Israel of God's love and urges a recommitment from them: "Circumcise therefore the foreskin of your heart, and be no longer stubborn" (Deut. 10:16). In the New Testament, Paul emphasizes the importance of spiritual over physical circumcision: "real circumcision is a matter of the heart, spiritual and not literal" (Rom. 2:29). Membership in the new Israel is signaled by the circumcision of the heart.

Solzhenitsyn's work similarly wounds the reader by means of the circumcision of the heart. *The Gulag Archipelago* leaves a scar on the heart of the reader. The scar is more than a way of remembering what would otherwise be forgotten. The scar is a way of re-membering in the sense of re-joining a community, being re-membered to Solzhenitsyn's own new Israel. By imprisoning, torturing, and working the prisoner to death, the state does more than enforce its law. It constitutes itself as a state; it founds its law. The state writes the fiction of its own power on the prisoner's body. The *Gulag* rewrites the fiction of power as the reality of individual suffering. But it also writes a new law, by means of which individuals are joined in a new community. Having restored speech to the collective body of Russia that has no tongue, Solzhenitsyn seeks to reforge his individual readers into a new collective.

The model for this new fellowship comes from his experience of the Gulag. In his account of the uprising at Kengir, for example, Solzhenitsyn describes how prisoners in the Gulag overcame its law, the law of the jungle ("you die today, but I'll die tomorrow") and their own "slave mentality" and founded their own law. Those participating in the hunger strike "were reborn." They neglected their own personal advantage and the risk of new punishments. The biblical allusions are overdetermined. The chapter is titled "Forty Days at Kengir." Israel wandered in the desert for forty years; Moses was on Mount Sinai for forty days and nights. In describing the hunger strikers' feeling of solidarity, Solzhenitsyn's language jarringly combines legal, religious, and Soviet diction, with its characteristic emphasis on the collective: "This was a law that was also unstudied—the law of the general inspiration of mass feeling, in spite of every rationality" *(zakon obshchego vzleta massovogo chuvstva)* (5:273).

The Gulag Archipelago not only describes the rebirth of a new collective; it attempts to enact this process in its readers. Solzhenitsyn founds his alternative law by symbolically wounding the body of the reader, who has no experience of the Gulag in the flesh. Reading the *Gulag* means submitting to a symbolic covenantal wounding by means of which we join the new chosen community.[33] We know we have gained membership when we are able to understand how the prison laborers excavating an archeological site at the Kolyma River could bring themselves to eat the frozen remains of a prehistoric salamander. When we comprehend that degree of starvation we become one with the inmates of the Gulag. In order to do so we must read the entirety of Solzhenitsyn's work and go back to the beginning. The structure of our reading mirrors the structure of religious conversion. The sinner returns to the beginning of his or her life with newfound knowledge.

---

33. Pervukhin also speaks of the "transformation" that Solzhenitsyn "expects" in the reader. See "Experiment in Literary Investigation," 500.

The reading of the *Gulag* produces the change in the reader. The Gulag formed the "tribe of zeks"; the *Gulag* tries to form a new community of readers.

The **Gulag** *as Monument*

In order to see more fully how the *Gulag* works on the reader, we must consider its formal qualities, one of the most obvious of which is its size. Solzhenitsyn's work is nearly eighteen hundred pages long. The scale of the suffering it describes, the numbers of individuals killed, is also enormous. But there need not be a relation of proportionality between an artwork and what it represents. Shalamov's *Kolyma Tales* are miniatures. The significance of the *Gulag*'s size must therefore lie elsewhere, not as "natural" result of its content. The meaning of the *Gulag*'s scale has to do with its aesthetic principle, which in part derives from socialist realism. As Igor Golomstock points out, Soviet architecture in the Stalin period emphasized enormity. Moscow State University is an example. The Palace of Soviets, which was never completed, was to have been the tallest building in the world. Golomstock writes: "The dimensions of this kind of architecture, rather than being based on the individual, were calculated from some super-personal point of view."[34] As we discussed earlier, Averbakh's theory of prisoner rehabilitation, which was itself informed by the art theory of its time, required that the prisoner's consciousness be transformed by "concentrated labor on gigantic objects, would shock the imagination by their grandeur." Solzhenitsyn's eighteen-hundred-page work also shocks the imagination—of the reader—with its enormity.

It is quite common to speak of *The Gulag Archipelago* as a monument to the dead. In an article for the *New York Review of Books* in October 1995, Tatyana Tolstaya, one of the best-known contemporary Russian writers, observes that in *The Gulag Archipelago* Solzhenitsyn "created a monument to the millions of innocent people who perished in the camps."[35] By examining more closely how monuments work, we gain a clearer understanding of how Solzhenitsyn's text works on the

---

34. Golomstock, *Totalitarian Art*, 281.

35. Tatyana Tolstaya, "Russian Lessons," rev. of *"The Russian Question" at the End of the Twentieth Century*, by Alexander Solzhenitsyn, *New York Review of Books*, October 19, 1995, 9.

reader. The text, in striving for monumental stature, seeks to create itself as an authoritative narrative of foundation.

The framing devices call attention to the text's monumental function. The *Gulag Archipelago* begins with an elaborate set of such devices. The first volume, containing parts 1 and 2, published in Paris in 1973, opens with a remark from the author about why he withheld publication of his work: "With constraint in my heart I withheld from publication for years." This remark, printed in boldface, comes before the title page. After the title page there is a dedication to the dead, printed as a prose poem, with each phrase on a separate line. The opening word is in uppercase letters: "I DEDICATE" (*POSVIASHCHAIU*). Then on two facing pages comes the author's account of his reading an article about excavations on the Kolyma River, printed in small type. The disclaimer about the factual status of the work, printed in boldface, follows on the next page. The author then acknowledges the 227 people, whose names he cannot mention, who supplied him with material for his study. He also mentions other published memoirs and stories of the Gulag, including those by Varlam Shalamov and Evgeniia Ginzburg. Next comes the triptych of photographs of Solzhenitsyn, and then finally part 1 begins. We can note immediately the strong visual qualities of the frame, especially in the juxtaposition of the different typefaces. The reader has to traverse a certain distance to get to the work itself.

There is another kind of distance that the work creates between itself and the reader. Because it is a monument to the millions who died in the camps, very few readers approach *The Gulag Archipelago* as a literary text with formal properties. Sidney Monas and Natalya Pervukhina, whose work I have already discussed, Vera Carpovich's "*The Gulag Archipelago*, Volume One: Notes on Its Lexical Peculiarities," and Alexander Schmemann's "Reflections on *The Gulag Archipelago*" may be cited as exceptions.[36] Schmemann, whose writing on Solzhenitsyn is for the most part concerned with the author's religious philosophy, gives another reason for this absence. He, like many others, both at the time of the book's original publication in the West in 1974, and its more recent first publication in Russia in 1989, calls the book "an *event*" (522).

---

36. See Vera Carpovich, "*The Gulag Archipelago*, Volume One: Notes on Its Lexical Peculiarities," and Alexander Schmemann, "Reflections on *The Gulag Archipelago*," in *Aleksandr Solzhenitsyn: Critical Essays and Documentary Materials*, ed. John B. Dunlop, Richard Haugh, and Alexis Klimoff, 2d ed. (New York: Macmillan, 1975), 527–33 and 515–26.

Lidiia Chukovskaia, a prominent Russian literary critic, writing in 1974, declared the book's publication to be an "event" comparable to the death of Stalin.[37] The 1989 publication of the *Gulag* in Russia has been similarly characterized, but this time comparable to the "colossal" events of perestroika and glasnost.[38] It seems petty to be concerned with the literary properties of a work that attains the extraliterary stature of an event. Ironically, Solzhenitsyn, who attacks "modernists" in the *Gulag*, achieves what the Russian avant-garde only hoped for: his book reaches beyond art to history. The aesthetics of his book share the aesthetics of the avant-garde and the socialist realist art of the 1930s and beyond.

As an event, Solzhenitsyn's book creates a magic circle around itself. It cannot be touched; it surrounds itself in the aura of the sacred. To go near it is to be changed by it, as we have seen. Roy Medvedev describes the experience of reading the *Gulag*: "No one will, I believe, rise from his chair after reading this book the same as he sat down to open it at page 1."[39] Reading the work, we leave the time frame of the historical and enter the realm of the eternal. We are asked to undergo the spiritual rebirth of its author. Schmemann writes that Solzhenitsyn appears as "a *martyr* in the deep and original meaning of this word: a *witness* to something great and high, pure and irreducible in man" (522). The distancing, the sacred aura, and the cyclical structure of initiation all help to construct the work as an act of founding, mysterious and awesome.

What is being described—the horror of the camps—and what is being founded—Solzhenitsyn's new Israel—surpass the imagination and comprehension of the single individual. What the work does cannot be represented. In the framing devices, Solzhenitsyn alludes repeatedly to the theme of the unrepresentable. He dedicates his work to the dead, of whom he asks forgiveness for not seeing everything, not remembering everything, and not guessing at everything. He cannot fulfill his debt to them because of the remainder of the not seen, not remembered, and not guessed at things, and therefore he asks forgiveness, that is, release from his debt. The dead, of course, cannot answer.

---

37. Chukovskaia, "Breakthrough," in Dunlop, Haugh, and Klimoff, *Aleksandr Solzhenitsyn*, 456.

38. S. Zalygin, "God Solzhenitsyna," *Novyi mir* 1990, no. 1 (January): 238.

39. Roy Medvedev, "On Solzhenitsyn's *The Gulag Archipelago*," in Dunlop, Haugh, and Klimoff, *Aleksandr Solzhenitsyn*, 460.

The work in its entirety is a breach of contract, a violation of the law that Solzhenitsyn made between himself and the living and the dead. It is a breach because, as Solzhenitsyn tells us in the closing frame to part 7, it can never be finished. There will always be something more to say. Here again the law comes to his rescue—not the law of the state, but "the laws of proportion," which the work is already in danger of violating:

> Let me not be accused of incompleteness: there is no end to the supplements. . . . But there are laws of proportion. . . . to add one bit more would topple the whole structure. (581)

These comments are included in an afterword to the afterword, which already indicates how the work exceeds its boundaries. The author's obligation and obedience to the laws of aesthetics release him from his obligations to his fellow inmates. But a surfeit of debt remains, and with it, guilt.

In the framing device to part 2, which contains his history of the operation of the camps, Solzhenitsyn writes that "what ought to find a place in this part—is immeasurable" (2:8). To paraphrase, in order to describe everything that takes place in the camps, to grasp it all, one would have to spend several lifetimes there, but lasting even one lifetime is impossible without special privileges. His perspective cannot be that of one posted at a watchtower. What must be represented escapes the categories of understanding, that is, the categories of time and space. The Gulag is infinite. As we have seen, the author's representation of his conversion experience culminates in a new understanding of religion and history. But the Gulag shatters the certainty and totality of the author's knowledge.

The all-pervasive theme of the unrepresentable makes the individual reader feel dwarfed.[40] The writer and reader of the *Gulag* share a similar feeling of individual powerlessness. These conditions and effects, taken together, permit us to see this text as a particular form of the sublime.[41] When an idea presents itself that surpasses the capacity

---

40. For another discussion of the significance of the unrepresentable, see Mikhail Yampolsky, "In the Shadow of Monuments: Notes on Iconoclasm and Time," trans. John Kachur, in *Soviet Hieroglyphics: Visual Culture in Late Twentieth-Century Russia*, ed. Nancy Condee (Bloomington: Indiana University Press), 94–95.

41. For a discussion of Kant's sublime upon which my simplistic account relies, see

of the imagination, we feel a lack or absence. But in that very lack, we feel ourselves to be bound together with our fellow humans. We are propelled by this gap toward something that is larger than ourselves. The theme of the unrepresentable in Solzhenitsyn's text serves to bind individual readers together. In contrast, the icons of Soviet culture, its massive architecture, the pumped-up bodies of its worker heroes and heroines, the gigantic constructions that Averbakh describes, attempt to fill in the gaps of the unrepresentable, to embody in the here and now that heaven on earth promised by the revolution.[42]

In the third volume, in a chapter devoted to the forced collectivization of the peasantry, Solzhenitsyn once again discusses the problem of representation:

> Yes, I know that here what is needed is not a chapter, and not the book of a single individual. And I cannot even compose a thorough chapter. But nevertheless I will begin. I will place it as a sign, as a mark, as the first small stones, if only so that the place will be indicated for a newly restored cathedral to Christ the Savior. (6:368)

The Cathedral of Christ the Savior was destroyed under Communist rule. The never-completed Palace of Soviets, a building designed to celebrate the founding of the new Soviet order, was to stand in its place. In an article investigating the cultural significance of monuments in post-perestroika Russia, Mikhail Yampolsky shows that the destruction of the cathedral held particular significance for the establishment of Soviet legitimacy. The founding of the Soviet state, touted as a radical break with the past, "paradoxically demands a forerunner." The erection of a new monument in place of the old "instantly creates the illusion of continuity, organizes a genealogy, and introduces into the consciousness the very concept of a founder-father" (102). Solzhenitsyn's text, the verbal equivalent of a monument, operates in a similar fashion by offering itself in place of what was destroyed, and thereby linking itself to the religious tradition. The Soviet monument was a false substitute for the Cathedral of Christ the Savior, but Solzhenitsyn's work is the true substitute, the copy that is truest to the original.

Jean-François Lyotard, *The Differend: Phrases in Dispute,* trans. Georges Van Den Abbeele (Minneapolis: University of Minnesota Press, 1988), 164–67.

42. According to Lyotard, describing an idea as an object available for observation is a totalitarian way of thinking. See ibid., 5.

The act of founding depends on an act of violation. In the opening frame, the author speaks of himself as suspended between two debts: one to the living and one to the dead. The two debts contradict each other. The debt to the dead requires speech, requires that the silence surrounding the Gulag be broken. But the debt to the living, which outweighs the debt to the dead, requires silence. If Solzhenitsyn allows their testimonies to be published, he will endanger their lives. The author is in a double bind. He cannot found his new Israel without violating his obligations to those whom he seeks to memorialize. Ironically, the KGB provides a remedy and breaks the deadlock. When the book is confiscated, the debt to the living is canceled and Solzhenitsyn publishes his work. Later, in part 3, Solzhenitsyn emphasizes his indebtedness: "I write this book only out of an awareness of debt" (3:209–10).

Conclusion

The Gulag Archipelago has been hailed as an event. Yet the book stops short of representing itself as having completed anything. The author's personal testimony, his account of his experience of religious rebirth, emphasizes the closure and finality of his newfound certainty and knowledge. But this certainty is short-lived. The author's own spiritual rebirth does not lead to a new finalized condition of certainty or wholeness. Stories of how the author reinflicts the wound of the Gulag on himself follow his account of his religious conversion. The *Gulag* leaves innumerable gaps in its report, for which the author repeatedly asks forgiveness. To put it another way, there are no utopian moments in the *Gulag*. This lack is a necessary part of the law that Solzhenitsyn seeks to impose, a part of his testament. *Doing* means wounding; binding together depends on cutting into the heart of the reader and leaving a scar there. Healing, wounding, and rewounding are inextricably linked. Giving voice to the testimony that had previously been silenced, remembering, and thereby being rejoined to the new community means being separated from the old, albeit false one.

The testimony of suffering that we have traced, the testimony of religious conversion, and Solzhenitsyn's testament pull at each other in different directions. Solzhenitsyn cannot claim mastery over his subject. At the center of this massive work, which strives for monumentality, there is an ellipsis. There is no end, Solzhenitsyn tells us, to the supplements that could be added to it. Out of the work there emerges an image of its author broken and remade, but always scarred by the Gulag and by the writing of the *Gulag*.

In the afterword the author provides a history of the material conditions of the writing of his book:

> It is necessary to explain: there was not a single time that this whole book, with all of its parts, lay on one table. In the very heat of work on the *Archipelago* in September 1965, I was threatened with the destruction of my archive and the arrest of the novel. At that time the parts of the *Archipelago* that were already written and the materials for other parts scattered in different directions and were no longer gathered together. I wrote down where something had to be checked or deleted, and with these lists traveled from one place to another. (579–80)

Solzhenitsyn characterizes the work in general as unpolished and adds that it has a "spasmodic" quality because of these conditions. In imperial Russia, extraordinary crimes were sometimes punished by quartering the criminal. In Soviet Russia the body of the book suffers a similar fate. Solzhenitsyn ends this afterword with a plea to those readers who have the requisite knowledge to complete what he could not. In chapter 6, we will examine a theory of writing advanced by Derrida and Siniavskii that posits the author's separation from and lack of control over his or her text as a necessary condition of writing, imposed by forces in language. Here in Solzhenitsyn's history of the writing of the *Gulag* the separation and loss are realized in the most concrete way—by external political forces. The forced separation of the parts of Solzhenitsyn's book from each other and from him represent yet another example of the literalization that is part of the language of punishment. The history of the writing of the *Gulag* provides a fitting ending to the story of an author obsessed by the corporeality of letters and tormented by the violence they inflict on bodies.

Chapter 6

Siniavskii, Libel, and the Author's Liability

The trial and conviction of Iulii Daniel' and Andrei Siniavskii in 1966 is not a unique instance of the Soviet government's brutality toward its writers.[1] In 1964, the poet Joseph Brodsky was arrested. Without regular employment, Brodsky was in violation of the law requiring Soviet citizens to work. He was tried and sentenced to five years of hard labor on the charge of "parasitism." In the opening of the trial, the judge asked Brodsky to state his occupation. His answer—that he wrote poetry—provoked the following exchange:

Judge: Who identified you as a poet? Who ranked you as a poet?
Brodsky: No one. And who counted me as a human being?
Judge: Did you study this?
Brodsky: What?
Judge: Being a poet. Didn't you try to get a university education, where they prepare . . . where they teach . . .
Brodsky: I didn't think . . . I didn't think this is given by education.
Judge: By what then?
Brodsky: I think [looks dismayed] it's from God.[2]

This chapter is a revision of research that was first published as "The Case against Andrei Siniavskii: The Letter and the Law," *Russian Review* 53, no. 4 (October 1994): 549–60. Copyright 1994 Ohio State University Press. All rights reserved.

1. Catherine Nepomnyashchy's wonderful book on Siniavskii, *Abram Tertz and the Poetics of Crime* (New Haven, Conn.: Yale University Press, 1995) and my article contain several similar arguments, formulated independently, for example, the use of the term *habeas corpus,* discussions of Siniavskii and the criminality of art, and the importance of the concept of the realized metaphor. Nepomnyashchy has greatly enriched my reading of Siniavskii, and I will refer to her work throughout this chapter.

2. See Frida Vigdorova, "Pervyi sud nad Iosofom Brodskim," in *Luchshie publikatsii Ogonek 88 goda,* ed. L. Gyshchin, S. Kliamkin, and V. Iumashev (Ogonek, 1989), 263. Vigdorova, a journalist and writer, took notes during the trial; her transcript was one of the

Several observers have commented on the literary qualities of the trial. Lidiia Chukovskaia writes: "Life is a great artist, but seldom does it succeed in creating a phenomenon of such expressiveness and perfection."[3] A poet is put on trial not for anything he wrote, but because he is a poet. The court demands to know, as David Bethea puts it, who "authorized" his poetry.[4] The poet finds authorization in God. The exchange reveals a confrontation between two seemingly diametrically opposed forces: on one side law, official permission, procedure, certification, crime and punishment, and on the other side, poetry, God, and the hesitant, confused poet who says, perhaps not even seriously, that his poetry comes from God.

In 1966, two years after the Brodsky trial and one hundred years after the Suvorin case, the Soviet government tried and convicted two writers, Andrei Siniavskii and Iulii Daniel', on charges of attempting to weaken governmental authority. As in the Suvorin case, the two authors were prosecuted on the basis of evidence found in their literary texts, primarily works of fiction. To what extent their crime was a "crime of writing," in the special sense that Susan Stewart uses the term, that is, an "alternate form of authorial subjectivity" made punishable by the state—we shall explore in the pages that follow.

Before their arrests in 1965 Siniavskii was a literary critic and Daniel' a translator. In the Soviet Union, Siniavskii wrote on Mayakovsky, Babel, and other modern Russian writers and coauthored a book on Picasso. In 1959 a series of works began to appear in the West under Siniavskii's pseudonym, Abram Terts: an essay, "What Is Socialist Realism?"; a collection of short stories; two longer narratives entitled *The Trial Begins* and "Liubimov"; and a set of aphorisms, *Thoughts Unaware*. The pseudonym comes from the Jewish criminal world of Odessa in the 1920s, a fact that the prosecution made much of at Siniavskii's trial.[5] He was imprisoned for six years in Siberia. Far from ending with his imprisonment, however, Siniavskii's literary career as Terts blossomed. During the years 1966 to 1971 he wrote another collection of

---

earliest works to be circulated in samizdat. The remark in brackets is her description of Brodsky's appearance.

3. Lidiia Chukovskaia, "Sudilishche," in Gyshchin, Kliamkin, and Iumashev, *Luchshie publikatsii Ogonek 88 goda*, 262.

4. Bethea, *Joseph Brodsky*, 17.

5. See Nepomnyashchy, *Abram Tertz*, 1.

aphorisms *(A Voice from the Chorus)* and the controversial critical work *Strolls with Pushkin* and began working on *In the Shadow of Gogol.* In 1973 Siniavskii, together with his wife and their son, emigrated to France. Free from the political constraints of the Soviet literary process, Siniavskii published the works begun during his imprisonment, numerous essays, and a novel *Goodnight!* under his pseudonym, reserving "Siniavskii" for his more scholarly literary criticism. His study of Russian folklore, *Ivan-Durak,* is an example of the latter from 1991. As Catherine Nepomnyashchy observes, the pseudonym Terts, while "no longer a necessary cover . . . has come to entail a series of linguistic strategies and metaphors for the writer and writing."[6]

The content of the early Terts works and the fact of their publication abroad constituted the basis of the charge against Siniavskii. The tsarist government accused Suvorin of "libel" against the nobility; one hundred years later Siniavskii and Daniel' were accused of "libel" against the Soviet government. The charge is contained in article 70 of the Russian Criminal Code: "the dissemination, for the purpose of undermining or weakening Soviet power, of slanderous fabrications which defame the Soviet government and social system."[7] The most recent American equivalent of the Soviet law that convicted Daniel' and Siniavskii is the Sedition Act of 1798,[8] which ceased to have the force of law in 1801. We will come back to American libel law later in the chapter.

The Brodsky trial may be compared to a spare and elegant tragedy, written in the classical style, and performed without deviation from the plot. The exchange between the judge and Brodsky plays out a long-standing Russian scenario of the conflict between art and the state, in which the writer is the suffering vessel of the transcendent "word." As David Bethea puts it, "the charismatic poet . . . suffers in life for the sake

---

6. Ibid., 1–2.

7. Aleksandr Ginzburg, ed., *Belaia kniga po delu A. Siniavskogo i Iu. Danielia* (Frankfurt am Main: Possev-Verlag, 1967), 167.

8. The act made it a criminal offense to "publish . . . any false, scandalous, and malicious writing . . . against the government of the United States, or either house of the Congress . . . or the President . . . with intent to defame . . . or bring them . . . into contempt or disrepute; or to excite against them, or either or any of them, the hatred of the good people of the United States." Quoted in Richard Labunski, *Libel and the First Amendment: Legal History and Practice in Print and Broadcasting* (New Brunswick, N.J.: Transaction Books, 1987), 35.

of culture."[9] In contrast, the Siniavskii trial belongs to the genre of the fantastic. The performers, including the judge and the spectators, step in and out of their roles. For example, at one point the lights went out. One of the spectators asked the judge what to do, and he answered, "I am not an electrical repairman, but the judge." The trial and the campaign against Siniavskii in particular carries the Suvorin case to a fantastic extreme—to the extreme imagined in Akhsharumov's "juridical fiction," in which a fictitious character becomes "real" and tries to make her author pay for what his plot has done to her. The fictitious character who becomes real in the Siniavskii case is his pseudonym, Abram Terts.

In the 1866 Suvorin trial, as we have seen, the government denied that it was engaged in literary interpretation. The law must stand outside of what it judges. The same will hold true for the Siniavskii trial. As in the Suvorin trial, the prosecution will depend on, but deny, its involvement in a literary process. In a strange sort of habeas corpus the state will set in motion the fantastical transformation of a literary persona into a legal subject, bringing the persona before the court as if he had come to life in the body of the author. The state convicts and punishes Siniavskii as Terts.

In order to see how this transformation unfolds, it is necessary first to understand the government's argument in its own terms. Having described what the government calls "slanderous fabrications" in Siniavskii's work, we will be able to trace the underlying models of author and authority and the practices of reading that the government relies upon in order to make its case. I will show that the court's apparent simplicity, what can be called its literal-mindedness, is a deliberate strategy that serves to effect the transformation of Siniavskii into Terts.

The Crime

The case of Daniel' and Siniavskii was heard in the Supreme Court of the Russian Republic. The presiding judge was the internationally

---

9. See Bethea, *Joseph Brodsky*, 11. Bethea emphasizes the role of the people in the writer's suffering. Bethea points out that the repeated scenario of the writer's real suffering and death makes scholars of Russian literature "uncomfortable" with the poststructural model of the metaphorical "death of the author." It is my contention in this chapter that Siniavskii's writing is highly congenial to such a model.

known L. N. Smirnov. The prosecution was conducted by the assistant to the general procurator of the USSR and two specially appointed public prosecutors, both members of the Writer's Union. In his novel *Goodnight!* published after his emigration to France, Siniavskii compares the court to the jaws of hell, and the trial to a performance whose "plot" he ruins by not capitulating. The officials of the court, the judge, prosecutor, and his own defense lawyers come out of a Gogol story:

> They were all similar: in their proximity, reality disappeared. To this day, I have only to close my eyes to hear them start speaking, not in their own God-given voices. Like in a waxworks—you wouldn't believe it, was it for fun, or on purpose, in order to scare you?[10]

In the Soviet, as in the European, system, the judge plays an active role in a trial. The judge directly questions the accused and the witnesses on both sides. In this trial, none of the witnesses whom Daniel' requested was permitted to testify. Only one witness requested by the defense actually spoke in court.

Throughout the trial, the prosecution took Siniavskii's literary works to be nothing more than as a vehicle for his political views. For example, in his novella *The Trial Begins,* a character named Karlinskii describes a plan to develop the remains of human embryos produced by abortions as a food source. Canning factories could be established right next to the abortion clinics, and everything would be carried out, as Karlinskii says, "in accordance with Marxism." The prosecution singles out this particular phrase, suggesting that Siniavskii is attacking Marxism. Siniavskii argues that Karlinskii is a clearly negative character and goes on to say: "You have confused the hero with the author."[11] The judge goes on to another episode from *The Trial Begins.* Two individuals "in civilian clothes" discuss various devices to monitor the writing and thoughts of the inhabitants of Moscow. One would catch scraps of paper flushed down toilets and another, the "thought-o-scope," would track mental activity. The judge finds clear evidence of

---

10. Andrei Siniavskii [Abram Terts, pseud.], *Sobranie sochinenii v dvukh tomakh* (Moscow: Start, 1992), 2:366. Henceforward all references to this work will be given parenthetically by volume and page number.

11. Ginzburg, *Belaia kniga,* 225.

"libel" in this scene. "Doesn't this defame our society, our people, our system?" he asks.[12]

In order to follow the argument between the court and Siniavskii, we have to gain some familiarity with the novella in question. *The Trial Begins* has a complicated narrative structure. Set in the 1950s, on the eve of Stalin's death—as Siniavskii explains—it is told by a first-person narrator, called "the Writer," who appears most prominently in the opening and closing of the work. In the prologue the Writer is subjected to a search. His manuscripts are confiscated and the very letters are scraped from the pages. The letter z runs away but is caught and squashed under the fingernail of the KGB agent. The Writer makes intermittent appearances throughout the work, as for example, in the scene describing the "thought-o-scope." He is accused by the two agents of thinking something and admits his guilt. We read: "I won't deny it—I'm guilty. I am a despicable hireling of a certain foreign power." In the epilogue, the Writer and several of his characters end up in the Gulag in Kolyma. The Writer was charged on the grounds that he did not depict his positive heroes in a positive enough light, and that his negative characters did not repent their mistakes soon enough. At the real-life trial, the judge identified the figure of the Writer in Kolyma as the author Siniavskii. Siniavskii explained to the court that the "I" in the story is a "convention": neither Siniavskii nor Terts, but the "Writer." The scene in Kolyma is a fantasy on the part of the fictitious writer who lives under Stalin's fist in a state of "terror and rapture," as Siniavskii says.

The judge continued his effort to expose Siniavskii's politics. A protracted discussion of "Liubimov" ensued. The story chronicles how a whole town, the eponymous Liubimov, a provincial backwater, falls under the hypnotic control of a power-mad bicycle repairman, Lenia Tikhomirov, who discovered an old book of magic. There is little food in the town, and very little culture. Under the spell, the inhabitants of Liubimov greedily devour rotten cucumbers that they believe to be sausage. The judge found in Liubimov a negative, libelous portrait of the Soviet Union as a whole. He is troubled by the similarity between the first name of the repairman, Lenia, and the name *Lenin*, a similarity that had been pointed out by one of Siniavskii's translators. He also finds evidence of Siniavskii's negative attitude toward Lenin in the fantastical description of Lenin's nightly ritual of howling at the moon.

---

12. Ibid.

"Liubimov" is told by a first-person narrator, Savelii Kuz'mich Proferansov, Tikhomirov's confidante. The story contains many allusions to nineteenth-century Russian literature, including works by the satirist Saltykov-Shchedrin, Dostoevsky, and Pushkin. For example, in the opening, Tikhomirov usurps power from the general secretary of the municipal Communist power. The townspeople do not object: "the people are silent" *(narod bezmolvstvoval)* (1:22). This line is a direct quotation from Pushkin's *Boris Godunov,* a play about Russia's seventeenth-century dynastic crisis. Later we will see how this stylistic feature is counted as a form of literary criminality by the court.

Judge Smirnov's reading of "Liubimov" seems reasonable. However, his interpretation begs the question as to whether it is possible to attribute criminal intention on the part of the author on the basis of fantastical statements made by a fictitious character, even if the character is also the narrator of the work. The story itself challenges the process of attribution upon which Judge Smirnov's reading rests. It does so in part by creating a double of the narrator. In the opening of the narrative Savelii Kuz'mich denies responsibility for his writing:

> You write and you don't understand what is happening to you, and where all these words that you've never heard of and never thought to write are coming from. . . . I didn't do this! Honest, it's not me. . . . If I am brought before threatening judges, and my hands and feet are put in iron shackles, I warn you in advance: I will renounce everything. (1:18)

We learn that Savelii Kuz'mich is himself controlled by a mysterious figure with occult powers, his own ancestor, Samson Samsonovich Proferansov, who dictates the writing of "Liubimov." During several points in the story, Savelii attempts to regain control of his pen, which moves according to Samson's dictates. Small skirmishes erupt between the body of the text, in which Savelii protests his loss of control, and the footnotes, in which Samson urges Savelii to keep writing.

In the closing frame of "Liubimov," a mysterious "Author" appears to announce the approaching end of the story. The Author "races toward his goal" notwithstanding the "fruitless efforts of the heroes to prolong the burden of existence" (1:84). The work as a whole emphasizes the constructedness of the figure of the author. Again and again, the figure of the author is exposed as a device, a fiction. In chapter 2, we used Edward Said's term "molestation," the novelist's of the character's awareness of his "confinement to a fictive, scriptive realm." In "Liubimov," the sense of molestation is very strong: the reader is continually reminded of the fictive, scripted quality of the reality represented in the story. But at the trial, it seems to be lacking.

Like the judge in the Suvorin trial in 1866, the judge in the Siniavskii trial in 1966 argued that Savelii's recantation is tantamount to a confession of guilt on the part of Siniavskii. According to Judge Smirnov, the passage contains Siniavskii's own "fears and misgivings" and therefore indicates his awareness of his own wrongdoing.[13] Confession, the best form of evidence in Russia since the time of Peter the Great, lies at the surface of the text, plain for all to see. As in the Suvorin trial, the work, in speaking for itself, is made to pass sentence on itself.

In "Liubimov," the narrator Savelii is ventriloquized by Samson Samsonovich. Both are creations of the "author," who is the creation of "Terts," the creation of Siniavskii. "Savelii" is a mask of a mask of a mask in a series of regressions that by no means ends in the real-life Siniavskii. Play with the mask of the author is key to all of Siniavskii's Tertsian works. In "At the Circus" we find a passage in which a first-person narrator, a pickpocket, tells his victim:

> Instead of you, I will go to the "Kiev" restaurant and eat up your sardines and drink up all the cognac . . . on your tab, but to my complete pleasure. . . . You will think that I am a writer, a performer, a renown athlete. . . . But I am none other than a conjurer-manipulator. (1:116)

The author as trickster revels in his theft not just of another's property—"your money became ours"—but of the other's identity. In the Tertsian vision of the world, identity circulates as if it were cash.

"Graphomaniacs," a first-person narrative that tells the story of its own creation, is a particularly important example of the Tertsian play with identity. It depicts writing as a process by which identity is lost. The hero, a failed writer with the comical name of "Straustin," steals the idea for the story from another "graphomaniac," Galkin. For Galkin, writing is not a matter of "expressing the personality":

---

13. Ibid., 243.

Every writer is concerned with only one thing: self-dodgery [*sa-mo-us-tra-ne-ni-em*]! That's why we labor in the sweat of our brow ... with the hope of escaping, overcoming ourselves, giving access to the thoughts that hang in the air. . . . . It's not your property! (1:168)

The word *samoustranenie*, which in Galkin's credo signifies the writing subject's avoidance of itself, graphically represents the very process it describes. *Samoustranenie* figures the masking of the writing subject named Straustin, the hero of the story, by scrambling the letters *straus-* into *-ustra-*. In a further play on the theme of writing and impropriety, Galkin's credo enters into Straustin's delusion that his own works have been plagiarized by the great Russian writers of the twentieth century. What Siniavskii imagines as Tertsian play is taken literally by the state, which interprets the subtitle of "Graphomaniacs," "From Stories of My Life," to refer to the real historical person Siniavskii.

"Graphomaniacs" was published in 1960. In a speech given in 1988 Siniavskii invokes the same themes of the noncoincidence of the writer with the self and the importance of "estrangement" for art. "Estrangement" or "defamiliarization" refers to the concept developed by the Russian Formalist critic Viktor Shklovsky in the early 1920s. According to Shklovsky, conventional forms of representation make our perception of phenomena automatic. The purpose of artistic language, which according to the Formalists is separate from the language of everyday life, is to stimulate and prolong the reader's perception of phenomena.[14] In the speech, titled "In Praise of Emigration," Siniavskii uses the formalist term *ostranenie* for "defamiliarization" and not the exaggerated and comical *samoustranenie*. In the speech, Siniavskii says that in distinction from other émigrés, he feels no "nostalgia." Prison cured him of that, "or more precisely, the sensation, that you, as a person, do not belong to yourself."[15] The effect of writing and the effect of incarceration are similar. Writing, like prison, dislocates the stable subject. Perhaps that is one of the reasons that in *Goodnight!* Siniavskii compares Lefortovo, the Moscow prison, to prose. As we will see, the emphasis

---

14. For a discussion of defamiliarization, see Victor Erlich, *Russian Formalism: History-Doctrine*, 3d ed. (New Haven, Conn.: Yale University Press, 1965), 176–80.

15. Siniavskii, "Rech' pri vruchenii priemii 'Pisatel' v izgnanii' Bavarskoi Akademii iziashchnykh iskusstv," December 1988, reprinted in *Stolitsa* 40 (1992): 50.

on the autonomy of artistic language is crucial to Siniavskii's defense at his trial.

Who Is the Author? Who Is Speaking?

The Tertsian persona is always one of imposture. The state tries to pin it down. The government's basic goal, both in the court proceedings and in the press campaign, is to settle the question of true and false identity. The court attempts to unmask the pseudonym, which it views as evidence of guilt. The opening interrogation of Daniel' reveals this strategy. The prosecutor charged that Daniel' was aware of the anti-Soviet direction of his works and out of a desire to conceal himself chose the pseudonym Nikolai Arzhak.[16] The prosecutor asked Daniel' the following question: "What works were written by you and when under the pseudonym?"[17] Daniel' corrected him, saying that works are not written under but published under a pseudonym. The prosecutor's apparent slip of the tongue and his quick acknowledgment—he changed "written" to "published"—suggest that the slip is deliberate. The prosecution meant to suggest that Daniel' and Siniavskii each became someone else when they wrote their allegedly "anti-Soviet" works. The personae of "Arzhak" and "Terts" took over Daniel' and Siniavskii, much in the same way that the narrator of "Liubimov" was taken over by his ancestor.

The campaign in the press elaborates and develops the prosecutor's lead. Iu. Feofanov, writing for *Izvestia*, uses the same locution: Daniel' and Siniavskii "*wrote* their libels under pseudonyms" (emphasis added).[18] Another newspaper article goes a step further: the two did not merely "write" under pseudonyms; they "acted" under pseudonyms.[19] During the trial, Siniavskii argued that the use of a pseudonym in and of itself is not criminal: it is a "lawful literary phenomenon." Siniavskii takes the pseudonym out of the realm of action, in order to restore it to what he considers its rightful sphere, that of the literary phenomenon, which has its own autonomous "laws."

The government's re-creation of Siniavskii as Terts is a more radical reworking of identity than the comical struggle between the two fic-

---

16. Ginzburg, *Belaia kniga*, 171.
17. Ibid., 175.
18. Ibid., 208.
19. Ibid., 216.

titious narrators in Terts's "Liubimov." The copy usurps the place of the original. Terts is no mere pseudonym of Siniavskii. Siniavskii is a pseudonym of Terts. The fundamental imposture of which Siniavskii is guilty, according to the state, is that he had, until his exposure, pretended to the role of legitimate Soviet critic, that is, according to Eremin, one who "actively participates in the building of communism" by revealing the "greatness" of its ideas."[20] As Vasil'ev, one of the public prosecutors, put it at the trial: "For some part of his time he gave himself out as a Soviet literary critic."[21] But he turns out to be Terts, an obscene Jewish hoodlum, who betrays his country with anti-Soviet literature published abroad. In his speech before the court, Prosecutor Temushkin says, "it turns out that Siniavskii is not Andrei Siniavskii, but Abram Terts."[22] Of course it is the state itself that construes the imposture by identifying the pseudonym Terts as the true identity of Siniavskii. In *Goodnight!* Siniavskii is shown "a memorandum ordering that he is to be called by his own pleasant name and patronymic exclusively out of politeness, out of the goodness of our security organs. . . . but he, a hireling of imperialism, a double-dealer, a turncoat [*perevertysh*] must himself understand that he is neither Andrei nor Donatovich, but the proven and inveterate traitor, Abram Terts" (2:346).

The state explicitly draws on and manipulates cultural and literary norms in re-creating Siniavskii as Terts. In the newspaper articles that were part of the state's campaign against Siniavskii and Daniel', and in the text of the trial itself, the two authors are accused of attacking the government, the party, the history of the nation, "the people and its ideals," mothers and the institution of motherhood, Chekhov and Pushkin, and human values in general. The state's invective against Siniavskii and Daniel' falls into an identifiable pattern, which calls upon a cultural reservoir of negative images, all having in common the motif of illicit substitution and transformation. To put it another way, the government's campaign relies on the semiotics of demonic imposture.

In 1966 Dmitrii Eremin titled his article against Siniavskii and Daniel' "Perevertyshi." As Olga Matich points out, the term originally

---

20. Dmitrii Eremin, "Perevertyshi," in *Tsena Metafory, ili prestuplenie i nakazanie Siniavskogo i Danielia*, ed. L. S. Eremina (Moscow: "Iunonoa," 1990), 22. The article was originally published in *Izvestia*, January 13, 1966.

21. Ginzburg, *Belaia kniga*, 284.

22. Ibid., 288.

meant "werewolf" but was used by Eremin to mean "turncoat."[23] Eremin also uses the term "oboroten'" to describe Siniavskii and Daniel'. *Oboroten'*, according to Dal', the nineteenth-century ethnographer, means one who is changed or changes himself into a wolf or other animals."[24] Eremin's term as a political accusation goes back to Stalinist times. In 1953, when a group of Soviet doctors were accused of murdering high officials, the humor magazine *Krokodil* ran an article suggesting that the suspects "knew how to change the expression in their eyes to give their wolves' souls a human aspect."[25] We can also hear perhaps the more distant echo of Sukhovo-Kobylin's policeman, Raspliuev, who says in the last play of the trilogy that all of Russia is inhabited by wolves and other animals who have turned into people. Stephanie Sandler shows that Eremin's article provides an image "not only of the traitor, the one who turns against . . . but also of one who is twisted, perverted." Sandler quotes Eremin's characterization of Daniel' and Siniavskii as writers who "rummage around in sexual and psycho-pathological 'problems' with sick voluptuousness."[26]

Dal' lists in his dictionary after *perevertysh*, the term used by Eremin to characterize Siniavskii and Daniel', the related term *pereverten*, which means "a baptized Yid, a Russified German, a Frenchified Russian."[27] Siniavskii was overtly charged with anti-Semitism in the newspaper campaign and during his trial. For example, the government prosecutor Temushkin, citing unnamed "experts," said that Terts's works were characterized by "Freudianism, anti-Semitism, sex, and the search for God."[28] That Siniavskii is charged simultaneously with "Freudianism" and anti-Semitism reveals that the latter claim is not to be taken too seriously. What is more serious, but more muted, is the government's charge that Siniavskii as Terts is a hidden Jew, and as such is an enemy of Russian culture. The newspaper represents Siniavskii's physical appearance in such a way as to empha-

---

23. Olga Matich, "Sinjavskij's Rebirth as Terc," *Slavic and East European Journal* 33 (1989): 57.

24. Vladimir Dal', *Tolkovyi slovar' velikorussskogo iazyka*, vol. 3 (Moscow: Gosudarstvennoe izdatel'stvo inostrannykh i natsional'nykh slovarei, 1955), 611.

25. Quoted in Louis Rapoport, *Stalin's War against the Jews: The Doctors' Plot and the Soviet Solution* (New York: Macmillan, 1990), 159.

26. Stephanie Sandler, "Sex, Death, and Nation in the *Strolls with Pushkin* Controversy," *Slavic Review* 51 (1992): 305.

27. Dal', *Tolkovyi slovar' velikorussskogo iazyka*, 38.

28. Ginzburg, *Belaia kniga*, 289–90.

size his resemblance to a stereotypically demonic figure. Feofanov reports Siniavskii as saying, "yes, the works listed, published abroad, I wrote and sent there" and adds a gesture not found in Ginzburg's notes. According to Feofanov, Siniavskii stroked "his big red beard" as he said this.[29]

The state's campaign against Siniavskii also charged him with the sin of demonic laughter. In her article published before the trial, which served as her speech to the court, Zoia Kedrina characterizes Terts's style as form of literary "parasitism":

> Torn from the flesh of the most varied of other authors' works, turned inside out and underhandedly tacked together into a motley and tattered blanket of anti-Sovietism, they characterize the creative persona of Abram Terts as that of a person brazenly parasiting on the literary inheritance.[30]

Kedrina's imagery lends a concrete physicality to the literary technique she describes. The literary devices of parallelism, allusion, and hidden quotation—as in the line from Pushkin in "Liubimov"—become grotesquely embodied in her language of the flesh. Kedrina's language transforms what Bakhtin describes as the rich and complex process of the novelistic transformation and appropriation of multiple language styles into a bloody and perverse act. Kedrina is herself guilty of the very literary borrowing she so abhors in Siniavskii. She is borrowing from the fantastical and grotesque world of Abram Terts.

Implicit in Kedrina's criticism is the admonition that the literary inheritance should be preserved intact, like Lenin's corpse in its mausoleum—a fitting description of the mythomonumentalizing of nineteenth-century classics by twentieth-century Soviets. Terts is a literary vulture who tears the flesh from the sacred relics by exposing and challenging the structure of prohibitions that surround their use. In "What Is Socialist Realism" Siniavskii writes, "Gorky knew that everything that is other than God is the Devil."[31] According to the poet Blok, whom Siniavskii quotes, irony manifests itself as "attacks of exhausting laugh-

29. Ibid., 267.

30. Ibid., 110.

31. Andrei Siniavskii [Abram Terts, pseud.], "Chto takoe sotsialisticheskii realizm," in *Fantasticheskii mir Abrama Tertsa* (New York: Inter-Language Literary Associates, 1967), 430.

ter, beginning with a diabolically mocking, provocative smile and ending with violence and blasphemy."[32] For Siniavskii, Blok's definition of
irony is "the laughter of the superfluous individual at himself and at
everything that is sacred in the world."[33] Neither eighteenth-century
neoclassicism nor twentieth-century socialist realism with its positive
hero can tolerate this sort of laughter. Mayakovsky could no sooner
laugh at Lenin than Derzhavin, the eighteenth-century poet and states-
man could "ironize the empress" (Catherine the Great). Siniavskii continues: "But Pushkin wrote indecent verse even to the chaste and pure
Tatyana."[34]

In a speech made in 1881 Dostoevsky apotheosized Pushkin as
Russia's savior and prophet and characterized Tatyana, the heroine of
Pushkin's *Eugene Onegin* as the model of virtuous Russian woman-
hood. Pushkin became Russia's national poet. This image of Pushkin
became enshrined in Soviet culture. Siniavskii's hint that there was
an erotic side to Pushkin's writing troubled the prosecutor. He
charged Siniavskii with offending the "radiant name of Lenin" *(svet-*
loe imia Lenina) and, along the way, offending Pushkin as well.[35] The
question about Pushkin reveals a continuity between the Suvorin and
Siniavskii trials. In both cases, the prosecution and the defendants
engage in contestation about who Pushkin is, and who may claim to
inherit his legacy.[36] The prosecutor's charge that Siniavskii offends

---

32. A. Blok, "Ironia," quoted in ibid., 433.

33. Siniavskii, "Chto takoe sotsialisticheskii realizm."

34. Ibid.

35. "Utrennee zasedanie 11 fevralia," in Ginzburg, *Belaia kniga,* 237. The prosecutor
is A. P. Temushkin.

36. The title of one of the newspaper articles, "Slanderers" (Klevetniki) echoes the
title of Pushkin's poem "To the Slanderers of Russia" (Klevetnikam Rosii). This theme
resurfaces with particular virulence in what is referred to as Siniavskii's "third trial," the
controversy surrounding his *Strolls with Pushkin,* and the campaign against him in the
conservative press. Siniavskii wrote this work in the camps in the form of letters to his
wife. It was published under the pseudonym Terts in 1989. In the work, Terts debunks the
myth of Pushkin, emphasizing the role of parody and the erotic in his writing. Pushkin's
skill at imitating and appropriating the voices of other poets, which Dostoevsky had
lauded as Pushkin's all-embracing love for humanity, appears in Terts as something
closer to vampirism. In the late 1980s, Igor Shafarevich, a mathematician and dissident
who had published together with Solzhenitsyn, began to promulgate an extreme form of
Russian chauvinism. Shafarevich's response to *Strolls with Pushkin* closely resembles the
language of the trial in 1966. Shafarevich described *Strolls with Pushkin* as "filthy tittering
at the most radiant name in Russian culture." Control over the Pushkin story is a point of
contention between the writer and the law—not only the law of the government but the
unofficial laws promulgated by Russia's self-proclaimed cultural commissars. See Igor'
Shafarevich, "Fenomenon emigratsii," *Literaturnaia Rossiia,* 8 September 1989.

Pushkin and Lenin confirms the Tertsian vision of the culture of socialist realism. What Terts says in "What Is Socialist Realism?" about Soviet culture's intolerance of laughter is enacted at Siniavskii's trial. In "What Is Socialist Realism" the narrator gives a list of canonical nineteenth-century authors that includes Maupassant, Balzac, and Tolstoy, but then stumbles over one name: "what's his name, Che, Che, Che . . . oh yes, Chekhov." At the trial, the judge asks for an explanation of the stuttered "Che, Che, Chekhov," and when Siniavskii replies that this is "obvious irony," the spectators in the hall call out "it's obvious anti-Sovietism."[37] The Soviet state confers the name Chekhov with the status of the sacred. *Chekhov* signifies the glory of Russian culture and the touching concern of the Soviet state for the "little man." The sign *Chekhov* is less important as a reference to the author of *Uncle Vanya*, for example, than it is as an emblem of state power. To play with it, to engage the arbitrariness of the sign, is blasphemous, or, anti-Soviet.

As is fitting for a literary critic, Kedrina adds a literary reference to the cultural reservoir of devalued and negative images used to discredit Siniavskii and Daniel'. The speech she reads in the courtroom contains her article published in the literary newspaper. The article is titled "The Inheritors of Smerdiakov." Smerdiakov is the fourth and illegitimate brother in Dostoevsky's *The Brothers Karamazov*. Kedrina makes a rhetorical move characteristic of the trial in general. She imagines Smerdiakov not as Dostoevsky's fictitious creation, but as the creator of literary works:

> If Dostoevsky had not created Smerdiakov, putting into his image all of the force of his hatred for corrupters of the human spirit, but if Smerdiakov himself wrote novels, generalizing the phenomena of life from his Smerdiakovian position, we could without difficulty establish a direct relationship between Terts and such a "tradition."[38]

Kedrina could have chosen to establish a lineage between a negatively valued *author* and Siniavskii. But her emphasis is on Smerdiakov, a fictitious being whom she makes real in Terts, that is, Siniavskii. Furthermore, while Dostoevsky is not Smerdiakov, Terts-Siniavskii is "insepa-

---

37. "Utrennee zasedanie 11 fevralia," 233.
38. Ginzburg, *Belaia kniga*, 111–12.

rable from the vileness that his characters inhabit" and from Daniel'
and Siniavskii as a pair:

> there is no limit to the moral fall and decay which these worthy
> inheritors of Smerdiakov would fear in their effort to besmirch and
> trample all that is human in the Soviet person: friendship, love,
> motherhood, the family.[39]

Smerdiakov hates Russia and wishes Napoleon had conquered it,
despises Russian folk speech and literature; he resembles a eunuch, is
unclean; he "comes from the bathhouse rot" and suffers from epilepsy,
a disease associated with demonic possession. For the Soviet state,
Smerdiakov is perfect twin to Siniavskii; he is the consummate image of
all the "perversions" of which Siniavskii is accused: political, sexual,
and supernatural.

There is, however, one more flaw in Smerdiakov that cannot be
acknowledged, because it too closely mirrors the state's own strategy of
deliberate literal-mindedness. Smerdiakov is too literal-minded to read
literature. He cannot suspend his disbelief and complains that Gogol's
stories are untrue. He cannot understand poetic language, because, as
he says, no one speaks in rhyme. Finally, Smerdiakov literalizes Ivan's
hypothesis that "all is permissible."

The government's goal is to unmask Siniavskii as an impostor. In
pursuit of this goal, it deploys a set of tropes and metonymies well
established in Russian and Soviet culture. The Jew, the parasite, and the
traitor form one associative chain, to which Kedrina adds the new link
of Smerdiakov. Another, positive associative chain runs from Pushkin
to Lenin and the party in general. Siniavskii, in response, does not
directly confront the government's smear tactics by professing his loyalty. Instead, he stands back and analyzes them. We can say, using a
term from Russian Formalism, that he "lays bare the device." Siniavskii
names the hidden operation by means of which the state creates the
illusion that he is Terts. He calls it the realization of a metaphor.

Siniavskii into Terts: The Realization of a Metaphor

During his trial Siniavskii was asked what he meant by writing "Stalin
realized Lenin's metaphors." He answered:

---

39. Ibid., 112.

If we realize metaphors, there will be complete chaos. We say "it's raining" [*dozhd' idet*, literally, "rain is coming"] "a meteor shower" [*zvezdy padaiut*, literally, "stars fall"] and so forth. Lenin spoke of the enemies of our ideas, he used metaphor. Stalin realized the metaphors, and thus began the horrors of 1937. Stalin turned the metaphors inside out, but Lenin is not responsible for Stalin, just as language is not responsible for the realization of metaphors.[40]

In his later work *Soviet Civilization* (1988), Siniavskii explains. Lenin used terms like "agents of the bourgeoisie" to describe the Mensheviks, but, according to Siniavskii, did not believe that they "were literally in the pay of the world bourgeoisie." Stalin acted as if they were. If when we say "the rain is coming" we "imagine the rain strolling across bridges, striding through puddles . . . the result is a live grotesque—not unlike what happened to Lenin's metaphors in the 1930s."[41] The state's "device" of the realized metaphor is key to Siniavskii's understanding of the Stalinist epoch as a whole.[42] In the 1988 work, Siniavskii attributes some greater degree of responsibility to Lenin than earlier at his trial. According to Solzhenitsyn, however, Lenin's metaphors were realized during his own lifetime at the Solovki concentration camp. Siniavskii's perplexing near absolution of Lenin bears the traces of the revolutionary Romanticism of his childhood.

Siniavskii sees his own trial as a continuation of the Stalinist epoch, as the realization, or the making literal, of a metaphor. A metaphor is, among other things, a word used in such a way that its referential status is suspended. In saying "you are the sun, the moon, and the stars," I do not assert that you are the same as those real entities. Similarly, the "I" spoken by a fictional character does not refer to anyone in the real world who says "I." If we assert that the hero's "I" is the same as the author's "I," in other words, that the hero's "I" has the author as its referent, we are making a mistake that resembles the mistake of taking "the sun, the moon, and the stars" in the previous sentence to be meant to refer to the real heavenly bodies that bear those names. This mistake can be called literal-mindedness, even though the hero's "I" is not a metaphor.

40. Ginzburg, *Belaia kniga*, 239.

41. Andrei Siniavskii, *Soviet Civilization: A Cultural History,* trans. Joanne Turnbill (New York: Little, Brown, 1988), 88.

42. See Catherine Theimer Nepomnyashchy, "An Interview with Andrei Sinyavsky," *Formations* 6, no. 1 (spring 1991): 19–20. I am grateful to Cathy for pointing this out to me.

In his closing statement Siniavskii says that the trial itself could come right out of Terts's dark underground: "Here, truly, in a very terrible and unexpected way, the artistic image loses its imaginary quality and begins to be taken literally."[43] To put it differently, the fiction is being made to have referential status by being enacted in the real world. In order to pursue its goal of fixing identity and unmasking Siniavskii's imposture, the state forces the word—his own word, phantasmagoric and unreal—to take on flesh at his trial. In *Goodnight!* for example, Siniavskii writes that riding in the car to prison, his "dark hero" Terts mocks and comforts him by reminding him of "all those comparisons, metaphors, that had to be brought to conclusion, to the truth, for which the author, naturally, ought to pay with his head" (2:346).

In "What Is Socialist Realism" Siniavskii describes Soviet culture as fundamentally "teleological." Every action is evaluated according to whether it advances or undermines the purpose of building communism. Siniavskii quotes the very familiar revolutionary slogan, "Who is not with us is against us,"[44] the origin of which can be found in Jesus' saying "He who is not with me is against me" (Matt. 12:30). To be either for or against are the only possibilities: there can be no "neutral sphere." One can be either with God, "or with Satan, go to heaven or to hell."[45] In *Ivan the Fool* (Syntaxis, 1991) his profession of faith in the Russian people (whom he is accused of hating), Siniavskii argues that the laughter deployed by the fools and thieves of Russian folk culture is in its own way an artistic practice that has no purpose other than its own aesthetic pleasure, even though it was perceived as demonic by ecclesiastical and secular authorities. In making this argument, Siniavskii retroactively makes a case for his own artistic embodiment as a third term, a tertium quid, or, in other words, an Abram Terts.[46]

The question is whether this third term is possible. Siniavskii tries to delimit a space outside the either/or of Soviet culture; at the trial, the prosecution sought to reinscribe that separate artistic realm back within the realm over which the law adjudicated. As we will see in the concluding sections of this chapter, this aspect of Siniavskii's struggle with

---

43. Ginzburg, *Belaia kniga*, 301.

44. Siniavskii, "Chto takoe sotsialisticheskii realizm," 429.

45. Ibid., 413.

46. In a series of essays published in 1992, Iu. Lotman, who characterizes Russia's image of itself as fundamentally binary, juxtaposes this self-image to that of cultures in the West, whose self-understanding is *ternary*. See *Kul'tura i vzryv* (Moscow: Gnosis, 1992).

the law is not unique to Russia or the Soviet Union. I will argue more generally that literature and the law each attempt to define a realm outside the other's jurisdiction. During the trial, was asked to explain what he meant in "What Is Socialist Realism" by comparing the West and the Soviet Union with the line: "What sort of freedom from God could the believer want?" Siniavskii answers that for the "teleological individual" there is no free choice. Soviet writers face no question about a choice. "Either you believe or, if not, [looking at the bench where the defendants sit] sit in prison." His words and his gestures are significant. The gesture of looking at the defendants' bench indicates that for Siniavskii the trial itself as it is unfolding at the moment confirms his vision of the teleology of Soviet culture. The gesture also indicates a playful mark of authorship. Everything that takes place at the trial is being quoted from his own script, performed according to his directions. Ironically, Terts the hoodlum, the anti-Soviet, the parasite—this figure authors, founds, and authorizes the terms of Siniavskii's trial. The gesture teasingly contests Judge Smirnov's authority over the proceedings.

The concept of the realized metaphor may derive in part from the theater of Vladimir Mayakovsky, the revolutionary poet and playwright about whom Siniavskii writes in his officially authorized literary criticism. In his experimental theater performances Mayakovsky used sets as "realized metaphors." For example, in one production, the metaphor of sinners roasting in hell was realized on the stage with giant frying pans. In his play from 1913, *Vladimir Mayakovsky*, the poet, playing himself, is surrounded by an adoring crowd, who bring him their tears and shower him with kisses. The "tears" were represented by sacks of various sizes covered in foil; the "kisses" were the same foil covered sacks shaped like pursed lips.[47] The process of making conventional phrases crudely concrete and literal was to serve the function of scandalizing "bourgeois" theater in order to refashion it, to generate more artistic forms, and in so doing to make art—and life—anew. The line between "art" and "life" in Mayakovsky is far from clear, as Siniavskii and Jakobson point out.[48] The realization of the metaphor at

---

47. See B. Rostotskii, "Teatral'nyi debiut Vladimira Maiakovskogo" *Teatr* 7 (October 1937): 117, and more generally 111–18.

48. Siniavskii writes of the Futurists' desire, as he puts it, "to turn art into life and life into art" (*Soviet Civilization*, 42). His characterization of Mayakovsky's work steers clear of any direct link between it and Mayakovsky's life and death, an avoidance which may be traced to his insistence on the separation between artistic language and everyday

Siniavskii's trial serves another purpose. The transformation of Siniavskii into Terts the criminal freezes the play with signs, the play with
the marks of authority and authorship that are characteristic of Terts's
literary imposture. It is another forced embodiment, kindred to the
branding of the criminal in prereform Russia, and part and parcel of the
Gulag system of punishment.

The Defense: No One Is Speaking

To recapitulate, the government constructed a chain of equivalences
between hero, pseudonym, and author with the goal, or telos, of fixing
identity. Siniavskii's defense disconnected the links in the chain and
put them back into play. To some extent, the Siniavskii trial replays the
Suvorin trial. In 1866, Suvorin said that he was "identified" by the government with the characters of his tale, but that in his opinion, such
identification was "pointless," because if it were applied to all writers,
there would not remain a "single book or a single author whom it
would be impossible to call a criminal." Suvorin lists as examples
Pushkin, Griboedov, and Gogol. One hundred years later, those who
came to Siniavskii's defense said the same thing. The linguist Viach-
eslav Ivanov, for example, patiently explained (in a "declaration" to the
Legal Advice Office) that most of Abram Terts's works are written in
the *skaz* style, in which the "narration is conducted by a hero who in no
way coincides with the author."[49] Siniavskii himself, in his final statement before the court, recited what he called the "elementary abc's" of
literature: "the word is not a deed, but a word; the author is not identical to the hero."[50]

It seems that at various moments in the trial, Judge Smirnov
understood the lesson. He said quite directly, "Of course I understand
that the author's discourse and the character's discourse are different
things."[51] His concession did not amount to much, given the far-reaching implications of Siniavskii's claims, and that is perhaps why he was

---

life. Jakobson confronts the issue more directly. He writes: "Is there anyone of us who
doesn't share the impression that the poet's volumes are a kind of scenario in which he
plays out the filmed story of his life?" (Roman Jakobson, "On a Generation That Squandered Its Poets," in *Major Soviet Writers*, ed. Edward Brown (New York: Oxford University Press, 1973), 22.

49. V. V. Ivanov, "Zaiavlenie v iuridicheskuiu konsul'tatsiiu," in *Tsena metafory*, 460.
50. Andrei Siniavskii, "Poslednee slovo," in *Tsena metafory*, 475.
51. Ginzburg, *Belaia kniga*, 182.

able to make it. Siniavskii's defense extends beyond the "abc's of literature" to a far-reaching defense of fiction as a unique language irreducible to legal regulation. In her study of Siniavskii, *Abram Tertz and the Poetics of Crime*, Catherine Nepomnyashchy has elaborated Siniavskii's position, and my discussion of it for the most part follows her argument. Unlike Nepomnyashchy, I use a passage that comes earlier in the trial. Siniavskii says:

> As far as "Liubimov" is concerned, it is difficult to define its precise logical meaning in accordance with the rules of jurisprudence, because an artistic image is always polyvalent. I consider a judicial analysis of an artistic text impossible because it is impossible juridically to define the univocal meaning of an artistic work. . . . Nonetheless, for me as the author it is easier to understand the logical meaning of my own works. Terts's works are very complex and multilayered and it would be difficult for me to analyze them. The court is interested in the political side. But I want to explain the literary aspect, defending specifically the literary text. (251)

The literary text is distinct from legal language because of the multiplicity of literary signification. The "rules of jurisprudence," (*iuridicheskii poriadok,* which can also be translated as "the regime of the law)," deal only with univocality. What hermeneutic method guides the judicial determination of meaning is left unclear, but Siniavskii suggests a complete overlap between politics and the law: "the court is interested in the political side." As we have already seen, Siniavskii's analysis of Soviet culture in general stresses that there is no tolerance of irony or ambiguity. One is either for or against. Every utterance, regardless of its context, either confirms or denies what Siniavskii calls the "purpose" of building communism. Siniavskii lays claim to a language that can say something other than "yes" or "no." He lays claim to a space for literature free from politics.

Nepomnyashchy explains Siniavskii's distinction between literary and legal language as follows:

> The essence of the language of the law court is to strive for transparent referentiality; the nature of literary language is to strive to unsettle semantic boundaries. Literature is criminal, but untriable,

because it challenges the illusion of the unambiguous relationship between signifier and signified on which legality depends.[52]

My discussion of libel law will later show that this model of legal language requires certain qualifications. As we have seen in the introduction, recent work on law argues that metaphor is a crucial part of legal discourse. For now, however, I will emphasize again Siniavskii's dependence on the Russian Formalist theory of literary language. The Formalist critic Roman Jakobson wrote in 1933 that "the function of poetry is to point out that the sign is not identical with its referent." As Victor Erlich shows, the distinctive characteristic of poetry for the Formalists "lies . . . in the multiplicity of meanings."[53] Jakobson, it should be pointed out, was a good friend of Daniel' and wrote a letter to the court defending him. Siniavskii generalizes the Formalist position for all artistic language, poetry and prose.

What is more, he shifts the emphasis from the autonomy of artistic language to the autonomy of the artist, who as artist has no identity in the real world, but escapes into a purely literary realm. The Formalist explication of poetic language, heightened, transformed, and exaggerated becomes the basis for Siniavskii's legal defense and ultimately the grounds upon which he contests the authority of the law. The loss of a unified literary language results in the loss of the author. Literary language fragments and multiplies the authorial self. The author is no longer the unified bearer of an intention expressed in language.

The impostor, who figures prominently in Sukhovo-Kobylin's cultural milieu and in his plays, and who serves as the romantic protagonist of Akhsharumov's "Another's' Name," becomes textualized as Siniavskii's literary modus operandi. It is significant in this regard that in his later novel *Goodnight!* Siniavskii fleshes out the impostor with references both to the seventeenth-century historical figure and his own fictitious twentieth-century invention, a False Lenin by the name of Aron Solomonovich Kats. The impostor, who perpetually improvises his script, appropriating and transforming another's language, ceaselessly defers the question of identity. As Nepomnyashchy writes: "The ability of language to name unities reliably is placed in doubt and with it all conventional taxonomies, including the integrity of identity

---

52. Nepomnyashchy, *Abram Tertz*, 37.
53. Victor Erlich, *Russian Formalism: History, Doctrine*, 3d ed. (New Haven, Conn.: Yale University Press, 1981), 185.

itself."[54] I would stress here, as Nepomnyashchy herself does, that the language that causes this doubt, according to Siniavskii, is literary language. Siniavskii's position is not only that the author is not equal to the hero; it is the far more radical claim that the author is not equal to himself. He writes in his postprison novel *Goodnight!* that the author's "style" is not the same thing as his "fingerprints," or his "character," or his "way of life" (2:413). If Siniavskii were asked "who wrote these works," he would answer, as Odysseus answered the Cyclops "no one," with the emphasis on the "one." No single person is the author. No one is speaking, and therefore no one can be held accountable. As in the episode from Homer, artistic writing is form of disguise, trickery, and flight—from the self as much as from one's adversaries.

For Siniavskii literary language defines an almost ontologically distinct world in which the author's self disappears. The specific nature of this realm emerges with particular clarity in his postprison aphorisms entitled *A Voice from the Chorus,* published under "Terts." Siniavskii elaborates further on the problem of authorship, specifically on the paternal relation between author and text. The lines of paternity move in an unexpected direction. A book can take the form of

> a road going out along which the author journeys as long as the story flows, and he follows as a trace left by the text, until he disappears from view. . . . in short the author writes himself out into the material formation of the book, which bears him behind itself and is lost in silence. (1:643)

We can use Said's model of the realist author as a yardstick against which to measure Siniavskii's image of the relation between author and text. According to Said, in the classical realist novel the author generates, founds, and prolongs the life of the text. In Siniavskii's model, the flow of power from author to text is reversed. The author is the creature of the text, which sustains his existence as the author so long as the story continues. We may infer that this means so long as the text is being read by somebody. Each time the work is read, another "author" is generated and sustained until that reading is completed. There are as many authors as there are readings. Of all the fictions generated by a work of fiction, the most fictitious is the single authoritative author. The

---

54. Nepomnyashchy, *Abram Tertz,* 37.

author nonetheless retains the authority to delimit this fictive realm in which these reversals of power take place. Within this realm, the author has no liability. This is precisely the point on which Siniavskii and the Soviet court disagree.

For Siniavskii, the literary text is not the vehicle of an author's message and not even the expression of the author's "self." The text is more properly described as a space or a field, in which words and meanings collide, commingle, and refract one another. In *A Voice from the Chorus* Siniavskii writes that the "text as a spatial problem cannot be a static square or a band that moves in one direction" (1:479). He compares the space of the text to ripples in water. Artistic language is not organized into a system of dichotomies but is instead a "place of meetings: the author with the love object, spirit with matter, truth with fantasy" (1:482). People are "not people, but expanses, not characters, but spaces, fields" (1:485). The writing subject disappears into the literary text, gets lost in the woods, as we read in *Goodnight!* The author's intention, which "clings" to language, is broken by it.[55] The specific operation of literary language renders the author incompetent before a court of law. The literary author is beyond the reach of the law.

Fiction as Fabrication Reconsidered: Libel Law

Siniavskii defends himself brilliantly and eloquently, offering what is ultimately not a defense of himself personally, but a defense of the art of fiction. Siniavskii claims that the models of author and authority evidenced in his works are utterly at odds with those of the government. Whereas the government charges Siniavskii with slanderous fabrications, Siniavskii defends his own writing, and by extension all fiction, as fabrication. Fiction as fabrication cannot slander because it is not true, but all slander is not true. Artistic images do not signify in terms comprehensible by the law. We have already discussed the question of authorial responsibility in Akhsharumov's "juridical fantasy." In that fictionalized account of the writer's contest with the law, fiction wins. Fiction contaminates and destabilizes the process of judgment.

---

55. Siniavskii's theory of authorship clearly resonates with recent literary theory. A connection may be drawn to Wayne Booth's "implied author," Bakhtin's concept of the author's right not to be himself, and Foucault's and Barthe's "death of the author." For Siniavskii and Barthes, see Nepomnyashchy, *Abram Tertz*, 38–39. See also chapter 3 of the present study. I will discuss Siniavskii and Derrida later in the next section of the chapter, and come back to the issue in greater detail in the conclusion.

In revisiting the issue of authorial responsibility in this chapter, I shift the focus of the discussion. The charge of libel against Daniel' and Siniavskii, though without legal merit in an American court in this century, nonetheless provides a new dimension to the central issues of this study: the relation between law and the operations of narrative fiction and the contest and overlap between legal and authorial authority. All authors claim the authority to describe a fictive, imaginary realm in their works. Dostoevsky and Solzhenitsyn seek an extraliterary authority, one that authorizes them not only to describe an alternative Russia, but to bind their readers to it and to them. The law is like narrative, for example, when in the execution of corporal punishment, it writes the story of the state's power on the prisoner's body. The law does not only write; it reads, and in so doing, it relies upon a certain fiction of an all-powerful author—as the trial of Suvorin reveals.

The case of censorship is only an instance, and a fairly specialized one, of the law's regulation of narrative fiction. Libel law, which may serve the same purpose as censorship, adds significantly to our understanding of this problem. In contemporary American law, a work of literary fiction that allegedly contains false and defamatory statements about a particular identifiable individual may be cause for action in a libel suit. Siniavskii defends fiction as a unique class of statements irreducible to legal analysis. Siniavskii's model of the author resists and undermines the notion of authorial liability—and not only in a totalitarian court. As Nepomnyashchy argues, Siniavskii's publication as Terts outside the former Soviet Union suggests that the writing practices signified by "Terts" have implications beyond the confines of Soviet culture. In order to tease out these implications, it is useful to explore what libel is outside the Soviet Union. The broad implications of his claim—in terms of the writer's contest with the law—may be tested against the reading practices that have evolved in American libel law.

In trying a literary libel case in the United States, the court examines the author's intentionality with regard to the literary work; it brings to bear specific tests of truth; it develops standards for resolving ambiguity; it explores, for example, the status of parody. The law pins down the referent by establishing whether the author's fictitious character can be identified as the plaintiff. The literary work is subjected to a regime of reading practices that take very little account of its special status as literary work. As we have just seen, during his trial and in his writing more generally, Siniavskii makes no attempt to meet the law in its own terms. Siniavskii instead defines his own regime, his own language, namely, fiction, which operates independently from the regime of the law. Reconsidering Siniavskii's claims against the competing claims of libel law opens up a new dimension to the contest between the regime of fiction and the regime of the law. It reveals that Siniavskii's claim about fiction approaches the claim that the law would make about itself. Each side claims autonomy from the other.

I begin by going back to the Siniavskii trial, in order to flesh out how the two sides addressed the specific question of libel. Early in the trial Judge Smirnov read the definition of libel from the legal code: "the circulation of what is known to be false and defamatory information."[56] Daniel' responded with what in the United States since the mid-nineteenth century has been a fully adequate defense against a libel suit: the truth of the defamatory information. Daniel' defended himself and Siniavskii on the grounds that the statements they made in their literary works were true. One of the stories that led to Daniel's arrest was "Moscow Is Speaking," in which the Soviet government, following the model of "Astronaut's Day," "Women's Day," and so forth, proclaims a "Day of Killing." This representation of the government, is, according to the judge, libelous. Siniavskii's line in "What Is Socialist Realism"—"in order that not one drop of blood be spilled we kept on killing and killing and killing"—received the same interpretation. In his closing statement before the court, Daniel' asserted that these representations were true. He gave a list of fifteen artists killed by the Soviet government, including Babel, Mandelshtam, and Meyerhold. The judge dismissed Daniel's assertion as irrelevant and offensive.

In this country, the question of the truth of potentially libelous statements is highly complex. Protecting individuals from false and defamatory statements competes with protecting the right to free speech. Common law and constitutional law conflict with each other. In these two competing arenas, truth receives a different level of priority.[57] The First Amendment is not interested in truth. A statement doesn't have to be true to receive protection. Beginning in the latter part of this century, the truth or falsehood of allegedly libelous statements may not be used as a means of inhibiting speech protected by the First Amend-

56. Ginzburg, *Belaia kniga*, 186.

57. For a discussion of this point, see Heidi Stam, "Defamation in Fiction: The Case for Absolute First Amendment Protection," *American University Law Review* 29 (1980): 574–75.

ment. In the landmark *New York Times v. Sullivan* case of 1964, the U.S. Supreme Court held that libel "must be measured by standards that satisfy the First Amendment."[58] To paraphrase the court, demanding truth from factual assertions on pain of libel judgments leads to self-censorship. Knowledge of the falsehood of these assertions or "reckless disregard" of the truth must be shown in order to satisfy the criterion of malice in a libel suit.

Critics of American libel law argue that the Sullivan standard is difficult to apply in works of fiction, which does not purport to state facts. At his trial, Daniel' made a similar claim. He suggested that a distinction can be made between statements that no one could take as alleging facts, statements that are exaggerated and fantastical, and those that can. Judge Smirnov described a hypothetical case. Mrs. Ivanova quarrels with Mrs. Sidorova. If Mrs. Ivanova writes that a certain woman is ruining the life of another woman, that is a hint or "allegory" *(inoskazanie)*. But if Ivanova writes that Sidorova puts garbage in the soup, that is grounds for legal action. Daniel' changed the hypothesis. If Ivanova writes that Sidorova rides on a broomstick, or changes herself into an animal, that is not libel, but, to use Daniel's words, "a literary device." For Daniel', the fact that his allegedly libelous statements belong to the genre of the fantastic means that they cannot be interpreted as asserting false and defamatory facts.[59] Siniavskii's claim about the polyvalence of literary language and the univocality of legal language makes a related point.

Since the Sullivan ruling, American courts have considered the impact of the literary device on the question of the assertion of fact. The courts have considered statements made in a work of fiction, the literary and rhetorical devices of parody, metaphor, and hyperbole, and the related distinction between assertions of fact and opinion. In all of the types of statements listed, the question is whether the author is asserting a defamatory fact about the individual claiming libel. Is the language used to refer to the plaintiff or is it used to arouse a particular reaction in the reader? Or again, is the target of the statement the plaintiff or another statement, as in parody, in which an author uses another author's characteristic language or style?

---

58. *New York Times Company v. Sullivan* 84 S. Ct. 710 (1964): 720. I am grateful to Professor Allan Brownstein of the University of California at Davis Law School for providing me with an introduction to this area of constitutional law.

59. For a discussion of the judge's failure to honor a "fictional contract," see Gary Saul Morson, *The Boundaries of Genre*, 44–45.

The *Hustler v. Falwell* libel case of 1988 takes up the question of parody. The magazine *Hustler* featured on its inside front cover an "interview" and picture of nationally known minister Jerry Falwell's "first time," referring to a series of Campari ads in which celebrities described their "first times." Falwell was depicted drunk in an outhouse in an incestuous relationship with his mother. The magazine listed the parody in its table of contents under the "fiction" heading. A disclaimer on the bottom of the parody read "do not take seriously." The jury in the lower court found that since the parody of the ad "could not reasonably have been interpreted as stating actual facts about the public figure involved," Falwell could not win libel damages. The jury did award damages for "emotional distress," but the Supreme Court overturned that decision. In this case, no one disputed that the figure depicted in the parody ad was Falwell. But since the frame devices, that is, the table of contents and the disclaimer, warned readers that the representation was a parody and not the truth, the content of the parody—Falwell's drunken incest with his mother—could not be interpreted as purporting to state facts about Falwell. However, the use of a frame device such as this does not guarantee the author immunity, as we will see.

For the Supreme Court, the crucial question is how to determine which statements purport to assert facts. In the mid-1980s the Court produced a set of criteria for distinguishing between fact and opinion: "the specific language used; whether the statement is verifiable; the general context . . . and the broader context."[60] The meaning of a specific word may change depending on its context. The leeway given by the standard of what a reasonable reader may conclude, given these factors, means that judgment may vary widely from case to case. *Milkovich v. Lorain Journal* (1990) is a case in point. A high school wrestling coach brought suit against a local newspaper for suggesting that he had perjured himself at an investigation of a postgame altercation. The lower court found that the specific and broader contexts of the article in question argued against the assertion of fact. According to the lower court, the broader context was the sports page, "a haven for cajoling, invective, and hyperbole," and the specific context was a headline reading "TD Says," which in the lower court's language, "would indicate even to the most gullible reader that the article was . . . opinion"

---

60. *Milkovich v. Lorain Journal* 110 S. Ct. 2695 (1990), 2700.

(2700). The Supreme Court disagreed. It found that the language used in the article was not "loose, figurative, or hyperbolic" (2707). Whether or not the coach actually perjured himself could be objectively determined, and, therefore, what the newspaper article alleged fell under the category of fact, not opinion. Finally, opinion in and of itself should not constitute a separate category of statement deserving First Amendment protection.

In a similar ruling, the California Supreme Court had in 1979 decided that the inclusion of a statement in a work of fiction does not protect its author from liability. In the *Bindram* case, a journalist attended a marathon group nude therapy session run by a psychologist and published a fictionalized account in which the psychologist uses obscene language and engages in unprofessional behavior. The author claimed that since the book was a novel, no claim that its author was asserting facts about actual persons could be made. The court found otherwise: fiction is no defense. "The test is whether a reasonable person, reading the book, would understand that the fictional character therein pictured was in actual fact, the plaintiff acting as so described."[61] The court gave a counterexample of a biography containing an episode that no reasonable person would regard as purporting to be true, since "no actual facts were known" about that episode. A comparison of the novel and taped group therapy session revealed that the novel was close enough to what the tapes recorded—close enough, in other words, so that a reader could not interpret the conduct and language represented to be "mere fictional embroidering," to use the court's language. The plaintiff was recognizable in the novel by a characteristic phrase he used in the sessions. The differences in physical appearance between the plaintiff and the fictitious character were not significant.

The dissenting opinion in this case found a circular logic in what can be called the "close enough" test. The statements about the plaintiff that are close enough to his practices make the identification between the fictitious character and the plaintiff, but the "practices which are unlike plaintiff's are called libelous because they are false" (86). The dissent also found that fiction may be an adequate defense. The book's publication as a novel means that none of the statements in it purport to be the truth. To quote the opinion, "when the publication purports to

---

61. *Bindram v. Mitchell* 92 Cal. App. 3d 61, 78.

be a fiction, it is absurd to infer malice because the fiction is false" (88). When fiction is the context for allegedly libelous statements, it is difficult to assess the author's intention with regard to the truth. We can hear echoes of Siniavskii here. The author may claim, as Siniavskii did at his trial, that his or her only intention was to create fiction, neither regarding nor disregarding the truth.

The *Bindram* case and others like it have led critics to argue for a modification of libel law with regard to fiction. All of the arguments in favor of making fiction a special case rest on some definition that marks fiction as distinct from other kinds of statements because it does not claim to be true. Some have argued for absolute protection for fiction and some for "quick dismissal" of libel suits in cases involving fiction. Since fiction does not purport to be true, the defendant is deprived of the defense of truth.[62] This discussion lacks a dimension. Fiction may not claim to contain assertions of fact. It is not "true" literally. But it may claim to be true metaphorically, that is: this event did not take place, but something like it could have.[63] It is on this level that the Soviet government responded to Daniel's "Moscow Speaks." The Soviet government was saying, in effect, that Daniel' alleged that the government could do something like the "Day of Killing." We will return shortly to the question of an absolute distinction for fiction as a unique type of speech.

The American Supreme Court, unlike the Soviet court, recognizes that the meaning of words depend on their context and also recognizes that the rhetorical devices of hyperbole, metaphor, and parody modify what otherwise might be taken as assertions of fact. Characterizing the legal model of language as one of "transparent referentiality" is too simple.[64] Nonetheless, like the Soviet court, and the imperial Russian court that convicted Suvorin, the Court views ambiguity with suspicion. In the *Greenbelt* case, the Supreme Court found that the term "blackmail" used in a newspaper article was merely a "vigorous epithet," and not a libelous assertion of fact. In his concurring opinion, Jus-

---

62. See Martin Garbus and Richard Kurnit, "Libel Claims in Fiction Should Be Lightly Dismissed," in *Brooklyn Law Review* 51 (1985): 409.

63. See Steven Yeazell, "Convention, Fiction, and the Law," *New Literary History* 13 (1981): 88–102.

64. In his dissenting opinion in the *Milkovich* case, Justice Brennan quotes Oliver Wendell Holmes: "A word is not a crystal, transparent and unchanged, it is the skin of a living thought and may vary greatly in color and content according to the circumstances and time in which it is used."

tice White observed that "double meaning in normal usage is itself some evidence."[65] He further observed that journalists were professionals who could be expected to master their craft sufficiently so as to avoid ambiguity. What is more, the Supreme Court, like the Soviet court, does not designate fiction as a special category of protected statements. It subjects fiction to the same tests of truth that it uses for other forms of writing in determining whether the words used in the author's text refer to the plaintiff. The court gages the author's intentionality with regard to the plaintiff. From Siniavskii's perspective, the process of discovering the author's intention with regard to determining the truth or falsehood of his statements collapses against the operations of literary language, which carry the author's intention in unforeseen directions. On balance, there is a great deal of continuity in terms of the model of the author between the three legal contexts that we have been exploring. For the American Supreme Court there is no tertiary realm in which the meanings of words cannot be determined. The realm that Siniavskii as Terts inhabits has no standing in an American court—which is not to say that an American court would have convicted Siniavskii.

However, there is something wrong with this perspective. Notwithstanding the effort to pin down the author's referent, American libel law is more open-ended in its approach to meaning than I have suggested thus far. In order to see this other side of the law, we have to move beyond the rather blunt distinction between fiction and truth that Siniavskii and the American legal authors rely upon. To do this we need a set of terms that characterize the operations of language on both sides of the law/literature divide. Derrida's concepts of iterability and recontexualization can be helpful.

Parasites and Performatives

In order to explore these concepts and their usefulness for our discussion about law and meaning in libel cases, I turn to a debate well known to literary critics, between Austin, his follower Searle, and Derrida. The debate concerns the problem of defining a boundary that would separate fiction, among other forms, from some notion of "serious" or "normal" language. In chapter 5, I used Austin's notion of the

---

65. *Greenbelt v. Bresler* 90 S. Ct. 1537 (1970), 1546.

performative to characterize Solzhenitsyn's testamentary writing. Solzhenitsyn says that words should do something, in contrast to Siniavskii, who says that a word is not an act. In Austin's theory of speech acts, a performative is a statement whose utterance effects what it says, as in the wedding ceremony. Performatives are neither true nor false. Austin distinguishes this type of statement from constatives, which describe things and are true or false. We may note parenthetically that some literary critics use the notion of the performative to define the fictionality of fiction. It is not what is being described that is neither true nor false, but who is performing the description, or telling the story. All the telling and saying in fiction is neither true nor false.[66] Austin limits the application of his distinction between performatives and constatives to nonfiction, what he calls the serious use of language:

> a performative utterance will, for example, be *in a peculiar way* hollow or void if said by an actor on the stage, or if introduced in a poem, or spoken in soliloquy. . . . Language in such circumstances is in special ways—intelligibly—used not seriously, but in ways *parasitic* upon its normal use.[67]

We have already seen the term *parasite* used with regard to the poet Joseph Brodsky, charged with sponging off the Soviet body politic and performing unauthorized work. We have also seen the term used to refer to the characteristic writing style of "Terts." Here the parasite is a metaphor for the dependence of literary language on everyday, or "normal," language. The notion that fiction imitates the real is crucial to Searle's principle of exclusion. The nonserious, "pretended form of behavior," such as fiction, poetry, and theater, as Searle characterizes it, depends on the prior, "serious," real use of language. This distinction fails to account for legal language, which uses metaphor and other literary devices that fall under the rubric of the mimetic but is nonetheless "serious."

Derrida responds to Austin and Searle by taking the metaphor of the parasite seriously. The parasite of fiction cannot be separated from the host, serious language. The host depends on the parasite. Both the

---

66. See Barbara Hernstein Smith, *On the Margins of Discourse: The Relation of Literature to Language* (Chicago: University of Chicago Press, 1978).

67. J. L. Austin, *How to Do Things with Words*, quoted in Jonathan Culler, "Convention and Meaning: Derrida and Austin," *New Literary History* 13 (1981): 20.

serious and the nonserious use of speech, whether oral or written, depend on what Derrida calls "iterability," that is, the possibility of the speech being repeated. Derrida writes that a performative could not "succeed if its formulation did not repeat a 'coded' or iterable utterance." He goes on to say, "The wedding ceremony or the contract, in order to function as such in a serious context has to confirm to and repeat some protocol or convention. "[68] This principle of repeatability is at work in all language use: iterability "renders possible *both* the 'normal' rule or convention *and* its transgression, transformation, simulation, or imitation."[69] To put it another way, if we could utter only unique, unrepeatable statements, we would lose the possibility of understanding each other. The repetition, however, alters what is being said, and the iterated message is never identical to itself. The nonidentity of the message to itself is the condition of possibility, according to Derrida, of the capacity of the message to function. There is no single, pure originary moment in which the author of any kind of speech, fictitious or not, is able to articulate and sustain his or her intention, if indeed intention is ever univocal. What we say depends on the possibility of recontextualization, which alters its meaning. The identity of the speaker, the listener, the intention, and the effect are all fragmented. At the initiation of every speech act is a multiplicity, and not a single author, and this multiplicity bears limited liability for what has been said. Siniavskii characterizes artistic speech in very similar terms but, again, draws a boundary around artistic speech as unique and separate from other kinds of speech. As Nepomnyaschchy argues, what for Siniavskii is specific to literary language is universal for deconstruction. Derrida, in contrast, characterizes all language in these terms: "conventions are by essence violable and precarious in themselves and by the fictionality that constitutes them even before there has been any overt transgression."[70]

It is significant that one of the examples Searle gives of the claim or promise that is void in advance, by definition, is the claim that an author makes in a work of fiction about his fictitious characters. Searle says that we don't make the same demands on the author's claim about his characters that we do when it comes to statements made in other

---

68. Quoted in Culler, "Convention and Meaning," 21.

69. Jacques Derrida, "Limited Inc abc. . . ," *Glyph: John Hopkins Textual Studies* 2 (1977): 241.

70. Ibid., 250.

contexts. We have already seen that this distinction does not hold for libel law. A whole apparatus is brought to bear precisely on the question of how the author decided to give the character particular traits. The cases that we have discussed, particularly *Milkovich* and *Bindram*, reveal the difficulties in establishing and sustaining the boundaries that would separate serious from nonserious contexts. The law attempts, however crudely, to determine the author's intention with regard to the truth.

Thus far we have argued that such attempts reflect the law's interest in fixing meaning. However, Derrida's concept of recontextualization helps to show the law's approach to meaning in a different light. The law's philosophy of literary interpretation looks far more open-ended when we shift our perspective from the tests of truth we discussed in the previous section to a consideration of the factors that set the case in motion. We can use Derridean recontextualization to describe what makes a libel case happen. Plaintiffs find that their statements or aspects of their behavior or image have been "recontextualized" by the defendant, the author, in a defamatory way. Authors find their opinions, conjectures, "vigorous epithets," or works of fiction recontextualized as assertions of fact. The jury then decides which version of the story to accept. In this process, the meaning of words is not fixed in advance. Statements are repeated in different contexts, and each citation brings a shift in meaning.

Again, if we must shift our perspective from the individual case to a series of cases taken as whole, the chain of recontextualization we have just described does not end with the jury's finding. The Supreme Court has stated that it will not provide any single all-encompassing definition of libelous speech The only universal standard is the concept of the average reader. Justice Brennan, in dissenting from the majority in the *Milkovich* case nonetheless agreed "that the statement that the plaintiff must prove false . . . is not invariably the literal phrase published but rather what a reasonable reader would have understood the author to have said."[71] The reasonable reader is a deliberately vague and open-ended standard. The emphasis on the reader rather than on some already given definition or even the author's "literal statement" means that the text is subject to any number of recontextualizations and reinterpretations. The emphasis placed on the reader is both antiteleo-

---

71. *Milkovich v. Lorain Journal*, 2708.

logical, since no greater "purpose" is thereby served, and it is also antitheological in the sense that it dethrones the author as the divine origin of the text's meanings. This is not to say that the author's liability is thereby limited; the author still has to pay for the reasonable reader's interpretation.

The penalty imposed on the defendant/author secures for the plaintiff the possibility of self-authorship. But even this form of authorial liability shows that libel law is more open-ended than we previously considered. The totalitarian society in which Siniavskii found himself recognized only one reputation worth protecting, that of the state, embodied in its many metonymies, including such cultural figures as Pushkin, and, of course, the figure of the ruler. Solzhenitsyn describes, for example, the hypersignificance attached to Stalin's image. In contrast, American society recognizes a multiplicity of individuals with reputations to be protected. Criticisms of the concept of the individual as the basis for a legal system, beyond the scope of our discussion, do not militate against what are at least the grounds for a plurality of authorial self-expression, not only on the part of authors in their literary works, but on the part of persons in their daily lives.[72]

Furthermore, in articulating what constitutes defamation, libel law defines identity not as an essence, but as a construction, a process of self-authorship. The truth, falsehood, or ambiguity of statements made about a particular individual is only one side of the story. The other side is who gets to tell the story, true, false, or ambiguous. The law takes an interest in determining who is the authorized author of the self, and how this authority may be protected and, when lost or stolen, compensated for. In his treatise on constitutional law, Laurence Tribe writes that the state "vindicates the individual's control over what others are told about his or her life. Such control constitutes a central part of the right to shape the self that any individual presents to the world."[73] Slander is equivalent to psychic "mutilation," according to Tribe. The writer Sukhovo-Kobylin, as we have seen, considered slander to be the equivalent of the *branding* of his name. Even when statements are made that are falsely favorable, the individual has the right to seek redress. In the world imagined by libel law, each individual is the sovereign owner of

72. See for example Jennifer Nedelsky, "Laws, Boundaries, and the Bounded Self," *Representations* 30 (spring 1990): 162–89.

73. Laurence Tribe, *American Constitutional Law*, 2d ed. (Mineola, N.Y.: Foundation Press, 1988), 887. I am grateful to Professor Kevin Johnson for directing me to this source.

his or her name. In the world imagined by "Terts" identity, property, and originality come under question. The outcome, however, is not a joyous performance of multiple identities. Siniavskii had to pay for Terts.

Testament and Tattoo

Siniavskii's conflict with the law leads him to posit an authority that is fundamentally similar to the authority of Dostoevsky, Solzhenitsyn, and the other writers in this study: the authority to draw a line separating his writing from all external forms of regulation. What Siniavskii does on his side of the line, however, is clearly distinct. For Siniavskii the encounter with the law, and with the specifically Soviet master narratives that the law depends on, is a chance to engage in the pleasure of literary hide-and-seek and masquerade. Siniavskii uses the literary work to escape the clutches of the law. In *Goodnight!* the narrator says that what enabled him to survive was "Terts, my dark double."

> I see him as if he were here now, the thief, the cardsharp, the son of a bitch, with his hands in his pockets, with tender expletives of an indecent sort on his dried lips, his thin body, sharpened in many years of stylistic polemics and stylistic disagreements. (2:345)

Siniavskii's alter ego, his authorial being as "Terts," cannot be contained by the law, since "Terts" is after all, a metaphor, a play with words, a body honed by literary polemics. For all his Tertsian play with boundaries, Siniavskii insists on one boundary above all: the boundary between literature and life. As Nepomnyashchy argues, this insistence is a defense against the Soviet government's repeated and relentless policy of forced embodiment—the forced embodiment that Solzhenitsyn chronicles in *The Gulag Archipelago* and that transforms Siniavskii into Terts at his own trial. It is against this condition of force that Siniavskii makes his small, precarious, and comic gesture of resistance as Terts. Against the tremendous power of the Soviet state, Siniavskii juxtaposes the lack of will and powerlessness of his own authorial image. He is powerless not only before the law, but before his own works. We return to Brodsky's trial and its image of an otherworldly, holy foolish author.

    Siniavskii's Tertsian oeuvre allows us to reexamine a problem that we have been tracing throughout this study: how the encounter with the law serves as a crucial moment in the writer's self-fashioning, and the resulting tension between writing as a form of transgression and writing as an extension, transformation, and appropriation of legal and paternal authority. For Sukhovo-Kobylin, law, progress, and reform are a false substitution for a mythologized one-to-one relationship between aristocrat and tsar. Writing itself is a hollow effort to reestablish a gentlemanly freedom and autonomy no longer guaranteed by an absolutist center. All is imposture, and imposture is damnable. Dostoevsky borrows the paternal authority of the law to fashion himself as Russia's moral center. While rejecting the injustice of Soviet law, Solzhenitsyn imagines an alternative community, remade from its encounter with *The Gulag Archipelago,* as he has been remade from the Gulag itself, bound together and to Solzhenitsyn by the "circumcision of the heart." For Siniavskii, art is criminal in its very nature. But Siniavskii's "play" is as serious as Dostoevsky's and Solzhenitsyn's work. In the final section of this chapter, I will reconsider this tension in Siniavskii's prison aphorisms, *A Voice from the Chorus.*

Written in the form of letters to his wife during his imprisonment, *A Voice from the Chorus* is, in the Pushkinian sense, a "motley collection" of folktales, aphorisms, weather reports, literary criticism, vignettes, reminiscences, and linguistic ethnography. It is a "writer's diary" like Dostoevsky's, but unlike Dostoevsky, Siniavskii makes no paternal claims over his reading audience or his text. The epistolary form its itself an abdication of authorial control, since the author is denied the certainty that his letters will reach his addressee. Unlike Solzhenitsyn's magisterial *Gulag Archipelago,* Siniavskii's fragmented and miniaturistic aphorisms offer no testimony of the author's suffering and rebirth.

In one section, Siniavskii reflects on the difference between speech and writing:

> Truth is careless about the future; all of its thoughts are about what is close, what is local, about this heap of familiar, short-term/eternal meetings—like a father who while communicating with his son, playing with him, teaching him will not start writing down dates and rules. The testament is another matter; it is not communication, but preservation, memorial, law, chronology, the precision of codes, facts, names—the testament is fulfilled usually by those who are left without the testator, without a father. (1:642)

The passage does not reject writing per se, but rather the kind of writing exemplified in the legal testament. That writing strives to fix what is being said for all time, to convey itself into the future without possibility of alteration. It is unapproachable, because its originator, the testator, is no longer there but requires from the grave that his word be fulfilled. This is the monumentalizing that characterizes socialist realism and Solzhenitsyn. In contrast, Siniavskii's artistic work is willing to accept the repeated staging of the father's absence. It more closely resembles the free and easy book that, as he says a few lines above the passage we quoted, "will interact with the first comer." A written work can be picked up by any reader, in contrast to the speaker who designates his interlocutor.

The writing that binds, that leaves its unalterable mark for all time, is also the writing on the body as a form of punishment. We have already commented on the use of this writing in imperial Russia. It originates in early Byzantine law, which, as Peter Brown writes, "treated the human body as a 'blazon,' on which society might leave permanent marks of punishment."[74] The sentence of the court is announced and enacted at once, so that the words of the sentence become the punishment itself. In rending the prisoner's flesh the words are rendered as physical instruments of punishment. This language leaves nothing left to the imagination except the horror of its pain. It is John Freccero who best captures this sense of the language of punishment: "the ordinary dynamism of language is turned back on itself, immobilized in literalisms that are ironically irreducible."[75] Freccero goes on to quote Vico, who characterizes ancient law as "a severe poetry," an apt description of the language of punishment in a number of contexts, including the Soviet Gulag.

We can juxtapose the state's "severe poetry" written on the prisoner's body with the prisoner's own body writing, that is, the tattoos popular among the ordinary criminals in the Gulag. Siniavskii describes or, perhaps, invents one such tattoo in *A Voice from the Chorus:*

---

74. Peter Brown, *The Body and Society: Men, Women, and Sexual Renunciation in Early Christianity* (New York: Columbia University Press, 1988), 441. I am grateful to Bruce Rosenstock for pointing this out to me.

75. John Freccero, *Dante: The Poetics of Conversion,* ed. and introduction by Rachel Jacoff (Cambridge, Mass.: Harvard University Press, 1986), 106.

> A tattoo: in front—an eagle pecking at the chest of Prometheus; in
> back a dog, using a woman in a barbaric fashion. Two sides of the
> same coin. The front and the back. Light and darkness. Tragedy
> and comedy. And parody of one's own feat. And the closeness of
> sex and laughter. Sex and death. (1:475)

The images represented here unite what is normally kept separate.
Prometheus, who steals fire from the gods and thus brings the possibility of culture to human beings, violates the boundary between the
human and the divine. The image of the dog and the woman is another
unnatural mixture. The juxtaposition of the images front and back, their
position on the body—sets in motion a dynamism that the language of
punishment freezes. Prometheus's noble feat is parodically undercut
by the image of the woman and the dog. What is serious and what is
funny, what is first and what is second, what is back and what is front
are called into question. Siniavskii's gloss on the tattoo emphasizes the
transmutability of human experience from one condition to its antithesis. The tattoo both in these particular images and as a whole offers a
series of recontextualizations. The prisoner's body, marked by punishment, becomes nothing more than a suffering body. The tattoo, a remarking, makes the body back into a metaphor. It is in its own way a
Tertsian use of language. Like Solzhenitsyn, Siniavskii in the Gulag
turns to the testimony of the body, but unlike Solzhenitsyn, he leaves
the reader not a testament that binds, not a scar on our heart, but this
near obscenity, the visual joke of this tattoo.

Conclusion

In writing this work, I have been nagged by the thought that no matter how interesting or compelling the materials I describe may be, their import may be dismissed because I am talking about Russia, and the target of discussion in the law-and-humanities field is invariably America. The law-and-humanities writers analyze Kafka, and Dostoevsky, and Bakhtin, but their goal is how to make American law better. How can the particular configurations of Russian law, narrative, and authority that I have described contribute to a broader discussion of these relations outside of Russia? In thinking about this question, I have decided to forgo the usual summarizing conclusion. Instead, I will reformulate some aspects of my argument as a response to James Boyd White's 1994 *Acts of Hope: Creating Authority in Literature, Law, and Politics*. As his title indicates, White is concerned with a set of problems similar to the ones I have considered. The specific legal, literary, and philosophical texts that he analyzes are drawn primarily from the Western European and American tradition. They include, for example, the *Crito*, Shakespeare's *Richard II*, the Supreme Court case *Planned Parenthood v. Casey* (1992), the poetry of Emily Dickinson, and Nelson Mandela's speech at his trial in 1963 for sabotage, at which he was sentenced to life imprisonment. Although there are many other possible responses to White—on a more theoretical plane, for example, Stanley Fish would make a suitable sparring partner—I will try to see how the Russian texts, both legal and literary, engage with the issues that White raises.[1]

The nodal point of White's book is the problem of authority. Authority is not a force beyond us; it in some limited sense makes us

---

1. For another discussion of White's method of reading, see Susan Mann, "The Universe and the Library: A Critique of James Boyd White as Writer and Reader," *Stanford Law Review* 41 (1989): 959–1009. Mann finds that White's New Critical approach tends to neglect the role of social, political, and economic forces in the formation of communities and authorities.

what we are, but, more importantly for White, we create and modify authority, even as we struggle against it, and we do so, for the most part, through language. Language is itself a system of authority, White remarks, and we may be concerned about our capacity to transform it. For White, authority is diffused throughout the social fabric, but it is not so diffused as to be invisible or insurmountable. Authority is not a given, but something we make. The agency of particular individuals in this process is something White hardly calls into question, although he does speak of the way that already existing authorities have a "purchase" in our minds. The act of writing is crucial to the creation and modification of authority:

> The authority of the law, or the church, or the poetic convention, or whatever institution the writer addresses, does not simply exist in unproblematic form in the external world . . . but is constituted in one's writing. (276)

The authority of a particular institution is represented by the author, constituted in his or her text in a particular way, and the claims the author makes on the reader—to obey or disobey this or that law—are based on the author's way of constituting the authority. Because we can imagine the law, or the institution, or the authority to be other than it is, and because we can describe it thus in our writing, we can make it thus in the world.

Authority is a quality attached to a written work, in part dependent on the specific nature of the writer's voice, which, as White puts it, "can range from authoritarian and dictatorial to the open and dialogic" (277). But more often for White the relation created between writer and reader and among readers, in the act of reading and interpreting a text and responding to its claims for or against a particular authority, is one of "community." White's consistent use of the first-person plural is one of the ways that he seeks to create a community with his readers. In *When Words Lose Their Meaning* (1984), White writes that communities are defined and constituted by "shared conceptions of the world, shared manners and values, shared resources and expectations and procedures for speech and thought."[2] A "textual community" is the

---

2. James Boyd White, *When Words Lose Their Meaning: Constitutions and Reconstitutions of Language, Character, and Community* (Chicago: University of Chicago Press, 1984), 193.

relation created between writer and reader. White makes the very important point that all literature, whether fictional or not, has an ethical and political dimension because it creates this relationship.

But not all texts seek an intimate community with their readers. For example, what Sukhovo-Kobylin wants from his theater is not a sense of community with his audience, but a restoration of the social distance that his encounter with the law and changes within the law have destroyed. The play within the play, the transformation of one character into another, the multiplication of roles performed by a single actor are all devices that produce the effect of distance. His theater does not model an egalitarian community, but a hierarchical structure of power, because it is that structure of power that allows him to fashion and refashion his aristocratic façade.

Nonetheless the concept of a "textual community" is useful in refuting Austin's dismissive characterization of literature as nonserious discourse, that is, discourse that does not make us do anything. According to White, all texts ask us to respond to them in a particular way: "a text asks its reader to become someone and . . . by doing so, it establishes a relationship with him."[3] All reading and writing is thus a form of social action that involves the reader in a process of self-transformation. Again, "to engage with a text is to become different from what one was." For White literature is serious business in Austin's sense of the word.

White points out that certain works may not live up to his standard of creating positive change in the reader. He writes that literary texts can provoke "aggressive or destructive impulses, not in order to subject them to understanding, to an integration with a larger context of impulses and values, but in order to give them free rein."[4] White calls this phenomenon a "momentary disintegration of the reader." Later I am going to suggest that disintegration and reintegration may be linked.

For White the meaning of the text is not to be found in the relationships it depicts, but in those that it creates with its readers. The terms *text* and *writer* are interchangeable. If the writer describes certain values in the world of the text but does not demonstrate them in the writer's relation to us, "what matters is who the writer actually is in his

---

3. Ibid., 15.
4. Ibid., 16–17.

relationship with us, not who he pretends to be."[5] The concept of the literary persona does not have a place in White's discussion. For Bakhtin, as we recall, being a novelist is exercising the right not to be who one actually is. Are irony and ambiguity examples of a bad faith relation between a writer and a reader? We have argued that Siniavskii's ironic and ambiguous performances as "Terts" are as serious, in Austin's sense, as Solzhenitsyn's covenant with his readers.

What if anything is specific to literary or narrative authority? For White the term *literary* is quite broad and means something rather different from the narrower term *narrative*. Narrative can be an extremely effective means of argument when it resonates with our sense of the "probable":

> If we find the movement of the story probable, we will be committed to it and to the sense of human nature and of the world by which it works. This is why narrative is so effective a means of argument, and why it can usually be met only by a competing narrative. (71)

We can raise a question as to where or how the literary work can effect a transformation in the world if we accept only those narratives that confirm our already present sense of what the world is.

The transformative capacity of the artistic work comes across more clearly from White's discussion of the literary, by which he means not just a collection of written artistic works, but a way of thinking and writing that is opposed to the linear and the scientific. *Richard II* shows a mode of thinking "not in propositions asserted through the elaboration of a system, but in tentativeness, in the capacity to hold in the mind at once, or in rapid succession, a variety of incompatible ways of talking, none of which could be a master language" (76). The literary art is the art of bringing together "for the moment at least, in the mind and in the text," these incompatible ways of talking (148). In his discussion of *Planned Parenthood v. Casey*, White argues that the law too may rely on a nonlinear, integrative mode of argument, which brings together a multiplicity of perspectives. For White, law is like literature in that in its overall structure of argument, of hearing two sides of the story, it too creates and sustains a multivalent form of communication and dis-

---

5. Ibid., 17.

course. The agreement to disagree is of profound cultural significance for White.

The world, the text, the self, and culture are all mutually constituted in such a way as to allow for a significant degree of transformation for each, without any appreciable cost. White counts on the integrity of individuals and the endurance of institutions even in the face of tremendous upheaval. In *Richard II*, according to White, Richard abdicates his own identity without losing the inner core of his selfhood. White speaks of "a reduction of the self to an irreducible core that can maintain a kind of integrity in the face of its own dissolution" (72). To give another example, even "when words lose their meaning," as White argues they do in Thucydides' *History of the Peloponnesian War*, when, as he says, the actors in the world described by the *History*, the readers of text, and Thucydides himself faces a "loss of language, a loss of the world, that threatens to become a loss of identity as well"—White recuperates from this loss a positive lesson in how "culture can change without collapsing."[6]

In White's world, the space allotted to individuals for self-invention and reinvention is vast, even though the literal space in which they live their lives may be extraordinarily limited, as in Mandela's prison cell and Emily Dickinson's confinement to domesticity. The space in which they create and re-create structures of meaning, authority, and community for themselves and others is equally so.[7] The slate is clean, and it is always morning in the Emersonian sense that the moment is bursting with possibilities and we are fully awake to them.[8] Listen to Emerson on "self-reliance": "Every true man is a cause, a country, and an age; requires infinite spaces and numbers and time fully to accomplish his design."[9] For White, the space for invention, both public and

---

6. Ibid., 90–91.

7. We can juxtapose Fish's far bleaker assessment of the possibilities for the creation of new meanings and new selves. In Fish's view, "all thought is totalizing in that its successive incarnations always deliver a fully articulated world, a world without gaps or spots of unintelligibility." The self is never left on its own, so to speak, but "is always and already constrained by the contexts of practice (interpretive communities) that confer on it a shape and a direction." See Stanley Fish, *Doing What Comes Naturally: Change, Rhetoric, and the Practice of Theory in Literary and Legal Studies* (Durham, N.C.: Duke University Press, 1989), 16, 26.

8. This is Stanley Cavell's reading of *Walden*. See his *The Senses of "Walden"* (New York: Viking, 1974), 35–67.

9. Ralph Waldo Emerson, *Essays and Lectures* (New York: Literary Classics of the United States, 1983), 267.

private, is by and large uninhabited by already-lived meanings and structures of authority and community. We get to make ourselves up as we go along. In this respect, White's vision is unabashedly American and closer to nineteenth- than to twentieth-century America.

I want to consider in more detail the assumptions behind White's concept of the writing self. On the first page of *When Words Lose Their Meaning,* White shows how the Declaration of Independence and Thoreau, each in different ways, create new structures, Thoreau creating a new life and a new language "when he goes to live by the pond in the woods."[10] The woods are an unmarked territory in which a new self and new structures can be created in the act of writing the book about the sojourn in the woods.

For Siniavskii, in contrast, a walk in the woods is another adventure entirely. In the first place, the woods have ears. In *Goodnight!* the narrator accompanies his father for a walk in the woods, but the father, just released from prison, is afraid to speak, because he believes the KGB has implanted a listening device in his brain. According to White's vision of Thoreau, the woods are a space for a willed and deliberate self reinvention. In Siniavskii, the woods as metaphor for writing define a space for the abdication of self and will:

> you forget yourself and live, not thinking about anything. How wonderful it is! Finally, you don't exist. You are dead. There is only the woods. And we depart into the woods. Into the text.[11]

The writer loses himself and delights in doing so. The writer takes no responsibility for his self-resurrection. With the death of the self comes the pleasure of the text. Not all writing takes up the civic burdens that White ascribes to literature.

The fundamental starting point for White and indeed the law-and-humanities field as a whole is that law is not a specialized quasi-scientific technique, cut off from the rest of culture, for the resolution of disputes.[12] As Austin Sarat writes, it is not "simply power patterned through rules."[13] Even when the profession of law does take the form of

---

10. White, *Words,* 3.

11. Siniavskii, *Sobranie sochinenii v dvukh tomakh,* 2:497.

12. See Clifford Geertz, "Local Knowledge: Fact and Law in Comparative Perspective," in *Local Knowledge,* 167–234.

13. Austin Sarat and Thomas R. Kearns, "Editorial Introduction," *The Rhetoric of Law,* 27.

a simple exercise of power, as in the Siniavskii trial, the exercise relies on a characteristic language, a specific history, and the self-conscious construction of relations to other aspects of cultural production. As we have seen, the government's campaign against Siniavskii exploited the semiotics of "Pushkin" and the semiotics of imposture. For White, law is an arena in which meaning is created and new possibilities of human interaction are imagined. I also start from this proposition and, like White, argue for the mutual constitution of authority in law and in literature. But at the same time, I contemplate the other extreme, examining how law, and in particular the language of punishment, forecloses possibility and reduces meaning to absolute literalization, as the example of branding the prisoner's face reveals. My sense of how the constitution of authority in law and in literature takes place, what it does to the shape of a literary text and to the personae of the author, is therefore quite different.

To get at these differences, I'm going to discuss each one of White's basic terms in light of my own readings, beginning with his concepts of language and the literary. According to White, although language imposes certain constraints, it nonetheless can be used to make new meanings, new authorities, and new ways of being in the world. My conclusions, both about language as an authority, and especially literary language as a means of subverting authority, are less optimistic. This more guarded sense arises from the specific historical world that I examine, nineteenth- and twentieth-century Russia, but I do not claim that these conditions are unique. I stress the way that language reproduces and repeats already established meanings and forms of social relations instead of creating new ones. The nearly universal metaphor of the letter and the spirit in late-nineteenth-century debates about the Russian jury provides an example of this tendency. Even as the Russian public created a new form of authority in the jury, the heavily New Testament language used to describe the jury repeated and even enhanced traditional biblical stereotypes about the Jew as the hated Pharisee.

This example also raises some questions about Robert Cover's discussion of the relation between nomos and narrative. Cover writes: "No set of legal institutions . . . exists apart from the narratives that locate it. . . . For every constitution there is an epic, for each decalogue a scripture."[14] For Cover, the nomos/narrative relation offers the

---

14. Cover, "Supreme Court 1982 Term," 4.

opportunity to live the law and not merely obey it. My point is not to deny the relation between law and story, but to show some of the negative implications of its power. In late-nineteenth-century Russia, fragments of the New Testament opposition between the old and the new law are incorporated into a national narrative about the Russian jury as the ministers of the spirit. The biblical story helps to make the new legal institution meaningful. Scripture is called upon in the creation of a specifically Russian national scripture. We can see the interweaving of these threads in Dostoevsky's *Diary,* in debates in the press about the jury, and in the frequent criticisms of the legal profession. But even as the biblical language is embroidered into the narrative of reform and progress, the Jew remains locked into a traditional mythologized role and thus excluded from the narrative of progress. Precisely because the relation between nomos and narrative is so powerful, the narrative can sanction discrimination against groups whose role is that of villain. More resonance and meaningfulness for some can lead to violence against others.

The ways in which language creates or enhances meaningfulness may have consequences that are unforeseen, not only from the prospective of insider versus outsider groups, as in the example we have just discussed, but for the individual authors, the "selves" deploying the language. We have seen examples of how literary language challenges legal interpretation. For example, in the 1866 Suvorin censorship case, the prosecution alleged that the author's afterward, an address to the censor, was tantamount to a confession of guilt. The prosecution read the line "I know very well that I take a risk in publishing this work" as a statement of the author's intention to commit a crime. This line can also be read as an instance of Bakhtin's "word with a loophole." This type of discourse does not articulate the speaker's knowledge, emotion, or intention but is more like a move on a chessboard, because it is oriented toward what the interlocutor will say. The word with a loophole anticipates and tries to invalidate what the interlocutor will say by saying it for him or her. As a word with a loophole, "I know very well that I take a risk" does not equal "I know that I hereby commit a crime" but could equal, for example, "I know that you think my act is criminal," a statement that does not disclose the speaker's own evaluation of the act but purports to disclose the interlocutor's.

There are several implications of the word with the loophole for the study of law and narrative. Legal interpretation seeks to capture the intention, knowledge, or psychological state that is thought to be expressed in the speaker's statement. While the word with a loophole points to the pitfalls of this approach, it does not lead to a greater sense of meaningfulness in White's terms of an integral core of self. The sense of meaningfulness of such statements moves to second place. What counts above all is the game. Bakhtin's theory of language shows that language may undermine the core of selfhood upon which White's vision depends—a vision of individuals interacting with the law to create new meanings and new ways of being in the world. The agonistics of the speech situation create the necessity of speaking in the other's language in order to forestall the next move. The consequence may be a diminution, fragmentation, or distortion of "self."

Siniavskii's case reveals another aspect of this problem. Siniavskii explicitly theorizes the ways in which literary language fragments authorial intention and destabilizes meaning. Literary language is thus inaccessible to the law. This alternative way of using language is not a way of being in the world, but a way of escaping from it. For Siniavskii, literary language does not and ought not to lead to new possibilities for justice, but only to more possibilities for literature. In this respect, his position is distinct from Dostoevsky's or Solzhenitsyn's. The specific conditions of totalitarian society account at least in part for Siniavskii's insistence on literature's autonomy. This insistence and the reasons for it can help shed light on a basic and obvious assumption of much of the work in the law-and-humanities movement, which is that victims want their complaints to be heard by the law, and not in some other venue. Those who have been excluded want to find ways of telling their stories before the law. We are looking for new legal idioms (Lyotard's term) to express the complaints that present legal language obscures or even condones. Robin West, for example, describes the law's allowance for a private space in which the strong dominate the weak, as in a repressive, patriarchal marriage. West argues that in this case, less private space and more law is desirable in order to protect the weak.[15] But what Siniavskii wants is less law and more private space. Several questions arise. Law is an appropriate language in which these previously

15. Robin West, "Invisible Victims: A Comparison of Susan Glaspell's 'Jury of Her Peers,' and Herman Melville's 'Bartleby the Scrivener,'" *Cardozo Studies in Law and Literature* 8, no. 1 (1996): 203–49.

excluded stories can be made audible because it offers the possibility of relief. What are the implications and costs of this move toward more and more law? What will become, for example, of the variety of incompatible ways of talking, to use White's terms—that is, the multiplicity of languages, identities, and selves that the law is supposed to protect?

For White, multivoicedness is a distinguishing feature of the literary, which the law can also incorporate. Although he does not use the term, what he means by a multiplicity of ways of talking corresponds in some ways to Bakhtin's concept of heteroglossia. One of the controversial acquittals that I discuss in chapter 2, the case of the murdered old woman, reveals precisely this multiplicity of incompatible ways of talking. We find juxtaposed the technical medical testimony of the coroner, the prosecution's careful logical exposition of the contradictions in the various statements given by the defendants and by key witnesses, particularly the father of the alleged murderer, and finally, the monosyllabic testimony of the defendants and the witnesses, who for the most part seem to be terrified of what is taking place around them. Theirs might be called a testimony of silence. In chapter 2, I described the Zherekhov trial of 1873 as an example of judicial heteroglossia, but it is by no means a unique instance. All jury trials incorporate some aspects of multivoicedness. But the question arises as to whether the jury trial is meaningful in these terms for any of its participants. Are any of the participants holding all these incompatible ways of talking together in such a way as to create new meanings for themselves? Some may not be talking at all.[16] White briefly considers the failure of language and the failure of legal language, but not to any significant extent. The participants at a jury trial may be speaking at cross-purposes, leaving the gaps between their languages intact. Under what conditions could a multiple and contradictory enunciation take place? In order for multivoicedness to have meaningful consequences for social transformation, it cannot remain a static object of some outsider's aesthetic contemplation but must lead to some change.

Richard II, according to White, exemplifies the possibility of multiple ways of talking, to use his exact language, "not by the principle of

---

16. Lyotard calls the failure of language the "differend" and argues that it is not an accidental or exceptional feature of litigation, but an essential one. In the situation designated by the term *differend*, the plaintiff is deprived not of a favorable outcome of her or his case but instead "is divested of the means to argue and becomes for that reason a victim." *The Differend*, 9.

noncontradiction, the ruling doctrine of modern exposition, but an opposite one, the principle of controlled and progressive countersaying" (78). Dostoevsky's *Writer's Diary* also exemplifies this principle, questioning how the knowledge of the lawyer and the doctor are constituted in for example, in the Kornilova case, and suggesting that knowledge of human behavior might be constituted otherwise. In the Kairova case, he uses a specifically novelistic technique to explore other possible outcomes to Kairova's attack on her lover's wife. What if she had not stopped after inflicting wounds to Velikanova but had gone on to cut off her head, nose, and lips? The question remains as to whether this form of "countersaying" opens up new possibilities of understanding or repeats old stereotypes about the dangers of uncontrolled female sexuality. In addition, how different is Dostoevsky's countersaying from the defense lawyer Utin's speech? The only difference may be in the choice of literary models: Utin casts Kairova in the role of Lermontov's Arbenin, whose jealousy transforms him into a raging torrent, and Dostoevsky perhaps casts Kairova in the role of Euripides' Agave.

White argues that narrative can be a persuasive form of argument when it resonates with our sense of how people really behave in the world. This type of narrative corresponds to the Russian realist aesthetics of the 1860s. As we recall, the attorney for the plaintiff in Akhsharumov's story stated that aesthetics does not tolerate a character who is completely new. The characters of fiction must be "taken entirely from life." I also make a claim for narrative as a particularly effective form of argument, but not in these terms. For Camus literary testimony has the power to make the reader an eyewitness because the literary work gives the reader the imaginative capacity to perceive what has happened to others in the reader's own body. Solzhenitsyn's "experiment in artistic investigation" argues that narrative fiction can provide knowledge of what is otherwise inaccessible, but not when the fiction conforms to our preexisting sense of the world. Solzhenitsyn has to *destroy* his readers' sense of the probable in order to convince them of the truth of his testimony. Although they are very different writers, both Solzhenitsyn and Siniavskii make the case for the reality of the grotesque and the fantastic in Soviet history.

Both White and I argue for the efficacy of narrative fiction as a means of persuasion, but for different reasons. The difference has little to do with the specific histories we consider. Some aspects of these histories are comparable. The terror of apartheid corresponds in some ways to Stalin's terror. The difference comes from the way we read these histories. White neglects the dimension of the traumatic. The term *trauma* has been used by scholars to suggest the problems of representation related to the Holocaust. Trauma cannot be described in the conventions of realist narrative. Trauma is, among other things, the suspension of the victim's sense of reality, continuity, and coherence. In an article on Claude Lanzmann's *Shoah*, Gertrude Koch describes Reinhart Koselleck's "plea for an analysis of historical dreams as historical material," referring to the "'inescapable facticity of the fictitious' that is reflected in terrifying dreams experienced during the National Socialist period."[17] Solzhenitsyn and Siniavskii do not refer to the sense of the facticity of the fictitious in dreams, but in daily life, upon which a nightmarish and grotesque facticity intrudes. Siniavskii's trial in particular shows how fantastical fictions—his own—were made fact. The politically imposed traumas of Nazism and Stalinism are far from unique in the twentieth century, the last years of which are replete with the traumas of "ethnic cleansing," genocide, and mass dislocations all over the globe. Finally, any trauma, and not only those that are the result of catastrophic historical events affecting huge numbers of people, can necessitate for its representation a story that accords with no one else's sense of what is likely or probable.

The need to destroy the reader's sense of the probable in order to establish the writer's authority has consequences for the particular feel of the writer's authority, for the dynamics of the text, and for the possible sense of community established between the writer and the reader. Solzhenitsyn's *Gulag Archipelago* provides a clear example of the interaction of all these factors. In order to disseminate knowledge of the Gulag, Solzhenitsyn must destroy a whole set of concepts, habitual ways of thinking, knowledge—of the past, of the great heroes of the revolution—and even the reader's sense of that in which daily life is made. For example, he takes the reader's familiar knowledge of what it is to be hungry and transforms it into an unfamiliar and horrifying knowledge of how it feels to be starving to death. The process of destroying the reader's habitual knowledge is another sense in which Solzhenitsyn's narrative works by wounding. Its calculated effect of shock on the reader on the reader can be compared to the grotesque rehabilitation theory promulgated in the 1930s by I. L. Averbakh. Being

---

17. Gertrude Koch, "Trauma and Memory," *History and Memory: Studies in Representation of the Past* 3, no. 1 (spring 1991): 131.

initiated into the community of sufferers is a wrenching, world-destroying process. The process by which the author emerges as an authority is similarly destructive for him. The regimes of the Gulag are indelibly etched in the psyche of the author of the *Gulag*.

For White, reading a literary text is a "process of assimilation and rejection, response and judgment, by which the reader becomes more fully one set of things that it is possible for him to be." We can contrast the author of such a text, who builds on what the reader is and what he or she knows, to Solzhenitsyn, who destroys what we know. To read the *Gulag* or some other similar testimony of trauma means to lose the capacity for judgment that White describes. Reading the *Gulag* means being engulfed by it. The process of gaining knowledge of the Gulag is not a process of becoming more fully one thing or another, but the inverse, a process of self-dissolution. As his sensitive reading of Emily Dickinson's poetry shows, White is aware that the process of establishing one's authority as a writer can mean exploding the concept of self and dismantling the normal patterns of language. The distinguishing feature of Solzhenitsyn's "experiment in artistic investigation" is that this process of unbecoming is deployed against the reader. Solzhenitsyn inflicts the trauma on the reader. In this respect his work is different from Dostoevsky's, whose linear narrative in the *Diary* absorbs the pain and violence of the beatings and assaults of the cases he describes. The "trauma" that some of the actors in these cases experience is masked in the story of Dostoevsky becoming a child of and then a father to a new Russia.

The world-destroying process in Solzhenitsyn is only a preliminary to its rebuilding. The danger here is that the re-created universe will repeat the totalizations that came before. The very conditions that create the Gulag and that shape the writing of the *Gulag* prevent Solzhenitsyn from creating a world that masks disorder, gaps in knowledge, and violence. The same may not be true of his more recent political writings.

The more general conclusion that I draw is that if listening to and telling stories in the law is going to have meaning, attention must be paid to the radical otherness of the story. In doing so, we may come up against the very limits of ourselves, our stories, and our law.

Bibliography

Abrams, M. H. *Natural Supernaturalism: Tradition and Revolution in Romantic Literature.* New York: Norton, 1971.

Afanas'ev, Alexander K. "Jurors and Jury Trials in Imperial Russia, 1866–1885." Trans. Willard Sunderland. In *Russia's Great Reforms, 1855–1881,* ed. Ben Eklof, John Bushnell, and Larissa Zakharova, 214–30. Bloomington: Indiana University Press, 1994.

Akhsharumov, N. D. "Naturshchitsa—Iuridicheskaia fiktsiia." *Otechestvennye zapiski* 164 (February 1866): 549–633.

———. *Chuzhoe imia: Roman v trekh chastiakh.* Part 2. *Russkii vestnik* 31 (January 1861): 166–307, (February 1861): 637–714; 32 (March 1861): 152–220, 601–67; 34 (August 1861): 464–526; 35 (1861): 2–133.

Arsen'ev, K. K. *Zakonodatel'stvo o pechati.* St. Petersburg, 1903.

Austin, J. L. *How to Do Things with Words.* 2d. ed. Cambridge, Mass.: Harvard University Press, 1962.

Averbakh, Leopol'd. *Kul'turnaia revoliutsia i voprosy sovremennoi literatury.* Leningrad: Gosudarstvennoe izdatel'stvo, 1928.

Bakhtin, M. M. "Discourse in the Novel." In *The Dialogic Imagination,* ed. Michael Holquist, trans. Caryl Emerson and Michael Holquist. Austin: University of Texas Press, 1981.

———. *Problems of Dostoevsky's Poetics.* Ed. and trans. Caryl Emerson. Minneapolis: University of Minnesota Press, 1984.

———. *Rabelais and His World.* Trans. Helene Iswolsky. Cambridge, Mass.: MIT Press, 1968.

Aleksandr Ginzburg, ed. *Belaia kniga po delu A. Siniavskogo i Iu. Danielia.* Frankfurt am Main: Possev-Verlag, 1967.

Belomor: An Account of the Construction of the New Canal between the White Sea and the Baltic Sea. Westport, Conn.: Hyperion Press, 1977. Reprint of 1935 edition. Orig. Russian 1934.

Bender, John. *Imagining the Penitentiary: Fiction and the Architecture of Mind in Eighteenth-Century England.* Chicago: University of Chicago Press, 1987.

Bernstein, Michael André. "When the Carnival Turns Bitter: Preliminary Reflections Upon the Abject Hero." In *Bakhtin: Essays and Dialogues on His Work,* ed. Gary Saul Morson, 99–121. Chicago: University of Chicago Press, 1986.

Bessarab, Maia. *Sukhovo-Kobylin.* Moscow: Sovremennik, 1981.

Bethea, David. *Joseph Brodsky and the Creation of Exile.* Princeton, N.J.: Princeton University Press, 1994.

Bhat, Girish. "Trial by Jury in the Reign of Alexander II: A Study in the Legal Culture of Late Imperial Russia, 1864–1881." Ph.D. diss., University of California at Berkeley, 1995.

Boborykin, P. "Voskresnyi fel'eton." *Sanktpeterburgskie vedomosti*, no. 32, February 1, 1876.

Brooks, Peter, and Paul Gewirtz. *Law's Stories: Narrative and Rhetoric in the Law.* New Haven, Conn.: Yale University Press, 1996.

Brown, Peter. *The Body and Society: Men, Women, and Sexual Renunciation in Early Christianity.* New York: Columbia University Press, 1988.

Burbank, Jane. "Discipline and Punish in the Moscow Bar Association." *Russian Review* 54 (1995): 44–64.

Burgess, Malcom. "Fairs and Entertainers in Eighteenth-Century Russia." *Slavonic Review* 38 (1959): 95–113.

Carpovich, Vera. "*The Gulag Archipelago,* Volume One: Notes on Its Lexical Peculiarities." In *Aleksandr Solzhenitsyn: Critical Essays and Documentary Materials,* ed. John B. Dunlop, Richard Haugh, and Alexis Klimoff, 527–33. 2d ed. New York: Macmillan, 1975.

Castle, Terry. *Masquerade and Civilization: The Carnivalesque in Eighteenth Century English Culture and Fiction.* Stanford, Calif.: Stanford University Press, 1986.

Cavell, Stanley. *The Senses of "Walden."* New York: Viking, 1974.

Cherniavsky, Michael. *Tsar and People: Studies in Russian Myths.* New Haven, Conn.: Yale University Press, 1961.

Chukovskaia, Lidiia. "Breakthrough." In *Aleksandr Solzhenitsyn: Critical Essays and Documentary Materials,* ed. John B. Dunlop, Richard Haugh, and Alexis Klimoff, 456–57. 2d ed. New York: Macmillan, 1975.

———. "Sudilishche." In *Ogonek 88: Luchshie publikatsii goda,* ed. L. Gyshchin, S. Kliamkin, and V. Iumashev, 262. Ogonek, 1989.

Clark, Katerina. *The Soviet Novel: History as Ritual.* Chicago: University of Chicago Press, 1985.

Conquest, Robert. *The Great Terror: A Reassessment.* New York: Oxford University Press, 1990.

Constable, Marianne. *The Law of the Other: The Mixed Jury and Changing Conceptions of Citizenship, Law, and Knowledge.* Chicago: University of Chicago Press, 1994.

Cover, Robert. "The Supreme Court 1982 Term, Forward: Nomos and Narrative." *Harvard Law Review* 97, no. 4 (1983): 4–68.

———. "Violence and the Word." *Yale Law Journal* 95 (1986): 1601–29.

Culler, Jonathan. "Convention and Meaning: Derrida and Austin." *New Literary History* 13 (1981): 14–30.

Dal', Vladimir. *Tolkovyi slovar' velikorussskogo iazyka.* 3 vols. Moscow: Gosudarstvennoe izdatel'stvo inostrannykh i natsional'nykh slovarei, 1955.

Danilov, Evgenii. "Tri vystreli v Lenina, ili za chto kaznili Fanni Kaplan." *Neva* 5–6 (1992): 307–24.

de Lauretis, Teresa. *Alice Doesn't: Feminism, Semiotics, Cinema.* Bloomington: Indiana University Press, 1984.

Delgado, Richard. "A Plea for Narrative." *Michigan Law Review* 87 (1988): 2411–41.

"Delo Very Zasulich." In *Sud prisiazhnykh v Rossii: Gromkie ugolovnye protsessy 1864–1917gg*, ed. S. M. Kazantsev, 281–316. Leningrad: Lenizdat, 1991.

Derrida, Jacques. "Limited Inc abc . . ." *Glyph: Johns Hopkins Textual Studies* 2 (1977): 162–254.

Dobrenko, Evgenii. "The Literature of the Zhdanov Era." In *Late Soviet Culture: From Perestroika to Novostroika*, ed. Thomas Lahusen with Gene Kuperman, 109–37. Durham, N.C.: Duke University Press, 1993.

———. *Metafora vlasti: Literatura stalinskoi epokhi v istoricheskom osveshchenii*. Munich: Verlag Otto Sagner, 1993.

Dostoevsky, F. M. *Polnoe sobranie sochinenii v tridtsati tomakh*. 30 vols. Leningrad: Nauka, 1972–90.

Emerson, Caryl. *Boris Godunov: Transpositions of a Russian Theme*. Bloomington: Indiana University Press, 1986.

Emerson, Ralph Waldo. *Essays and Lectures*. New York: Literary Classics of the United States, 1983.

Engelstein, Laura. "Combined Underdevelopment: Discipline and the Law in Imperial and Soviet Russia." *American Historical Review* 98, no. 2 (April 1993): 338–53.

———. *The Keys to Happiness: Sex and the Search for Modernity in Fin-de-Siècle Russia*. Ithaca, N.Y.: Cornell University Press, 1992.

———. "Revolution and the Theater of Public Life in Imperial Russia." In *Revolution and the Meanings of Freedom in the Nineteenth Century*, ed. Isser Wolloch, 315–57. Stanford, Calif.: Stanford University Press, 1996.

Eremin, Dmitrii. "Perevertyshi." In *Tsena metafory, ili prestuplenie i nakazanie Siniavskogo i Danielia*, ed. L. S. Eremina, 21–47. Moscow: "Iunona," 1990.

Erlich, Victor. *Russian Formalism: History, Doctrine*. 3d ed. New Haven, Conn.: Yale University Press, 1965.

Fanger, Donald. "Conflicting Imperatives in the Model of the Russian Writer: The Case of Tertz/Sinyavsky." In *Literature and History: Theoretical Problems and Russian Case Studies*, ed. Gary Saul Morson, 111–34. Stanford, Calif.: Stanford University Press, 1986.

Felman, Shoshana, and Dori Laub, M.D. *Testimony: Crises of Witnessing in Literature, Psychoanalysis, and History*. New York: Routledge, 1992.

Feoktistov, E. M. "Glava iz vospominanii." In *Atenei* 3, ed. B. L. Modzalevskii and Iu. G. Oksman, 106–14. Leningrad, 1926.

Fish, Stanley. *Doing What Comes Naturally: Change, Rhetoric, and the Practice of Theory in Literary and Legal Studies*. Durham, N.C.: Duke University Press, 1989.

Foinitskii, I. Ia. "Zhenschina-prestupnitsa." Pt. 1. *Severnyi vestnik* 1893: no. 2, 123–44.

Fortune, Richard. *Alexander Sukhovo-Kobylin*. Boston: Twayne Publishers, 1982.

Foucault, Michel. *Discipline and Punish: The Birth of the Prison*. Trans. Alan Sheridan. New York: Vintage, 1979.

———. "What Is an Author?" In *Language, Counter-Memory, Practice*, ed. Donald Bouchard, trans. Donald Bouchard and Sherry Simon, 113–38. Ithaca, N.Y.: Cornell University Press, 1977.

Frank, Joseph. *Dostoevsky: The Years of Ordeal, 1850–1859.* Princeton, N.J.: Princeton University Press, 1983.

———. Intro. to *The Diary of a Writer,* by F. M. Dostoevsky. Trans. Boris Brasol. Santa Barbara, Calif.: Peregrine Smith, 1979.

Freccero, John. *Dante: The Poetics of Conversion.* Ed. Rachel Jacoff. Cambridge, Mass.: Harvard University Press, 1986.

Freud, Sigmund. "A Child Is Being Beaten." In *Collected Papers,* trans. Joan Riviere, 2:171–201. New York: Basic Books, 1959.

Galtseva, Renata, and Irina Rodnyanskaya. "The Obstacle: The Human Being, or the Twentieth Century in the Mirror of Dystopia." In *Late Soviet Culture: From Perestroika to Novostroika,* ed. Thomas Lahusen with Gene Kuperman, 69–94. Durham, N.C.: Duke University Press, 1993.

Garbus, Martin, and Richard Kurnit. "Libel Claims in Fiction Should Be Lightly Dismissed." *Brooklyn Law Review* 51 (1985): 401–23.

Geertz, Clifford. "Centers, Kings, and Charisma: Symbolics of Power." In *Local Knowledge: Further Essays in Interpretive Anthropology.* New York: Basic Books, 1983.

Gernet, M. N. *Soslovnaia organizatsiia advokatury 1864–1914.* Vol. 2 of *Istoriia russkoi advokatury.* Moscow: Izdanie sovetov prisiazhnykh, 1916.

Gessen, I. V. *Advokatura, obshchestvo i gosudarstvo 1864–1914.* Vol. 1 of *Istoriia russkoi advokatury.* Moscow: Izdanie sovetov prisiazhnykh 1914.

———. *Sudebnaia reforma.* St. Petersburg, 1905.

Glad, John. Foreword to *Kolyma Tales,* by Varlam Shalamov. Trans. John Glad. Middlesex, England: Penguin, 1994.

Golomstock, Igor. *Totalitarian Art in the Soviet Union, the Third Reich, Fascist Italy, and the People's Republic of China.* Trans. Robert Chandler. New York: Harper-Collins, 1990.

"Sudebnaia khronika: Delo Kairova." *Golos,* no. 118, May 11, 1876.

Gromnitskii, M. "Advokat ob advokatakh." *Nedelia* 1875, no. 52, 1758–65.

Grossman, Leonid. *Prestuplenie Sukhovo-Kobylina.* Leningrad: Izdatel'stvo priboi, 1928.

———. *Teatr Sukhovo-Kobylina.* Moscow: Izdanie V. T. O., 1940.

Grossman, Viktor. *Delo Sukhovo-Kobylina.* Moscow: Gosudarstvennoe izdatel'stvo khudozhestvennaia literatura, 1936.

Groys, Boris. *The Total Art of Stalinism: Avant-Garde, Aesthetic Dictatorship, and Beyond.* Trans. Charles Rougle. Princeton, N.J.: Princeton University Press, 1992.

Gutkin, Irina. "The Legacy of the Symbolist Aesthetic Utopia: From Futurism to Socialist Realism." In *Creating Life: The Aesthetic Utopia of Russian Modernism,* ed. Irina Paperno and Joan Delaney Grossman, 167–96. Stanford, Calif.: Stanford University Press, 1994.

Holquist, Michael. "How Sons Become Fathers: *The Brothers Karamazov.*" In *Dostoevsky and the Novel.* Evanston, Ill.: Northwestern University Press, 1977.

Hunt, Lynn. *The Family Romance of the French Revolution*. Berkeley and Los Angeles: University of California Press, 1992.

Iur'in, M. "O novom sude." *Den'*, no. 7, February 16, 1863.

Ivanov, V. V. "Zaiavlenie v iuridicheskuiu konsul'tatsiiu." In *Tsena metafory, ili prestuplenie i nakazanie Siniavskogo i Danielia*, ed. L. S. Eremina, 460–62. Moscow: "Iunona," 1990.

Jackson, Robert Louis. *Dostoevsky's Quest for Form—a Study of His Philosophy of Art*. New Haven, Conn.: Yale University Press, 1966.

———. "The Triple Vision: 'Peasant Marei.'" *Yale Review* 67 (winter 1978): 225–35.

Jakobson, Roman. "On a Generation That Squandered Its Poets." In *Major Soviet Writers*, ed. Edward Brown, 7–32. New York: Oxford University Press, 1973.

Kantorowicz, Ernst H. *The King's Two Bodies: A Study in Medieval Political Theology*. Princeton, N.J.: Princeton University Press, 1957.

Karabchevskii, N. P. *Okolo pravosudiia: Sta'ti, soobshcheniia i sudebnye ocherki*. St. Petersburg, 1908.

Kholodov, E. G., ed. *Istoriia russkogo dramaticheskogo teatra v semi tomkah*. 7 vols. Moscow: Iskusstvo, 1977–87.

Kistiakovskii. B. "V zashchitu prava." In *Vekhi: Sbornik statei o russkoi intelligentsii*. 2d ed. Frankfurt am Main: Possev, 1967.

Koch, Gertrude. "The Angel of Forgetfulness and the Black Box of Facticity: Trauma and Memory in Claude Lanzmann's Film *Shoah*." *History and Memory: Studies in Representation of the Past* 3, no. 1 (spring 1991): 119–34.

Koni, A. F. *Izbrannye proizvedeniia*. Moscow: Gosudarstvennoe izdatel'stvo iuridicheskoi literatury, 1956.

———. "Prisiazhnye zasedatelei." In *Sud prisiazhnykh v Rossii: Gromkie ugolovnye protsessy 1864–1917gg*. Leningrad: Lenizdat, 1991.

Konshina, E. N. "Vstupitel'nye zamechaniia." In "Pis'ma A. V. Sukhovo-Kobylina k rodnym," ed. E. N. Konshina. *Trudy publichnoi biblioteki SSSR imeni Lenina* 3 (1934): 203.

Kucherov, Samuel. *Courts, Lawyers and Trials under the Last Three Tsars*. Westport, Conn.: Greenwood Press, 1953.

Kuznetsov, E., ed. *Russkie narodnye gulian'ia po rasskazam A. Ia. Alekseev-Iakovleva*. Leningrad: Iskusstvo, 1948.

Kvachevskii, A. *Sud prisiazhnykh po russkim zakonam: rukovodtsvo dlia prisiazhnykh zasedatelei*. St. Petersburg, 1873.

Labunski, Richard. *Libel and the First Amendment: Legal History and Practice in Print and Broadcasting*. New Brunswick, N.J.: Transaction Books, 1987.

LaCapra, Dominick. *"Madame Bovary" on Trial*. Ithaca, N.Y.: Cornell University Press, 1982.

Lebedev, K. N. "Iz zapisok Senatora K. N. Lebedeva." *Russkii arkhiv* 1910. Vol. 7: 333–408; vol. 8: 465–524; vol. 10: 183–253; vol. 11: 353–76; vol. 12: 542–82.

Lermontov, M. Iu. *Izbrannye proizvedeniia v dvukh tomakh*. Vol. 2. Moscow: Gosudarstvennoe izdatel'stvo khudozhestvennoi literatury, 1963.

Levinson, Sanford. "Law as Literature." In *Interpreting Law and Literature: A*

Hermeneutic Reader, ed. Sanford Levinson and Steven Mailloux, 155–73. Evanston, Ill.: Northwestern University Press, 1988.

Liubavksii, A. "O krest'ianke Varvare Erkhove, suzhdennoi za sozhzhenie v pechke svoego rebenka," in *Russkie ugolovnye protsessy.* St. Petersburg, 1867.

———. *Novye russkie ugolovnye protsessy.* 2 vols. St. Petersburg, 1868.

Lotman, Iu. M. "Agreement and 'Self-Giving' as Archetypal Models of Culture." In *The Semiotics of Russian Culture,* ed. Ann Shukman, 125–40. Ann Arbor: University of Michigan Press, 1984.

———. "The Decembrist in Everyday Life: Behavior as a Historical-Psychological Category." Trans. C. R. Pike. In *The Semiotics of Russian Culture,* ed. Ann Shukman, 71–123. Ann Arbor: University of Michigan Press, 1984.

———. "Gogol's Chlestakov: The Pragmatics of a Literary Character." Trans. Ruth Sobel. In *The Semiotics of Russian Culture,* ed. Ann Shukman, 177–212. Ann Arbor: University of Michigan Press, 1984.

———. *Kul'tura i vzryv.* Moscow: Gnosis, 1992.

———. "Russo i russkaia kul'tura XVIII-nachala XIX veka." In Jean Jacques Rousseau, *Traktaty,* ed. V. S. Alekseev-Popov, Iu. M. Lotman, et al. Moscow: Nauka, 1969.

———. "The Theater and Theatricality as Components of Early Nineteenth Century Culture." Trans. G. S. Smith. In *The Semiotics of Russian Culture,* ed. Ann Shukman, 141–64. Ann Arbor: University of Michigan Press, 1984.

Lyotard, Jean-François. *The Differend: Phrases in Dispute.* Trans. Georges Van Den Abbeele. Minneapolis: University of Minnesota Press, 1988.

Maikov, M. *Vtoroe otdelenie ego imperatorskogo velichestva kantseliarii 1826–1882.* Vol. 1. St. Petersburg, 1906.

"Manifest 14 Marta 1848." In *Epokha Nikolaia I,* ed. M. O. Gershenzon, 9. Moscow: Obrazovanie, 1910.

Mann, Susan. "The Universe and the Library: A Critique of James Boyd White as Writer and Reader." *Stanford Law Review* 41 (1989): 959–1009.

Masing-Delic, Irene. *Abolishing Death: A Salvation Myth of Russian Twentieth-Century Literature.* Stanford, Calif.: Stanford University Press, 1992.

———. "Creating the Living Work of Art: The Symbolist Pygmalion and His Antecedents." In *Creating Life: The Aesthetic Utopia of Russian Modernism,* ed. Irina Paperno and Joan Delaney Grossman, 51–82. Stanford, Calif.: Stanford University Press, 1994.

Massaro, Toni M. "Empathy, Legal Storytelling, and the Rule of Law: New Words, Old Wounds?" *Michigan Law Review* 87 (1988): 2099–3153.

Matich, Olga. "Sinjavskij's Rebirth as Terc." *Slavic and East European Journal* 33 (1989): 50–63.

Medvedev, Roy. *Let History Judge: The Origins and Consequences of Stalinism.* Rev. ed. Trans. George Shriver. New York: Columbia University Press, 1989.

———. "On Solzhenitsyn's *The Gulag Archipelago.*" In *Aleksandr Solzhenitsyn: Critical Essays and Documentary Materials,* ed. John B. Dunlop, Richard Haugh, and Alexis Klimoff, 460–76. 2d ed. New York: Macmillan, 1975.

Miller, D. A. *The Novel and the Police.* Berkeley and Los Angeles: University of California Press, 1988.

Miller, J. Hillis. "Laying Down the Law in Literature: The Example of Kleist." In *Deconstruction and the Possibility of Justice,* ed. Drusilla Cornell, Michael Rosenfield, and David Gray Carlson, 305–29. New York: Routledge, 1992.

Monas, Sidney. "Fourteen Years of Aleksandr Isaevich." *Slavic Review* 35 (1976): 518–26.

———. "GULag and Points West." *Slavic Review* 40 (1981): 444–56.

———. *The Third Section: Police and Society under Nicholas I.* Cambridge, Mass.: Harvard University Press, 1961.

Morson, Gary Saul. *The Boundaries of Genre: Dostoevsky's "Diary of a Writer" and the Traditions of Literary Utopia.* Austin: University of Texas Press, 1981.

———. "Commentary: Traditions and Institutions." In *Literature and History: Theoretical Problems and Russian Case Studies,* ed. Gary Saul Morson, 263–74. Stanford, Calif.: Stanford University Press, 1986.

———. "Introductory Study: Dostoevsky's Great Experiment." In *A Writer's Diary,* by Fyodor Dostoevsky, trans. Kenneth Lantz, 1–117. Evanston, Ill.: Northwestern University Press, 1993.

———. *Narrative and Freedom: The Shadows of Time.* New Haven, Conn.: Yale University Press, 1994.

Murav, Harriet. "The Case against Andrei Siniavskii: The Letter and the Law." *Russian Review* 53 (1994): 549–60.

———. "Dostoevsky in Siberia: Remembering the Past." *Slavic Review* 50 (1991): 858–66.

———. *Holy Foolishness: Dostoevsky's Novels and the Poetics of Cultural Critique.* Stanford, Calif.: Stanford University Press, 1992.

Naiman, Eric. "Of Crime, Utopia, and Repressive Complements: The Further Adventures of the Ridiculous Man." *Slavic Review* 50 (1991): 513–20.

Nechaeva, V. S. *Zhurnal M. M. i F. M. Dostoevskikh "Epokha" 1864–1865.* Moscow: Nauka, 1975.

Nepomnyashchy, Catherine. *Abram Tertz and the Poetics of Crime.* New Haven, Conn.: Yale University Press, 1995.

———. "Andrei Sinyavsky's 'Return' to the Soviet Union." *Formations* 6, no. 1 (1991): 24–44.

Neuberger, Joan. "Popular Legal Cultures: The St. Petersburg *Mirovoi sud.*" In *Russia's Great Reforms, 1855–1881,* ed. Ben Eklof, John Bushnell, Larissa Zakharova, 231–46. Bloomington: Indiana University Press, 1994.

"Neznakomets." *Birzhevye vedomosti,* no. 31, February 1, 1876.

Nikitin, V. "Neestestvennyi dualizm." *Molva* 1876, no. 7.

Orshanskii, I. G. *Russkoe zakonodatel'stvo o evreiakh.* St. Petersburg, 1877.

Orshanskii, M. "L. N. Tolstoi i pravosudie." *Iurist* 1902: no. 6, 235.

Paperno, Irina. *Chernyshevsky and the Age of Realism: A Study in the Semiotics of Behavior.* Stanford, Calif.: Stanford University Press, 1988.

Paperno, Irina, et al. "Symposium." *Slavic Review* 53 (1994): 193–224.

Pashin, Sergei. "Rossiskii sud prisiazhnykh vchera i segodnia." *Znamia* 6 (1996): 177–88.

Pervukhin, Natalia. "The 'Experiment in Literary Investigation' (Čexov's *Sax-*

alin and Solženicyn's *Gulag*." *Slavic and East European Journal* 35 (1991): 489–502.

Peterburgskaia gazeta, no. 17, January 25, 1876.

Politicheskie protsessy nikolaevskoi epokhi: Petrashevtsy. Moscow, 1907.

Polnoe sobranie zakonov Rossiiskoi Imperii, series 2 1825—81, vol. 39. St. Petersburg, 1867.

Polozov, N. "Neskol'ko slov ob ugolovnykh sledstviiakh." *Russkii vestnik* 31 (1861): 715–77.

Pomerants, Grigorii. "Real'nost' fiktsii." *Znamia* 7 (1996): 234–36.

Pomorska, Krystyna. "The Overcoded World of Solzhenicyn." *Poetics Today* 1, no. 3 (1980): 163–70.

Posner, Richard. *Law and Literature: A Misunderstood Relation*. Cambridge, Mass.: Harvard University Press, 1988.

Rappaport, Louis. *Stalin's War against the Jews: The Doctors' Plot and the Soviet Solution*. New York: Macmillan, 1990.

Reformy Petra pervogo: sbornik dokumentov. Ed. V. I. Lebedev. Moscow: Gos. sotsial'no-ekon. izd-vo, 1937.

Rev, Istvan. "*In Medacio Veritas* (in Lies There Lies the Truth)" *Representations* 35 (summer 1991): 1–19.

Review of "Vzgliady russkogo ministra pervoi polovinoi XIX stoletiia." *Otechestvennye zapiski* 164 (February 1866): 271–88.

Reyfman, Irina. "The Emergence of the Duel in Russia: Corporal Punishment and the Honor Code." *Russian Review* 54 (1995): 26–43.

Riasanovsky, Nicholas V. *A History of Russia*. 2d. ed. New York: Oxford University Press, 1969.

Rice, James L. "Psychoanalysis of 'Peasant Marei.'" In *Russian Literature and Psychoanalysis*, ed. Daniel Rancour-Laferriere, 252–54. Philadelphia: John Benjamins, 1989.

Roosevelt, Priscilla. *Life on the Russian Country Estate: A Social and Cultural History*. New Haven, Conn.: Yale University Press, 1995.

Rose, Mark. "The Author as Proprietor: *Donaldson v. Becket* and the Geneology of Modern Authorship." In *Of Authors and Origins: Essays on Copyright Law*, ed. Bram Sherman and Alain Stroud, 23–55. Oxford: Clarendon Press, 1994.

Rosenshield, Gary. "Dostoevskij and the Kroneberg Case." *Slavic and East European Journal* 36 (1992): 415–34.

Rossiev, Pavel. "A. V. Sukhovo-Kobylin i Frantsuzhenka Simon." *Russkii arkhiv* 6 (1910): 315–19.

Rostotskii, B. "Teatral'nyi debiut Vladimira Maiakovskogo" *Teatr* 7 (1937): 111–18.

Roth, Philip. *The Counterlife*. New York: Penguin Books, 1986.

Rowe, William. *Dostoevsky: Child and Man in His Works*. New York: New York University Press, 1968.

Ryklin, Mikhail. "Tela Terrora (tezisy k logike nasiliia)." *Bakhtinskii sbornik* 1 (1990): 60–76.

Said, Edward W. *Beginnings: Intention and Method*. New York: Basic Books, 1975.

Sandler, Stephanie. "Sex, Death, and Nation in the *Strolls with Pushkin* Controversy." *Slavic Review* 51 (1992): 294–308.

Sarat, Austin, and Thomas R. Kearns, eds. *The Rhetoric of Law*. Ann Arbor: University of Michigan Press, 1994.

Scarry, Elaine. *The Body in Pain: The Making and Unmaking of the World*. New York: Oxford University Press, 1985.

Schapiro, L. "The *Vekhi* Group and the Mystique of Revolution." *Slavic and East European Review* 34, no. 82 (December 1955): 56–76.

Scheppele, Kim Lane. "Forward: Telling Stories." *Michigan Law Review* 87 (1988): 2073–98.

Schmemann, Alexander. "Reflections on *The Gulag Archipelago*." In *Aleksandr Solzhenitsyn: Critical Essays and Documentary Materials*, ed. John B. Dunlop, Richard Haugh, and Alexis Klimoff, 515–26. 2d ed. New York: Macmillan, 1975.

Sedgwick, Eve Kosofsky. "Jane Austen and the Masturbating Girl." In *Questions of Evidence: Proof, Practice, and Persuasion across the Disciplines*, ed. James Chandler, Arnold Davidson, and Harry Harootunian, 105–24. Chicago: University of Chicago Press, 1994.

Semenov, Nikolai. "Graf Viktor Nikitich Panin." *Russkii arkhiv* 10 (1887): 538–66.

Shafarevich, Igor. "Fenomenon emigratsii." *Literaturnaia rossia*, September 8, 1989, 4–5.

Shaikevich, S. "O polozhenii ugolovnogo pravosudiia v Rossii v techeniia 1864 goda." *Iuridicheskaia gazeta*, no. 6, September 15, 1866, 3–4.

Siniavskii, Andrei. "Rech' pri vruchenii priemii 'Pisatel' v izgnanii' Bavarskoi Akademii iziashchnykh iskusstv." *Stolitsa* 40 (1992): 50.

———. *Soviet Civilization: A Cultural History*. Trans. Joanne Turnbill. New York: Little, Brown, 1988.

——— [Abram Terts, pseud.]. *Sobranie sochinenii v dvukh tomakh*. 2 vols. Moscow: Start, 1992.

Solzhenitsyn, Aleksandr. *Arkhipelag GULag, 1918–1956: Opyt khudozhestvennogo issledovaniia*. 3 Vols. Paris: YMCA Press,1973–75.

Spivak, Gayatri Chakravorty. "Constitutions and Culture Studies." In *Legal Studies and Culture Studies: A Post Modern Critical Theory*, ed. Jerry D. Leonard, 155–73. New York: State University of New York Press, 1995.

Stallybrass, Peter, and Allon White. *The Politics and Poetics of Transgression*. Ithaca, N.Y.: Cornell University Press, 1986.

Stam, Heidi. "Defamation in Fiction: The Case for Absolute First Amendment Protection." *American University Law Review* 29 (1980): 571–41.

Starobinski, Jean. *The Invention of Liberty: 1700–1789*. New York: Rizzoli, 1987.

Stewart, Susan. *Crimes of Writing: Problems in the Containment of Representation*. Durham, N.C.: Duke University Press, 1994.

Straus, Nina Pelikan. *Dostoevsky and the Woman Question: Rereadings at the End of the Century*. New York: St. Martin's Press, 1994.

"Sudebnye ustavy i zakliuchenie ober-prokuratora po delam Mel'nitskikh i Sviridova." *Zhurnal ugolovnogo i grazhdanskogo prava* 5 (May 1884): 93–210.

Sukhovo-Kobylin, A. V. "Iz dnevnika A. V. Sukhovo-Kobylina." *Russkii arkhiv* 5 (1910): 284–88.

———. *Trilogiia*. Moscow: Iskusstvo, 1986.

Suvorin, A. S. *Vsiakie: Ocherki sovremennoi zhizni*. St. Petersburg, 1866.

Tagantsev, N. S. *Russkoe ugolovnoe pravo*. 2 vols. 2d ed. St. Petersburg, 1920.

Taylor, Katherine Fischer. *In the Theater of Criminal Justice: The Palais de Justice in Second Empire Paris*. Princeton, N.J.: Princeton University Press, 1993.

Timofeev, Lev. "Poetikia lagernoi prozy: Pervoe chtenie *Kolymskikh rasskazov* V. Shalamova." *Oktiabr'* 3 (March 1991): 182–95.

Timofeev, M. P. *Sud prisiazhnykh v Rossii. Sudebnye ocherki*. Moscow, 1881.

Tolstaya, Tatyana. "Russian Lessons." Review of *"The Russian Question" at the End of the Twentieth Century*, by Alexander Solzhenitsyn. *New York Review of Books*, October 19, 1995, 9.

Tribe, Laurence. *American Constitutional Law*. 2d. ed. Mineola, N.Y.: Foundation Press, 1988.

Tunimanov, V. A. "Publitsistika Dostoevskogo *Dnevnika pisatelia*." In *Dostoevskii khudozhnik i myslitel': Sbornik statei*. Moscow: Khudozh. lit., 1972.

Unkovskii, A. "Novye osnovaniia sudoproizvodstva." *Sovremennik* 95 (April 1863): 529–56.

Uspenskii, B. A. "Tsar and Pretender: *Samozvanchestvo* or Royal Imposture in Russia as a Cultural-Historical Phenomenon." In *The Semiotics of Russian Culture*, ed. Ann Shukman, 255–92. Ann Arbor: University of Michigan Press, 1984.

Vengerov, S. A. *Kritiko-biograficheskii slovar' russkikh pisatelei i uchenikh*. Vol. 1. St. Petersburg, 1889.

Venturi, Franco. *Roots of Revolution: A History of the Populist and Socialist Movements in Nineteenth Century Russia*. Trans. Francis Haskell. Chicago: University of Chicago Press, 1960.

Vigdorova, Frida. "Pervyi sud nad Iosofom Brodskim." In *Ogonek 88: Luchshie publikatsii goda*, ed. L. Gyshchin, S. Kliamkin, and V. Iumashev, 263. Ogonek, 1989.

Vladimirskii-Budanov, M. F. *Obzor istorii russkogo prava*. 6th ed. St. Petersburg, 1909.

Voitinskii, V. *Dvenadtsat' smertnikov: Sud nad sotsialistami-revoliutsionerami v Moskve*. Berlin: Izdanie zagranichnoi delegatsii P. S. R., 1922.

Volgin, I. L. *Dostoevskii—Zhurnalist. Dnevnik Pisatelia i Russkaia obshchestvennost'*. Moscow: Izdatel'stvo Moskovskogo universiteta, 1981.

———. "Pis'ma chitatelei k F. M. Dostoevskom." *Voprosy literatury* 9 (1971):173–96.

Volodimirov, V. Introduction to "Sudebnye ustavy i zakliuchenie ober-prokuratora po delam Mel'nitskikh i Sviridova." *Zhurnal ugolovnogo i grazhdanskogo prava* 5 (May 1884): 89–92.

Walicki, Andrzej. *Legal Philosophies of Russian Liberalism*. London: Oxford University Press, 1987.

Weisberg, Richard H. *The Failure of the Word: The Protagonist as Lawyer in Modern Fiction*. New Haven, Conn.: Yale University Press, 1984.

Weisberg, Robert. "The Law-Literature Enterprise." *Yale Journal of Law and Humanities* 1, no. 1 (1988): 1–67.

West, Robin. "Invisible Victims: A Comparison of Susan Glaspell's 'Jury of Her Peers,' and Herman Melville's 'Bartleby the Scrivener.'" *Cardozo Studies in Law and Literature* 8, no. 1 (1996): 203–49.

White, James Boyd. *Acts of Hope: Creating Authority in Literature, Law, and Politics.* Chicago: University of Chicago Press, 1994.

———. *Heracles' Bow: Essays on the Rhetoric and Poetics of the Law.* Madison, Wisconsin: University of Wisconsin Press, 1985.

———. *When Words Lose Their Meaning: Constitutions and Reconstitutions of Language, Character, and Community.* Chicago: University of Chicago Press, 1984.

Wilf, Steven. "Imagining Justice: Aesthetics and Public Executions in Late Eighteenth-Century England." *Yale Journal of Law and the Humanities* 5, no. 51 (1993): 51–78.

Wortman, Richard. *The Development of a Russian Legal Consciousness.* Chicago: University of Chicago Press, 1976.

———. *Scenarios of Power: Myth and Ceremony in Russian Monarchy.* Princeton, N.J.: Princeton University Press, 1995.

Yampolsky, Mikhail. "In the Shadow of Monuments: Notes on Iconoclasm and Time." Trans. John Kachur. In *Soviet Hieroglyphics: Visual Culture in Late Twentieth-Century Russia,* ed. Nancy Condee, 93–112. Bloomington: Indiana University Press.

———. "Vina-Pokaianie-Donos." In *Russian Culture in Transition: Selected Papers of the Working Group for the Study of Contemporary Russian Culture, 1990–1991,* ed. Gregory Freidin. Stanford Slavic Studies Vol. 7. Stanford, Calif.: Stanford University Press, 1993. 222–23.

Yeazell, Steven. "Convention, Fiction, and the Law." *New Literary History* 13 (1981): 88–102.

Zakharov, Alexander. "Mass Celebrations in a Totalitarian System." In *Textura,* ed. Alla Efimova and Lev Manovich, 201–18. Chicago: University of Chicago Press, 1995.

Zakrevskii, I. P. *Nastoiashchem i budushchem suda prisiazhnykh: Sbornik statei.* St. Petersburg, 1897.

Zalygin, S. "God Solzhenitsyna." *Novyi mir* 1990, no. 1 (January): 233–40.

Zhivov, V. M. "Istoriia russkogo prava kak lingvo-semioticheskaia problema." In *Semiotics and the History of Culture.* Columbus, Ohio: Slavica Publishers, 1988. 46–128.

Zhivov, V. M., and B. A. Uspenskii. "Tsar' i bog: semioticheskie aspekty sakralizatsii monarkha v Rossii," *Iazyki kul'tury i problemy perevodimosti.* Ed. B. A. Uspenskii. Moscow: Nauka, 1987. 47–152.

Index